A Century of Organized Labor in France

A Century of Organized Labor in France

A Union Movement for the Twenty-First Century?

Edited by

*Herrick Chapman, Mark Kesselman,
and Martin A. Schain*

St. Martin's Press
New York

ISBN 0-312-16497-1

Library of Congress Cataloging-in-Publication Data
A century of organized labor in France : a union movement for the
   twenty-first century? / edited by Herrick Chapman, Mark Kesselman,
   Martin Schain.
      p.   cm.
   A collection of some of the papers presented at the seminar : A
century of trade unionism in France, what type of trade unionism for
the 21st century? which was held in February 1996 and sponsored by
Columbia University and New York University.
   Includes bibliographical references and index.
   ISBN 0-312-16497-1
   1. Trade-unions—France—History—Congresses.   2. Trade-unions—
France—Political activity—History—Congresses.   3. Trade-unions—
France—Forecasting—Congresses.   I. Chapman, Herrick.
II. Kesselman, Mark.   III. Schain, Martin, 1940–.   IV. Century of
Trade Unionism in France, What Type of Trade Unionism for the 21st
Century? (1996 : New York, New York)
HD6684.C45 1998
331.88'0944—dc21   97–50524
                                                                      CIP

Design by Letra Libre

First edition: November, 1998
10   9   8   7   6   5   4   3   2   1

Contents

Acknowledgments

The editors and authors would like to thank the Center for European Studies and the Institute of French Studies at New York University and the Institute for Western Europe at Columbia University for supporting the conference at which most of the chapters of this volume were first presented. We would also like to thank Mary Carter, Ann-Marie Steiritz, and Matthew Golder, all graduate students at New York University, whose careful work editing and translating the text and creating the index has been an important contribution to this book.

Foreword

Georges Séguy

The idea for this book was born following a symposium organized by our friends from New York and Columbia universities. All the credit for making this project a reality is due to their friendly persistence and kindness. We came to New York at the very beginning of 1996, following the centenary anniversary of the General Confederation of Labour in 1995. This anniversary was an occasion for many conferences in France and elsewhere, but the New York meeting was an original and extremely useful highpoint.

However glorious and eventful the history of the Confédération Générale du Travail (CGT) may have been, our common aim was not to dwell on the past but more to discuss what the CGT means in the complex panorama of French trade union life. We wanted to have calm yet rigorous exchanges on the major problems and prospects of the trade union movement in a world in the midst of upheaval and chaos and undergoing profound transformations of a technological, social, and geopolitical nature. The title of the seminar, "A Century of Trade Unionism in France, What Type of Trade Unionism for the Twenty-first Century?" meant that we were obliged to look back, but we also were firmly invited to look ahead. I feel that the conference fulfilled the expectations of our American friends, because it focused on some of the extraordinary traits of the French trade union movement.

In our view, the conference revealed both strengths and weaknesses of the movement. Without claiming to be exhaustive, I would cite, on the *positive* side, its ability to mobilize at certain historic moments (1936, the Resistance, 1968) and to initiate huge movements such as the strikes at the end of 1995. On the *negative* side, the conference revealed division, which is certainly a factor of weakness. One of our most urgent tasks is to overcome division in order for workers and unions to be able to present a united front against numerous employers' attacks on decades of social victories and also to be in a position to deal with future challenges.

Four trade unionists[1] and three researchers[2] from France participated in this conference. They were sure of finding at this conference highly informed American research partners in a variety of disciplines who were knowledgeable about the trade union movement and social situation in France as well as AFL-CIO trade unionists, who were particularly interested in these issues. The large number of researchers and trade unionists who participated enhanced the quality of the conference.

It is interesting to note that this meeting took place at a very special and particularly invigorating time: only a few days after the three-week conflict of most railway workers and their unions against the management of the nationalized French railways and the conservative government. The government was implementing its free market program of social decline. The movement not only stopped attempts to weaken social programs but also forced authorities to negotiate and the government to retreat on important aspects. Without any doubt these outcomes were the result of a deep and growing desire among workers to take joint action and to go beyond trade union divisions.

In itself the event was important. But the sympathy, solidarity, and extraordinary understanding that the movement received from other workers and the great majority of French people—despite the difficulties the strike caused in their daily lives—was also essential. Railway workers have long been highly regarded; it is clear from opinion polls that many workers identified with the movement and supported the legitimacy of the struggle. Perhaps the clearest proof is the great success of solidarity demonstrations in small towns, which brought together thousands of people. It was also reflected in the exceptional number of messages of support from all corners of the world, including the United States.

Everyone in New York wondered about the significance and meaning of these events. Since the conference, there have been many analyses of the movement in France. They do not all agree on its significance, but few deny its influence and its impact (see chapter 8). I think now that the role we attributed to it at the time was not hasty speculation or simple satisfaction with a fleeting event but rather an accurate assessment—however fragile—of a *change in the social conjuncture* and an indication of growing conflict. The accuracy of this analysis has been demonstrated since then in various nonlinear forms, such as the truck drivers' movement for better working conditions and in the reaction to racist laws against immigrants, which the Juppé government promulgated. The support of numerous intellectuals in very different fields for criticism of the conservative government's program is also one of the signs of a renewal of critical thinking against the hypnotic effects of free market orthodoxy and a symptom of the government's growing difficulty in gaining success.

The contributions to this volume deal with such crucial questions as the consequences of economic restructuring and technological change, the state of militant activity, developments in public opinion, and relationships between trade unions and political parties. The processes of globalization and increased international competition engendered among workers, which represent a real economic war against people and which raise problems for the international trade union movement to meet the challenges of the twenty-first century, occupy an important place in these chapters.

I think that readers will find a rich expression of the discussions of the New York conference, and I am pleased about the book's publication. I am also pleased that several French universities and research institutions have decided to hold a follow-up conference in Paris, as we all hoped would happen. I am convinced of the importance of the discussions between researchers and academics on the one hand and trade union activists on the other—in full mutual respect for their respective identities—about new questions for which we all need to find answers to build a world of social progress and peace.

NOTES

1. Jean Magniadas, director of the CGT's Trade Union Research Institute; Jean Pierre Page, head of the CGT's International Department; Georges Séguy, former national CGT general secretary; and Jean Kaspar, then minister counsellor at the French Embassy in Washington, D.C., and former CFDT National Secretary.

2. Roland Cayrol, director of the Opinion Poll Institute C. S. A. and director of research; Guy Groux, director of research; and René Mouriaux, director of research, all at the Center for the Study of Contemporary French Political Life (CEVIPOF).

CHAPTER ONE

Introduction: The Exceptional Trajectory of the French Labor Movement

Herrick Chapman, Mark Kesselman, and Martin A. Schain

The decline of organized labor features prominently in most current analyses of advanced industrial society. On the one hand, students of "new social movements" have contrasted two modes of collective action: The first is a traditional mode, based on rational calculation, involving the strategic pursuit of preexisting (predominantly material—often class—based) self-interest. Organized labor played a key role in a society structured in this fashion. It helped to organize the previously dissident and unorganized, and thus facilitated rational, predictable class compromises.[1] Trade unions were the preeminent "old" social movement in this story. In the second mode, the trade union movement and social democratic regimes have gone on the defensive. Organized labor is no longer one of the key players. Trade unions have been eclipsed by a new mode of popular collective action—the new social movements—based primarily on ascriptive or ideological ties, not those of material self-interest. The power of class as a theoretical and affective source of collective identity began to be consigned to the dustbin of intellectual and social history sometime in the late 1960s or 1970s. New social movements represent a paradigmatic alternative to the old, primarily class-based, movements.[2]

On the other hand, the trade union movements of the West (and elsewhere) have been further weakened by economic and political globalization. Given the immense acceleration of global financial flows, many consider strong labor movements to be an obstacle to the project of attracting capital from abroad. In an era when deregulation and privatization are high on the agenda, organized labor is no longer on the side of progress. There are notable exceptions to the scholars' farewell to the working class; for example, some superb studies, several focusing on France, analyze organized labor's recent efforts to adapt to the brave new (and hostile) world.[3] But it is clear that studying organized labor has become a sunset rather than a sunrise industry.

At the same time, to paraphrase Galileo, like it or not, organized labor continues to move! This collection of essays on the French labor movement following the centennial of its creation provides a fine example of how neglecting a development does not make it disappear. We do not question that the French labor movement is in severe crisis. Indeed, we have analyzed the reasons in our own work. But analyzing the crisis is quite different from ignoring the labor movement altogether. Moreover, the public-sector strikes that immobilized France in late 1995, and whose effects continued to reverberate in fall 1996, testify to the continuing importance of organized labor. The chapters that follow are the product of an unusual partnership between two American universities (Columbia University and New York University) and the Confédération Générale du Travail (CGT). The three institutions, with the assistance of other agencies,[4] sponsored a conference in February 1996 on the topic: "A Century of Organized Labor: A Union Movement for the Twenty-first Century?" Participants included officials from the CGT as well as a former secretary-general of the Confédération Française Démocratique du Travail (CFDT), American trade union officials, and French and American specialists on the French labor movement. The papers presented at the conference have been revised and rewritten, and are presented in this volume, along with some additional chapters.

This introduction provides a theoretical and historical context for understanding the trajectory of the French labor movement. First, we analyze some key dimensions useful in classifying labor movements and locate France in a preliminary fashion on these dimensions. Then we use these dimensions as a point of departure to describe the historical trajectory of the French labor movement. Finally, we focus on the contemporary crisis of French labor.

KEY DIMENSIONS OF ORGANIZED LABOR

In order to understand the character of the French labor movement, and especially the extent to which it is exceptional compared to labor movements in other industrialized capitalist nations, it is useful to identify some key dimensions often used to characterize labor movements generally. Unions vary considerably on these dimensions; rather than variations on a theme, differences in quantity are often so great as to suggest quite fundamental qualitative differences. We distinguish between internal features of unions and their external relations. We define the labor movement in a fairly narrow sense as centering on the actions of trade unions. Although social historians and other scholars have rightly emphasized the need to study the complex ways in which social relations are structured in the workplace and communities, our task is sufficiently ambitious (given the number and complexity of French unions) that, for the most part, we focus on union organizations.

DIMENSIONS INTERNAL TO ORGANIZED LABOR

Organizational Features

Unity/rivalry. To what extent does a single labor confederation possess a de facto monopoly of representation for working people? At the extreme, all workers in a given work unit, industry, and/or national economy can belong to a single-union confederation. Or a number of confederations can compete for workers' allegiance. An important feature of the French labor movement has been plural and intensely divided unionism through most of its history. France occupies an extreme position in this respect, both because of the large number of major labor confederations and their bitter rivalry: Labor confederations frequently display greater hostility toward other confederations than toward employers.

Extent and characteristics of the potential constituency that unions seek to organize. Labor unions can define their constituency narrowly—manual wage earners, for example—or more broadly, to include wage earners in the public and service sector, supervisors, and so on. Obviously, the broader the constituency, the greater the potential size of the labor movement. But the more diverse the constituency, the more difficult it is to develop common demands linking members of a given union.

French unions generally have defined their potential constituency quite broadly, to include public-sector workers (notably teachers, postal workers, transportation workers, and civil servants), technicians, and lower- and middle-level supervisors. Thus, although until recently skilled crafts workers and semiskilled industrial workers were French labor's core constituency, French unions also have organized sectors often neglected by union movements elsewhere. The recent retrenchment of French unions has not occurred in uniform fashion across socioeconomic sectors; private-sector unions have been devastated, such that the contemporary French union movement is confined largely to public-sector workers.

Unions also develop priorities regarding the socioeconomic categories of workers they seek to recruit. Most labor unions traditionally have defined their core constituency as stably employed, native-born, white male workers. French unions are typical in this respect, having made little effort to organize "peripheral" workers (female, immigrant, part time, irregular, and unemployed workers).

Mode of organizing. Unions can aggregate workers by craft, industry, and region. These factors are not mutually exclusive, in that a union can be organized both "vertically," or functionally—by craft or industrial sector—and by locality or region, with union locals affiliated to both functional and geographic organizations. French unions typically have organized simultaneously on a sectoral/industrial basis (metalworkers, chemical workers, railway workers, and so on) and on a geographic basis, with all union locals of a given confederation federated in a given locality or department. This dual basis has been a source of strength in the labor movement, in that it has built on and promoted local solidarity; but it also has been a weakness, since it creates the basis for internal divisions based on the two modes of organizing.

Degree of centralization. Within a given union confederation, decision-making power regarding union strategy and action can be concentrated at the peak, rest primarily at the industrial/sectoral/federation level, or lie with union locals. Major decision-making power within French unions resides at the level of union federations. Union locals at the base and the peak confederations are significant but generally less powerful.

Extent of success in organizing: union density. A key indicator used to measure union strength is the proportion of the labor force that unions persuade to join them. The proportion varies from under 10 percent (or less) in France and the United States to 80 percent or higher in Scandinavia. French unions historically have displayed an unusually weak capacity to recruit members.

Ideology

Two elements determine whether a labor movement can be considered radical or moderate: (1) All unions must both defend the immediate interests of their members—notably by seeking to enunciate the classic material demands of higher wages, shorter hours, and improved working conditions—and act to develop class identity and solidarity, primarily by defending workers' nonmaterial interests (for example, honor, dignity, and autonomy).[5] But unions can place greater emphasis on the "business union" pole or the more "social union" pole. (2) The extent to which unions assume that a fundamental conflict exists between the interests of their members and those of employers and the state (that is, a zero-sum game) versus a situation in which interests are regarded as partially convergent and shared (a positive-sum game) must be determined. Concretely, when calculating their demands, do unions seek to safeguard the interests of employers and the state?

Given the situation of plural unionism, the French labor movement is highly fragmented ideologically. Different confederations have orientations that run the gamut from favorable attitudes toward employers (for example, the CFTC), to intense hostility toward employers and the organization of capitalist production (the CGT during certain periods). Indeed, the ideological diversity of the trade union movement is more noteworthy than the particular ideology of any given union; the result of this diversity is to weaken the possibility of the trade union movement developing common demands and acting in a solidaristic manner.

Strategy and Tactics

Do unions calculate that they can best pursue their strategic interests by seeking to extract benefits directly from employers, or do they seek to persuade the state to mandate benefits to unions and their members? Regarding tactics, do unions seek to achieve their goals through militant, direct action—notably strikes, demonstrations, factory occupations—or by more institutionalized means, involving negotiations with employers and the state?

Where does the French labor movement fall on these two continua? As with ideology, given the diverse character of the French union movement, unions do not share a common strategic or tactical orientation. Although all unions espouse a voluntarist approach (voluntarist in the American, not the French, sense), unions also have typically sought, even when using voluntarist means such as the strike, to obtain benefits from the state.

Mobilizational Capacity

The French labor movement has displayed quite a strong capacity to mobilize workers in support of its goals. Often it has been observed that unions enjoy wider support among workers than membership figures would suggest: Nonunionized workers often support union strike calls, vote for union nominees in works committee elections, and support union demands even while failing to take out a membership card. Thus the French labor movement is more powerful than its low union density and plural unionism suggest. However, often this power has consisted of being able to veto actions that the union movement opposes, as opposed to the proactive power to help shape arrangements and policies favorable to organized labor. (The strikes of late 1995 well illustrate the importance of this distinction.)

UNION RELATIONS WITH KEY ELEMENTS OF THE ENVIRONMENT

In order to understand the character of a labor movement, one must analyze the complex field of relations with the external environment. Internal and external factors are closely related. For example, a labor movement that has close and favorable relations with external actors is less apt to espouse a radical ideology and adopt militant tactics. Conversely, unions that display a radical ideology are less likely to develop cooperative relations with employers and the state.

The Organization of Capital and the Economy

Unions devote the bulk of their energies to day-to-day relations with employers. Whether unions have a "civilized" relationship with employers (the phrase is William Serrin's, describing the relationship of General Motors and the United Auto Workers in the 1950s and 1960s) or hostile relations depends in part on employers.[6] The character of union-employer relations is heavily conditioned by the organization of the economy. For example, firms that are sufficiently insulated from market competition can afford to grant unions concessions in order to "purchase" favorable relations and labor peace. French unions have had to operate in an unfavorable economic situation virtually throughout their entire history. French capital typically has been organized into predominantly small firms; most employers have opposed developing cooperative relations with unions.

The International Economy

The location of a national economy within the international division of labor heavily affects both employers and unions. For example, nations are more or less exposed to international competition and produce goods for export whose added value is highly variable. In general, the more favorably situated the economy, the more latitude employers have to grant concessions and the greater the incentive for labor movements to enter into cooperative relations with employers. But these factors do not operate in an unmediated fashion. For example, Peter Katzenstein's classic analysis describes how in the small nations of northern Europe with exposed economies, capital and labor are induced by the pressure of international competition to participate in corporatist relations.[7]

France may occupy the worst of both worlds. On the one hand, it has not enjoyed a favorable position in the international division of labor, and the result has been to labor's detriment. Given that the French economy has not been highly competitive, there is not a large economic surplus that could be redistributed to obtain cooperative relations with labor. On the other hand, France is not among the Benelux countries, whose economic fate so heavily depends on international trade that capital and the labor movement are forced into a marriage of convenience.

The State

Given the primordial importance of the state in regulating industrial relations, and the impact of state economic and social policies, relations between the state and labor are a key element in understanding the character of a labor movement. Unions can entertain close, cordial relations with the state or an arm's-length relationship that is cool or even hostile. French unions have had a varied relationship to the state, depending on the particular labor confederation and historical period. Moreover, even at a given moment, the same labor confederation typically has exhibited quite a diverse relationship to the state. For example, a confederation may sit on state councils, including the Economic and Social Council, on consultative commissions in given sectors, and on parapublic governing boards (for example, the social security system) while at the same time mobilizing members and sympathizers to strike.

Political Parties

If a labor movement has close relations with a major party, it is more likely to emphasize the value of seeking favorable state policies, usually through cooperative (corporatist) means. Conversely, labor movements without favorable access to a major political party are likely to emphasize more voluntarist actions to defend their interests as well as to pressure the state by demonstrations and other confrontational tactics.

Ever since the Chartre d'Amiens of 1906, the French labor movement officially has defended the importance of nonpartisanship and independence from political parties and the state. On the other hand, important elements of the labor movement—including the very confederations that have most strongly defended independent action—have entertained close relations with the state. Thus one must distinguish words and actions in this sphere. What this quick overview might suggest is that, given the variegated character of French labor—both at any given time and through time—generalization about the labor movement is less useful than is analysis of its historical trajectory.

THE WEIGHT OF THE PAST

French labor activists today can easily identify with late-nineteenth-century pioneers of the labor movement who struggled with the burdens of organizational disunity and factional conflict. Then as now, organizers held divergent views about what changes in the economy workers should aspire to and how unions should relate to parties and the state. In the 1880s and 1890s rival Socialist parties vied for control of budding unions, while many labor organizers, including a number of anarchists, sought to escape party affiliations altogether. Out of this disorder the CGT, founded in 1895 and strengthened by its merger in 1902 with Fernand Pelloutier's network of *bourses du travail* (labor exchanges), gradually emerged as the leading national organization for labor. With its decentralized structure and growing but still modest following, on the eve of World War I the CGT was relatively weak by Western European standards. Trade union membership hovered around 15 percent in France in comparison to about 25 percent in Germany and 40 percent in Britain. This weakness both reflected and reinforced a chronic case of organizational anemia in the French unions: Without many dues-paying members, the CGT could scarcely pay organizers, much less provide the technical staff, educational programs, and social services that made the labor movement as central to working-class community life as it was in Germany, Britain, the Low Countries, and Scandinavia.[8]

What the CGT did offer, especially under the influence of its anarchists, was a place to build a militant culture of revolutionary syndicalism as an alternative to both Jean Jaurès's parliamentary socialism and Jules Guèsde's more *marxisant* socialism that aimed at seizing state power to destroy capitalism. Revolutionary syndicalists looked instead to the general strike as their ultimate weapon, and despite their difficulties in building unions as organizations they demonstrated a remarkable ability to mobilize large numbers of workers in major strike actions. In 1906 they also reaffirmed their independence from political parties in what would long remain the major doctrinal reference point for the CGT, the Chartre d'Amiens, which enshrined trade union autonomy as a guiding principle. It soon became apparent, however, that despite the charter, discord on the question of parties and the use of state power continued to trouble the movement.

This early evolution of the CGT depended a great deal on the strategic choices of key leaders. But it also reflected the long-standing effects of economic change and political upheaval in the nineteenth century. The gradual pace of industrialization in France had kept the labor movement firmly rooted in the oppositional culture of skilled workers, with its Proudhonian emphasis on craft autonomy and working-class self-sufficiency.[9] A collective memory of state repression, especially associated with the June Days in 1848 and the destruction of the Paris Commune in 1871, had endowed workers with a deep suspicion of the state and political parties. By the same token, the achievement of universal male suffrage in France by the 1870s had removed the incentive workers felt in less democratic countries, such as Germany, to link unions and parties in the common pursuit of political rights.[10]

By 1914 several enduring characteristics of French trade unionism—organizational weakness, small membership, a dependence on a core of ideologically motivated activists, a capacity to enlist large numbers of nonmembers in major strike actions—had taken hold. Equally decisive for the future of the movement were the effects of the world wars and the Russian Revolution. On the eve of World War I some signs appeared of moderation within the CGT and of a growing interest in cooperating more openly with the Socialist Party (the SFIO). But a long, horrifying war, the Russian Revolution, and government repression of strike waves from 1917 to 1920 brought to the surface the underlying differences in outlook that divided revolutionaries and reformists in the unions. A war that initially strengthened many unions as interlocutors for workers in a wartime economy eventually served to pave the way toward a devastating schism in the CGT. The confederation's rupture in 1920 into a Communist-oriented CGTU and the non-Communist CGT was to cast a long shadow over the French labor movement for the rest of the century.[11]

What made interconfederational rivalry so enduring a feature of the union movement was the particular character of the Communist Party and its vision of the unions. To be sure, the labor movement had been factionalized before 1914. Religion and ideology had divided workers, as these matters did elsewhere in Europe, although not necessarily to the point of ensuring a permanent condition of organizational disunity. But division over Communist domination of the unions was of another order entirely. Despite their denials to the contrary, militants in the CGTU were forced in practice to violate the basic tenet of the Chartre d'Amiens by subordinating their unions to party authority. Communist trade unionism proved to be deeply divisive because it left no room for compromise on precisely those issues that had so inflamed passions before the war—the autonomy of working-class organizations, union independence from political parties, and the question of whether to combat or cooperate with the state.

Still, the Communist movement did equip militants ideologically and organizationally to respond to new opportunities to promote trade unionism in the 1930s and 1940s. For better and worse, the party gave militants a structure and a discipline. When the sitdown strikes of June 1936 ushered 3 million new members into a newly reunified CGT, Communist militants already had gained a stronger foothold in many industries as local organizers than had their Socialist, Catholic, and anarchist rivals—and they reinforced their position in the CGT accordingly. Communists likewise benefited from the Parti communiste français's (PCF) unambiguous commitment after mid-1934 to fighting fascism, its support for national defense, and its pragmatic approach to collective bargaining in the late 1930s.[12]

Much the same story could be told of the second great moment of CGT expansion—from the Liberation of France to the outbreak of the Cold War in 1947. The confederation quickly recovered the membership it had lost in the late 1930s and during the Occupation. Communist organizers, bolstered by the prestige of the Resistance and by the PCF's newfound electoral strength, gained a firmer grip on union leadership posts. Above all, for the first time the CGT acquired a major institutional role in the management of the economy. Union representatives secured seats on the governing boards of nationalized enterprises and on the planning committees of Jean Monnet's Commissariat du Plan. Workers became entitled to elect union delegates to the vast new network of plant committees and local social security boards that the Left-dominated government established after the Liberation. With Communist ministers in government, the CGT enjoyed an access to decision making in many areas of economic and social life that far exceeded what labor had won during World War I and the Popular Front of 1936.[13]

Just when the CGT finally had established itself as a power broker, however, the Cold War intervened. In 1947 Paul Ramadier's coalition government expelled its Communist partners. Tensions between Communists and Socialists had been building over the Indochina war and a policy of wage constraint that was putting the PCF in an increasingly compromised position. International polarization drove the wedge wider. Once the coalition broke down, the CGT rediscovered the debilitating effects of schism, factionalism, and the political ghettoization of the Communist Party. A new rival confederation emerged, the anti-Communist Force Ouvrière (FO), aided by subsidies from the French government and the American Federation of Labor. The FO and the Catholic confederation, the CFTC, embraced the hallowed principle of trade union autonomy, but in doing so suffered from the old weakness of having little political means, apart from the strike, to exert leverage on parliament and the ministries. Meanwhile, the Communist-dominated CGT bore the burden of its association with a pariah party, losing over half its members between 1949 and 1958.[14] Bitter hostilities between the Communist and non-Communist left in the Cold War France of the 1950s further reinforced the historical tradition of labor movement factionalism.

For French workers, the timing of this political catastrophe could not have been worse. If in other countries the economic boom of the 1950s led to a strengthening of labor movements and in northern Europe to an enlargement of the role unions played in national economic decision making, in France the extraordinary modernization of the economy and the further expansion of state regulatory authority did little to enhance trade union power. The CGT could take only indirect credit for wage hikes in the 1950s: Working-class incomes rose largely because the government chose to convert some of the period's productivity gains into higher wages in hopes of keeping workers out of a (stagnating) CGT.[15] After 1947, moreover, economic planning and public investment policy consolidated the partnership of business and the state through decision-making bodies that excluded the unions.

Much of labor's early postwar institutional influence vanished with remarkable speed.

It would take a period of renewed commitment to the cause of left-wing unity, beginning in the 1960s, to give labor activists an opportunity to escape from this cul-de-sac. Several factors converged to make greater labor unity possible. By the early 1960s a brightening of the Cold War international climate tempered the sectarianism of Communists and anti-Communists alike. Meanwhile, activists of various political hues forged a more ecumenical left-wing culture out of their common experience of protesting the Algerian war and the Gaullist domination of the new Fifth Republic. The electoral rules of the new regime, moreover, encouraged the Left to close ranks against the Right. And of special importance to labor activists, the "deconfessionalization" of the CFTC in 1964 into a secularized and more radical CFDT (Confédération Français et Démocratique du Travail) suddenly created a dynamic confederation that was more inclined, and better suited ideologically, than the FO to explore collaborative relations with the CGT. By 1966 the CFDT and the CGT struck a pathbreaking unity-of-action pact that committed both unions to joint support for workers' strikes at the local level. What made this gesture toward labor unity doubly significant was that it happened amid renewed grassroots fervor for worker mobilization. These breakthroughs for labor—greater unity in the movement, greater combativeness in the workplace—prepared the ground for that stunning surprise, May 1968, when 7 million workers took part in the largest strike wave in the country's history. Just as June 1936 gave birth to mass trade unionism, so May 1968 offered the labor movement an unanticipated opportunity to return to a position of central importance in French political and economic life.[16]

The period from May 1968 to the left-wing defeat in the parliamentary elections of 1978 proved to be as fateful a decade for the labor movement as any in the twentieth century. Not since the Liberation had trade unions had a better chance to make headway. The May strikes inspired a new generation of young workers, technicians, and even cadres to become labor activists. Membership lists swelled in every confederation. The political climate improved all the more in 1972 when the PCF and the new Parti Socialiste created a Common Program of the Left to serve as the basis of the first credible electoral alliance between Communists and Socialists since the Popular Front. Most surprising of all, some prospect of renewal blossomed within the PCF itself as the warm winds of Eurocommunism, of genuine de-Stalinization, swept across Western Europe. By 1974 the CGT even advocated *autogestion,* worker self-management, previously dismissed in Communist circles as so much *gauchiste* anarchism. Although the CGT and the CFDT remained rivals, unity of action brought grass-roots' credibility to both confederations through the mid-1970s.

Why did a decade so full of promise in the end fail to produce historic gains for the labor movement? For one thing, the two major confederations focused their hopes on an electoral victory of the Left. When the Communist-Socialist alliance broke apart in 1977 (mainly because the PCF feared its eclipse by the Socialist Party), labor's strategy collapsed. It is easy to understand how this happened. The CGT, of course, was still thoroughly entangled with the PCF, but even the formally autonomous CFDT had developed important informal links to the Socialist Party. Still relatively weak confederations with little institutionalized power in the workplace, the CGT and the CFDT pursued a state-centered strategy. They banked on using the French state's enormous influence over capital flows to improve labor's position in the modernizing economy. Under these circumstances political strategies continued to make sense, but they came at the high cost of keeping unions hostage to parties and underdeveloped as workplace-oriented organizations.

After losing the electoral gamble in 1978, turmoil broke out within both the CGT and the CFDT. Each confederation soon resorted to its traditional defensive posture—the CGT to rigid opposition, the CFDT to moderation—at the expense of trade union unity. As in previous periods of intensified rivalry, membership sagged. According to sociologist George Ross, from 1977 to 1979 the CGT lost 20 to 25 percent of its members, while the CFDT lost 12 to 15 percent.[17] By 1980 the rupture between the two confederations was nearly complete. The CGT, once again trapped by the sectarianism of a PCF on the defensive, found itself in the ludicrous position of supporting the Soviet invasion of Afghanistan and the imposition of marshal law against the Solidarity movement in Poland.

Equally damaging in the late 1970s was the failure of all the confederations to adapt adroitly to the *crise,* the enormous changes in the global economy that were undermining the competitive position, indeed the very structure, of the French (and European) economy.[18] By the late 1970s there was no gainsaying that the great postwar boom had ended. Manufacturing jobs disappeared, unemployment rates soared, and the male blue-collar workforce that had long been the mainstay of the labor movement dwindled in size. Sadly, none of the confederations had done enough in the 1970s (to say nothing of before then) to recruit the women, immigrants, white-collar employees, part-time service workers, and youth who would have counterbalanced the decline of the traditional male working class. Nor did they focus their strategies sufficiently on winning a voice for labor in corporate boardrooms and government committee (to say nothing of the European Commission in Brussels), where they might have influenced policy responses to the crisis. Although the CFDT welcomed such a role, as did an important minority of activists in the CGT, the latter confederation eventually rejected it (as did the FO for its more conservative reasons). When, for example, some CGT activists began to assert themselves in debate about how to restructure a flagging French steel industry, it was PCF hostility to participation in policy making, as much as business and government opposition to labor, that eventually silenced them.[19]

How much labor could have accomplished in the 1970s with better strategies, given the recalcitrance of employers and the strength of the political right, is hard to say. All the major confederations, including the CGT, tried to expand the use of collective bargaining in that decade, only to encounter employer and government hostility.[20] Still, by squandering the opportunities they did have to broaden their membership base and to make more of a place for themselves independent of parties, trade unionists faced the future with huge liabilities. The long-standing handicaps of weak organization, poor financing, interconfederational rivalries, and a feeble collective bargaining system at the firm level made French unions ill-equipped for the even more accelerated pace of deindustrialization they soon would face in the 1980s.

Was the modern French labor movement condemned to these weaknesses by dint of its initial development early in the century? In some ways, yes. The vicious cycle of small membership and heavy dependence on state intervention plagued the movement from the beginning. As long as the unions remained too weak to force employers to collaborate in cultivating a culture of collective bargaining, workers had little recourse but to rely on dramatic strike waves and brief moments of left-wing governments to get what they could not win otherwise.

Little in history, of course, is completely foreordained. In theory, at least, activists might have better used key moments of trade union resurgence—during World War I, the Popular Front, and the post-Liberation era—to cement trade union unity and to secure rights to union representation and collective bargaining at the firm and industrywide levels. Had labor leaders done so, perhaps the dependency on political strategies might have diminished. But the obstacles to such a stronger institutionalization of enterprise-level trade union power were formidable. Employers and unsympathetic governments fought it bitterly, and the Communist Party, ironically, impeded it as well. By keeping the CGT so tightly yoked to the party's political objectives, and by stressing nationalizations and the expansion of government authority over the economy after 1944, Communist leaders kept the CGT focused more on the strategic possibilities of state power than on the organizational imperatives of a union movement built for collective bargaining. Communist unionism, employer intransigence, and state dependency became mutually reinforcing after 1945, just when the labor movement might have had its best chance of breaking the vicious cycle of its early pattern of development. This legacy left the unions all the more poorly prepared to adjust to the era of deregulation that would shrink the state's role in the economy in the last two decades of the twentieth century.

THE CONTEMPORARY CRISIS

The period since the first election of François Mitterrand has been the best of times and the worst of times for the French labor movement. On one hand, two of the most important elements of trade union power have been eroding since the mid-1970s: membership and strike mobilization. Union membership, as a percentage of the workforce in union organizations, has been declining since between 1975 and 1977, and strike levels—the number of strikes and the number of workers participating in them—also have been falling. On the other hand, union stability, involvement in policy making, and—at times—influence over policy appear to have increased during the years of Socialist government. Although, like unions in many other industrial democracies, French unions have been unable to attract significant numbers of the young entering the workforce during this period, in contrast to those in other countries they have maintained surprising credibility among workers and among the population in general (see chapter 9).

Thus an evaluation of the importance of unions in France of the 1990s can be neither simple nor stagnant. For example, strike levels had increased modestly during the two years prior to the movement of 1995, and there were some indications that the membership decline had bottomed out. Does this indicate the beginning of a new cycle of union ascendancy, or does the tendency toward union change and decline continue? Increases in "normal" strike activity have been very small and almost completely in the public sector, however; even the strike wave of 1995, also limited to the public sector, was modest in comparison to similar waves in the past. Finally, although this strike movement did stimulate union membership growth, the increase was also small, and at least some of the tendencies of the past 15 years seem to have been reinforced.

Dimensions Internal to Organized Labor

Organizational Features

Unity/Rivalry. The Left's victory in 1981 served to intensify the rivalry among the three main confederations and within them. We might have expected that under the guidance of a more sympathetic and open government, there would have been a concerted attempt to develop greater cooperation, at least among those unions that were committed to the Left: the CGT, CFDT, and Fédération de l'Education Nationale (FEN), the teachers' union. Instead, the new opportunities that opened up provoked greater rivalry in several different ways.

Politically, a government of the Left presented problems as well as opportunities. Having been locked out of decision making for most of the Fifth Republic, national unions now competed for policy influence in Leftist governments. They also struggled among themselves and internally over how to deal with Leftist governments that pursued managerial policies that resulted in increased unemployment and few jobs in sectors in which unions had been historically important.

In a sense, unity was much easier when the Right was in power. National confederations could find common ground in opposing policies that could be understood as being against the larger interests of workers, and, in opposition, the parties of the Left could find common ground with their trade union counterparts. With the Left in power, developing a common position on promoting policy was far more difficult and finding agreement on actually opposing a government of the Left was virtually impossible. National unions competed for policy influence, on the one hand, and for support among workers on the other.

In the waning days of the Mitterrand presidency, unions were increasingly divided internally, often for different reasons. The CGT struggled to readjust its relationship with a withering PCF, and the CFDT was divided over its relations with other national unions as well as its strategy toward dealing with the evolving market economy. The consequences were most serious for the CFDT, whose dissident public service workers created what has become a new national union pole, Solidaires, Unitaires et Démocratiques, (SUD) that continues to attract militants who have deserted the confederation.[21]

Extent of potential constituency.   Although the extent of the potential constituency of the French labor movement remained broad even as the real constituency was contracting after 1981, mobilization success has varied considerably. The relative proportions of membership mobilization have hardly changed over the years. It has been greatest in the public sector (by about 2 to 1 compared to the private sector), relatively greater among blue-collar workers, and least successful among technicians and engineers. The union movement has made considerable efforts among technicians and engineers, but with only marginal success. Among immigrant workers, a significant source of membership and support in the past, unions generally have been unsure how to approach North Africans and have been unsuccessful in bringing them into the union movement.

Mode of organizing and degree of centralization.   While the mode of organizing has changed relatively little since 1981, the recent fragmentation that is evident in both the CFDT and the FEN has given greater weight to specific categorical unions in the public sector.[22] Also the tendency toward local bargaining encouraged by the Auroux laws has given new importance to UDs (departmental unions) and enterprise unions.

The same process also has given greater weight to the federations in each of the confederations. Although researchers have paid most attention to the confederations, the federations have been arenas of considerable instability in recent years. It is at the federal level that the challenge to the leadership of CFDT has emerged, but this is also true of challenges to the leadership of the CGT and the FO.[23] In this way, tendencies toward centralization have been consistently weakened by both the federations and the relatively diminished control that national officials have had over militants at the departmental and enterprise levels.

Union density. The core problem of the French trade union movement always has been density, and of course this problem has been growing worse since 1975 to 1977. French unions have lost more than half their membership in the last 25 years.[24] With some local exceptions, density is now so low that it is generally discounted as a measure of union support. Most analysts tend to use social elections (shop steward elections, *comités d'entreprise* elections, *prud'homme elections*) as more reliable indicators. In fact, Roland Cayrol gives us reason to adopt such an approach. At least for some purposes, it is more diffuse support that counts. Indeed, in the early 1980s, analysts such as Gérard Adam argued that, with the establishment of union representatives as stable bargaining agents under the Auroux laws, the functions of unions had changed and reduced membership was less consequential. However, by the end of the decade, the consequences of "unions without members" had become more apparent.

The most important consequence is that in comparison with the pre-1981 period, French unions are even more dependent on the "social climate" and their ability to mobilize, rather than organize, in order to achieve their goals. Generally, only in the context of relatively rare social movements have unions really counted in decision making or even bargaining. However, in a social climate in which there has been diminishing strike activity since 1981, unions are necessarily less powerful as social or political actors.

The decline of stable membership also has meant that union rivalry has been intensified by the search for relative support in the context of strike activity and in social elections. Union pluralism and competition in social elections has been complicated during the past decade by two factors: the sharp rise of nonunion lists and the fragmentation of the organized union movement in some sectors. In this crowded field, unions have tended to focus on their differences rather than to seek common ground.

IDEOLOGY

This tendency toward divisiveness has become most evident in the complex movement of ideological orientation. The more or less stable ideological orientations of the 1970s have been changing for some time. Before 1981 the FO was considered the privileged interlocutor for both the employers and the state. This status changed during the Mitterrand period, and the FO has never been able to regain this status. By 1996 its leadership had assumed a *protestaire* role that was most evident during the December strike movement. The CFDT, which was the core of the "second left" in the 1970s, sharply revised its ideological orientations between 1984 and 1988 away from *socialisme autogestionaire;* by 1996 it had taken over the old role of the FO under a government of the Right.[25] These two shifts left the CGT, which has been struggling to deal with its relationship to a declining Communist Party,[26] in confusion. It has been reluctant to surrender its protest role while it also has been under internal pressure to assume a more constructive role of initiating and "proposing new solutions."[27] This process of ideological repositioning also should be seen in systemic terms. With the breakthrough of the SUD on the left (in part related to the CFDT's repositioning on the right), all of the other national unions have been forced to reconsider ideological orientations in terms of their ability to mobilize workers and their access to the state.

STRATEGY AND TACTICS

This ideological movement therefore has been related to strategy and tactics. The balance between mobilization and access is related to the historic dependency of unions on various levels of state support. This support has been, and continues to be, manifested in direct subsidies and positions in the state and quasi-state apparatus and legislation that guarantees acceptance and indirect subsidies both from the state and private employers. In a system of unions without members, militants constantly are tempted to test the social climate.

MOBILIZATION CAPACITY

Thus mobilization capacity is often unpredictable. One result of this situation has been a volatile system of social relations and an unstable system of industrial/bargaining relations. In the 1990s, as in the 1980s and the 1970s, both the government and the employer have spoken about "modernizing" the bargaining system and have bemoaned the division and weakness of their union counterparts.[28]

UNION RELATIONS WITH KEY
ELEMENTS OF THE ENVIRONMENT

All of this is related, of course, to changing relations between the trade union movement and key elements in the environment since 1981. Union relations with French employers have been transformed surprisingly little by the implementation of the Auroux laws. Although one result of the legislation has been a vast expansion of collective bargaining at the plant level, unions have proven to be relatively weak in this process. The new rules have opened up new and direct modes of consultation between employers and workers, have encouraged fragmentation of and competition among worker representatives, and have absorbed the time of plant-level union militants to the detriment of their ability to maintain contact with workers (the traditional role of union militants). The decline of union membership has reduced the unions' effectiveness at the very level at which they are engaged in bargaining—a formula for accelerating weakness.

The new rules also have expanded union contacts with the state. With increased fragmentation and declining membership (and therefore diminished income), unions are more dependent on state subsidies than they have been in recent times. The ideological ambivalence that all union organizations have expressed toward the state only masks their dependent relationship.

During the period since 1981, the relationship between the major union organizations and political parties has changed considerably. The CGT has been going through (and continues to go through) a painful process of distancing itself from the PCF. While the PCF continues to maintain influence, perhaps a veto over confederal leadership, the relationship between union and party is limited and under question within the CGT.[29] The *recentrage* of the CFDT during the past decade has meant that its flirtation with the PS is clearly over. In 1985 the CFDT decided to no longer support any party in elections. Nevertheless, individual CFDT leaders have continued to be identified with currents (especially the Rocard current) of the Socialist Party. On another level, the *membership* (and support) of each of the three national confederations can be differentiated by party commitment: the CGT is largely Communist and Socialist; the CFDT is generally PS; and the FO is centrist and even right. We also should emphasize that none of the major unions is nonpolitical, even if it professes to be nonpartisan.

Recently, almost all Western trade union movements have suffered serious decline as a result of the globalization, reorganization of capital, and the attack on unions that has come from both business and the state. Confronting this common problem, each union movement has responded in ways that are related to its institutional and political environments. Compared with other union movements in Europe, French unions are among the weakest in organizational terms, and the historic problems of low membership density, weak organization, rivalry, and dependence on the state have been exacerbated during this period. However, because they seem to retain more legitimacy in public opinion than some other union movements, French unions also seem to have more mobilization capacity than their organizational strength would indicate. This is important in an environment in which global economic and political processes have generated social conflicts that offer new possibilities to unions as vehicles of mobilization.

NOTES

1. The historical and theoretical basis for this form of political and economic exchange has been subtly analyzed in Adam Przeworski, *Capitalism and Social Democracy* (New York: Cambridge University Press, 1985).
2. Note, for example, that Sidney Tarrow, in *Power in Movement: Social Movements, Collective Action and Politics* (New York: Cambridge University Press, 1994), devotes less than a page to trade unions in an analysis of collective protest and action in Western Europe and the United States in the nineteenth and twentieth centuries.
3. Anthony Daley, *Steel, State, and Labor: Mobilization and Adjustment in France* (Pittsburgh: University of Pittsburgh Press, 1996); Miriam Golden and Jonas Pontusson, eds., *Bargaining for Change: Union Politics in North America and Europe* (Ithaca, NY: Cornell University Press, 1992); Chris Howell, *Regulating Labor: The State and Industrial Relations Reform in Postwar France* (Princeton, NJ: Princeton University Press, 1992); Kathleen Thelen, *Union of Parts: Labor Politics in Postwar Germany* (Ithaca, NY: Cornell University Press, 1991); Lowell Turner, *Democracy at Work: Changing World Markets and the Future of Labor Unions* (Ithaca, NY: Cornell University Press, 1992).
4. Including the New York Consortium for European Studies, the Institute for French Studies at New York University, the Currier-Sterling Fund at Columbia, and the Embassy of France in New York.
5. See Claus Offe, *Disorganized Capitalism: Contemporary Transformations of Work and Politics* (Cambridge, MA: MIT Press, 1985), chap. 7.
6. William Serrin, *The Company and the Union: The "Civilized Relationship" of the General Motors Corporation and the United Automobile Workers* (New York: Knopf, 1973).
7. Peter Katzenstein, *Small States in World Markets: Industrial Policy in Europe* (Ithaca, NY: Cornell University Press, 1985).
8. For the early history of the CGT, see Michel Dreyfus, *Histoire de la C.G.T.: Cents ans du syndicalisme en France* (Paris: Editions Complexe, 1995), pp. 15–43; Val R. Lorwin, *The French Labor Movement* (Cambridge, MA: Harvard University Press, 1954), pp. 21–46; Jacques Julliard, *Fernand Pelloutier et les origines du syndicalisme d'action directe* (Paris: Seuil, 1971); Michel Pigenet, "Les Finances, une approche des problèmes de structure et

d'orientation de la C.G.T. (1895–1914)," *Le Mouvement social* 172 (July–September 1995). For an excellent analytic overview of workers, business, and the state in twentieth-century France, see Patrick Fridenson, "Le Conflit social," in André Burguière and Jacques Revel, eds., *Histoire de la France*, vol. 3, *L'Etat et les conflits*, ed. Jacques Julliard (Paris: Seuil, 1990), pp. 351–453, which includes an extensive bibliography.

9. The central role of skilled workers in the French trade union is emphasized in Bernard H. Moss, *The Origins of the French Labor Movement, 1830–1914: The Socialism of Skilled Workers* (Berkeley: University of California Press, 1980); Edward Shorter and Charles Tilly, *Strikes in France, 1830–1968* (New York: Cambridge University Press, 1974), pp. 175–179; Michael Hanagan, *The Logic of Solidarity: Artisans and Industrial Workers in Three French Towns, 1871–1914* (Urbana: University of Illinois Press, 1980); Joan Wallach Scott, *The Glassmakers of Carmaux: French Craftsmen and Political Action in a Nineteenth-Century City* (Cambridge, MA: Harvard University Press, 1974); and Leora Auslander, *Taste and Power: Furnishing Modern France* (Berkeley: University of California Press, 1996).

10. On the political and economic context of union building in the late nineteenth century, see Aristide R. Zolberg, "How Many Exceptionalisms?" in Ira Katznelson and Aristide R. Zolberg, *Working-Class Formation: Nineteenth-Century Patterns in Western Europe and the United States* (Princeton, NJ: Princeton University Press, 1986); and Adolf Sturmthal, *Unity and Diversity in European Labor: An Introduction to Contemporary Labor Movements* (Glencoe, IL: The Free Press, 1953). For a criticism of the influential Katznelson and Zolberg volume, see James E. Cronin, "Neither Exceptional nor Peculiar: Towards the Comparative Study of Labor in Advanced Society," *International Review of Social History* 38 (1993): 59–75.

11. The essential starting point for understanding the impact of World War I and the Russian Revolution on the CGT is Jean-Louis Robert, *Les ouvriers, la patrie et la révolution: Paris, 1914–1919* (Besançon: Université de Besançon, 1995); Annie Kriegel, *Aux origines du communisme français*, 2 vols. (Paris: Mouton, 1964); and Robert Wohl, *French Communism in the Making, 1914–1924* (Stanford, CA: Stanford University Press, 1966). See also Jean-Jacques Becker, *The Great War and the French People* (Providence, RI: Berg, 1985); Kathryn Amdur, *Syndicalist Legacy: Trade Unions and Politics in Two French Cities in the Era of World War I* (Urbana: University of Illinois Press, 1986); John Horne, *Labour at War: France and Britain, 1914–1918* (Oxford: Clarendon Press, 1991); and Laura Lee Downs, *Manufacturing Inequality: Gender Division in the French and British Metalworking Industries, 1914–1939* (Ithaca, NY: Cornell University Press, 1995).

12. On the emergence of mass trade unionism in the 1930s and the growth of Communist Party influence in the labor movement after 1934, see Antoine Prost, *La CGT à l'époque du front populaire, 1934–1939: Essai de description numérique* (Paris: Librairie Armand Colin, 1964); Herrick Chapman, *State Capitalism and Working-Class Radicalism in the French Aircraft Industry*

(Berkeley: University of California Press, 1991); Jean-Paul Depretto and Sylvie V. Schweitzer, *Le Communisme à l'usine: Vie ouvrière et mouvement ouvrier chez Renault 1920–1939* (Paris: Edires, 1984); Bertrand Badie, "Les Grèves du front populaire aux usines Renault," *Le Mouvement social* 81 (October-December 1972); Henry Ehrmann, *French Labor from Popular Front to Liberation* (New York: Oxford University Press, 1947); Raymond Hainsworth, "Les Grèves du front populaire de mai et juin 1936: Une Nouvelle analyse fondée sur l'études de ces grèves dans le bassin houiller du Nord et du Pas-de-Calais," *Le Mouvement social* 96 (July-September 1976); and Jacques Girault, ed., *Sur l'implantation du parti communiste francais dans l'entre-deux-guerres* (Paris: Editions Sociales, 1977).

13. On working-class experience and the resurgence of the CGT after the war, see George Ross, *Workers and Communists in France: From Popular Front to Eurocommunism* (Berkeley: University of California Press, 1982); Chapman, *State Capitalism;* Antoine Prost, "Les Effectifs de la C.G.T. en 1945," *Revue d'histoire moderne et contemporaine* 41, no. 1 (January-March 1994); Irwin M. Wall, "The French Social Contract: Conflict amid Cooperation," *International Labor and Working-Class History* 50 (Fall 1996): 116–124; Rolande Trempé, *Les Trois batailles du charbon, 1936–1947* (Paris: Editions La Découverte, 1989); Patrick Fridenson and Jean-Louis Robert, "Les Ouvriers dans la France de la Seconde Guerre mondiale: Un bilan," *Le Mouvement social* 158 (January-March 1992); and Roger Linet, *C.G.T.: Lendemains de guerre 1944–1947* (Paris: Hachette, 1995).

14. Dominique Labbé, "Trade Unionism in France since the Second World War," *West European Politics* 17, no. 1 (January 1994), p. 148.

15. Wall, "The French Social Contract," pp. 120–121.

16. On the resurgence of labor militancy and the search for interconfederation alliances in the 1960s and 1970s, see Martin A. Schain, "Relations between the CGT and the CFDT: Politics and Mass Mobilization," in Mark Kesselman, ed., with the assistance of Guy Groux, *The French Workers' Movement: Economic Crisis and Political Change,* trans. Edouardo Diaz, Arthur Goldhammer, and Richard Shryock (London: George Allen and Unwin, 1984). CGT and PCF strategy in this period is brilliantly analyzed in Ross, *Workers and Communists,* and George Ross, "The Perils of Politics: French Unions and the Crisis of the 1970s," in Peter Lange, George Ross, and Maurizio Vannicelli, eds., *Unions, Change and Crisis: French and Italian Union Strategy and the Political Economy, 1945–1980* (London: George Allen and Unwin, 1982). See also Dreyfus, *Histoire de la C.G.T.,* pp. 262–287; and Jeff Bridgford, *The Politics of French Trade Unionism* (Leicester: Leicester University Press, 1991). On the origins and early years of the CFDT, see Frank Georgi, *L'Invention de la C.F.C.T., 1957–1970. Syndicalisme, catholicisme et politique dans la France de l'expansion* (Paris: Editions de l'Atelier-C.N.R.S. Editions, 1995).

17. Ross, "The Perils of Politics," p. 65. The assessment of labor's predicament in the late 1970s draws heavily from Ross's analysis.

18. For a variety of views about how the unions responded to deindustrialization, unemployment, and political conflict within the Left in the late 1970s, see the chapters in Kesselman, ed., *The French Workers' Movement.* See also W. Rand Smith, *Crisis in the French Labour Movement: A Grassroots' Perspective* (New York: St. Martin's Press, 1987).

19. Ross, "The Perils of Politics," p. 63; Daley, *Steel, State, and Labor,* pp. 137–143.

20. Bridgford, *The Politics of French Trade Unionism,* pp. 168–172.

21. *Le Monde,* April 14–15, 1996, p. 6.

22. See *Le Monde,* February 9, 1995.

23. *Le Monde,* December 6, 1995; February 9, April 14–15, June 12, June 8, 1996

24. Dominique Labbé, *La Syndicalisation en France depuis 1945* (Grenoble: CERAP, 1995).

25. *Le Monde,* June 14, 1996.

26. *Le Monde,* April 6, 1996.

27. *Le Monde,* December 8, 1995, April 6, May 9, 1996.

28. *Le Monde,* August 13, 1993, February 11–12, 1996.

29. *Le Monde,* April 6, 1996.

PART I

Historical Trajectory:
Decline of Militantism, Interunion Relations,
and Relations with Political Parties

CHAPTER TWO

Strategies and Events:
The "Form" of the CGT
from 1936 to 1968

René Mouriaux

In the fall of 1995, French society was shaken up by a surge of collective action that was immediately given diverse and contradictory interpretations. A scholar, whose intention it is to be an "understander" (*ein Verstehender*), is required to relate the recent events to the trade union movement tradition, which has been both actualized and abandoned. If we examine the CGT alone, continuity can be seen in the union's plunge into mass mobilization. However, a major break occurred in its relationship to politics. Prime Minister Alain Juppé's authority certainly was questioned and his resignation envisaged, but his replacement would have been another right-wing figure. Despite criticism of the "politicization" of the movement, first pronounced by Nicole Notat and swiftly retracted since it turned so fiercely on its utterer, the November-December 1995 struggle, although strongly rooted in an opposition to economic liberalism, did not pose the question of power.

TRADE UNIONISM BASED ON MOBILIZATION

Three features of CGT trade unionism from 1936 to 1968 characterize its system. Except sporadically, union membership has been composed of only a minority of wage earners, its strength being based on a group of militants with a firm foothold in the life of industry. Professional elections provide opportunities to assess the audience it enjoys in the course of day-to-day union action. Except for rare sectors, such as printing or teaching, the union does not provide any services to its members other than those related to action, and although it plays a role in the management of social security or works councils, this role is indeed to help wage earners, but indirectly, from a distance. Trade union life reaches its peak during strikes, and the period under study includes the battles of June 1936, the insurrectional strike of 1944, the 1947–1948 conflicts, action in the public sector in 1953, the miners' struggles in 1963, and the events of 1968.

TRADE UNIONISM ON A SMALL SCALE

According to the dominant conception in the CGT at the beginning of the twentieth century, the union is the cognizant spokesperson for the working class. Revolutionary syndicalists first aimed to unite the angry and the audacious whose initiatives were unfettered by the do-gooders and the conformists. Through direct action, the "growing" minority (to use Emile Pouget's adjective) animates the masses who then overturn the relationships of domination and learn economic, political, and intellectual emancipation. Emile Pataud and Emile Pouget's novel, *Comment Nous Ferons la Révolution*, published in 1909, portrays the full dynamics of this strategy. The union is at once teacher, tutor, and midwife. From its minority status, its vocation is to become a majority once the general strike has led the masses on the road to true freedom. The pan-syndicalist problematic thus sees membership as a conscious and voluntary involvement in class struggle.

The exigent conception of revolutionary syndicalism that some have qualified as elitist was to endure throughout the interwar period. Despite contrary practices in the printing industry and among civil servants, the reformist CGT chose to unite only reliable supporters. The CGTU foresaw itself becoming a "widespread" organization. Its highly politicized watchwords, its often avant-garde practices, and its systematic recruitment of leaders among the Communists prevented it from enlarging its fairly tight circle.

Twice the CGT had an influx of members.[1] The reunification of the CGT and the CGTU, union struggles and their triumphs provoked a "union rush" that dwindled as early as 1938. The outburst of activity that came with Liberation also gave rise to a strong inrush of members to which the scission in 1947 brought an abrupt end.

While still the largest union organization, the CGT came out weakened, and its influence resided in its activists' potential. As dues collectors, worker delegates, elected representatives on works councils, and members of industrial sections, it was they who ensured union presence and by their devotion inspired confidence in the confederation to which they claimed allegiance. Distribution of tracts, discussions, taking the floor, delegations, demonstrations, work stoppages, and such are the usual form their action takes. Its activists' appeal is exemplified in the evolution of the worker-priests who became increasingly involved in the workforce after 1947. Most of the worker-priests joined the CGT and accepted great enough responsibilities to anger Rome, which authoritatively put an end to the experiment in 1954. The vigor of militancy does not mean that it is practiced without difficulty. Family life suffers. Repression occasionally strikes a blow. Discouragement looms, given the apathy of many workmates. Disappointment follows as well.

Among the political blows that shook the militants, the repression in Hungary in 1956 must be cited in particular[2] as well as the founding of the Fifth Republic in 1958. The years of strong economic growth deeply modified the labor world and the world in general. Mass consumption took hold and, with it, to use sociologist Raymond Aron's expression, so did "quarrelsome satisfaction." At the same time, unionism became to some extent institutionalized. The May 1968 movement brought with it a critique of traditional militancy and its share of dogmatism, desire for power, and renewal of union engagement.

Central to CGT-style unionism, the figure of the activist overshadows that of the union member; at the same time, it guarantees the organization's foothold on the turf of industrial life. Professional and social security elections provide a means of verifying the audience enjoyed by union organization. The elections for social security (1947, 1950, 1955, 1962) were nationwide. On a more routine basis, local elections for worker delegates, works councils, and, in the civil service, joint administrative commissions help to measure representativity. In 1968, in fact, the Labor Ministry began publishing the overall results of works council elections, to be used as a measure of the unions' general audience. The number of union members thus became secondary, if not in terms of concerns, at least in terms of assessing union strength.

Belated and Usually Mediated Services

When he created the *Mutualité Impériale,* Napoleon III put relief activities out of the French union movement's reach. The revolutionary syndicalist CGT harshly denounced the 1910 law on worker and peasant retirements, labeling it "a law for the dead." Such reservations faded in the interwar reformist CGT. Civil servants attempted to build up a broader-based unionism, in particular by creating a central purchasing facility. The printing sector pursued a tradition of mutual aid that made it exceptional. The CGTU examined the question of services in 1927, but the debate was virtually closed shortly thereafter.

Apart from some highly specific sectors, the trade union movement scarcely offers any collective advantages to its members. Its pluralism is a major obstacle to establishing a solid mutual aid network. Moreover, in the absence of union services, it has been the advocate of other forms of compensation. The social security system set up in France in 1945 is the result of a dual effort by the government in the person of Pierre Laroque and by CGT leader Ambroise Croizat. Social security, from its origins until the edicts of 1967, was managed solely by representatives of the insured, mainly union members. It is perceived as an achievement that belongs to the wage earners and is managed by the unions.

The second service—providing institution with which the unions have strong ties, although they are not synonymous, are the works councils. To simplify reality somewhat, works councils can be said to have two functions: consultants in economic matters and organizers of social activities. This second attribution receives an allocation of approximately 1 percent of the payroll,[3] thus allowing works councils to arrange a variety of activities, sports, cultural outings, and trips. From various amenities to special discounts, the facilities offered by works councils indirectly legitimize the unions, which themselves draw benefit in terms of men and means from these collective resources.[4]

ENHANCING STRIKE ACTION

The caricature is a familiar one. CGT activists are maximalists, refuse compromise, have great contempt for negotiations, and could not care less about the outcome. They seek out dispute for the sake of it and believe only in open conflict. General Charles de Gaulle was not the only one to denounce this nihilism, "this spirit that says no to everything." It should be pointed out that these criticisms usually are accompanied by stigmatization of the CGT's defense of social attainments, a defense that proves that CGT unionism shows no lack of interest in the outcome of its action. Certain CGT activists are not untainted by overextremism. In the sectarian phases at the beginning of the Cold War, during the quarrel over the establishment of economic planning and the "pauperization" debate (1953–1955), for instance, the union certainly took a hard-line attitude. The conviction that "action pays off" did not vanish, and the CGT has never neglected to underline retreats imposed and battles won. At times to the detriment of following through with issues, researching cases, and routine fieldwork, the emphasis is laid on the strength of mass movements.

Following the June 1936 conflicts, the working class won paid holidays, the 40-hour work week, and worker delegates. The insurrectional strike of 1944 paved the way to implementing the CNR's (National Committee of the Resistance) program, which led to the creation of works councils and of the social security system, nationalizations, and the statute establishing rights for civil servants. The battle of 1953 enabled unions to save the public sector's specific retirement plan. Miners obtained a substantial revaluation of their wages. The movement of May-June 1968 brought with it a harvest of satisfactions, particularly the creation of in-house union sections.[5]

The close connection between labor movements, with the CGT in the forefront, and general strikes does not exclude a possible breach between the rank-and-file and the organization's leadership. Dissension could be seen in 1936, in 1953, and even more so in 1968. Managing spontaneity is a delicate skill, and a superficial view of social movements leads one to be surprised at what are inevitable tensions. However, here we are attempting to grasp the meaning behind mobilizations. The mixed outcome of May 1968 has to do partly with the opposition between the demands of the state that fueled CGT activists and the libertarian culture of the youth movement at the time.[6]

TRADE UNION INVOLVEMENT
IN THE POLITICAL SPHERE

The "old" CGT carefully steered clear from the influence of workers' parties for several reasons: out of a concern for unity given their numbers prior to 1905; because of their disagreement with Jules Guèsdes's ideas; and because their general strike strategy enabled them to forgo partisan support. The outlook changed radically with the end of World War I. Reformists already had drawn closer to the SFIO (Socialists) in 1912, and they set up a joint action committee with the Socialist Party in 1914. While keeping his distance from Léon Blum's Socialist organization, in 1927 Léon Jouhaux declared, "I am a socialist in thought and spirit, but a party socialist I am not."[7] The CGT reformists later admitted that the October 1917 Revolution shattered their political solidarity, in the broad sense of the term, with the SFIO. Likewise, many revolutionary syndicalists turned to the Parti Communiste Français (PCF), and although the Bolshevization and the subordination of the union to the party that it implied prompted some resistance, the new rationale took hold on the CGTU.

SFIO-PCF Relations and Their
Repercussions on Union Activities

The CGT was reunified twice, in 1936 and in 1943. In both cases, union reconciliation was preceded and promoted by an agreement between the two main left-wing forces. The Popular Front, a response to the Depression and the fascist peril, created a context that the reformists were incapable of opposing. The dissidents of the CGTU—to abolish any reason for a split, what occurred in the party realm was organically imposed on the union framework—accepted the CGT's plan; affiliation with the FSI (the anti-Communist International Federation of Trade Unions), the proscription against holding multiple offices, and the maintenance of proportional representation as well as the statutes, generally speaking. The foreword to the statutes adopted at the Congress of Toulouse in May 1936 proclaimed that the union "reserves the right to respond affirmatively or negatively to appeals made by other groups to join in a given action. It also reserves the right to take the initiative in these temporary associations, feeling that neutrality with respect to political parties in no way implies indifference to dangers that threaten public liberties such as the reforms in force or to be gained." The text indicates a departure from the Amiens Charter, despite a previous assertion of union independence and the principle of trade union unity inscribed in the political entente of the Popular Front.

The April 17, 1943, reunification, decided by accords negotiated in Le Perreux, was facilitated by the ties established between the PCF and Free France in November 1942. The Socialist Party, dissipated after the armistice, belatedly put itself back together in June 1943. The understanding between the PCF and the SFIO was strengthened in 1944 when a committee was set up to explore paths of organic unity. Socialist resisters opted in favor of de Gaulle's leadership; as long as the Communists agreed to work with the general, the two left-wing parties maintained close ties, thus giving an impetus to discussions between the Jouhaux faction and the Frachon faction.

Cooperation between the PCF and the SFIO fostered two reunifications. Conversely, the deterioration of SFIO-PCF relations resulted in splits. What happened in 1921 with the breakup into the CGT and the CGTU recurred in 1939 when the German-Soviet pact was signed. The exclusion of Communists from the CGT struck the final blow to collapse the Popular Front, prompted by disagreements on economic and foreign policy. Within the CGT, solidification of the former Unitarians' positions worried the ex-Unitarians. The Hitler-Stalin accord caught the Communists in a snare. This event alone was not the cause of the break between Socialists and Communists. The feud went back much further. It basically lay in the Communists' accusation of Socialist moderatism and the Socialists' reproach against the Communists' Leninist-style Blanquism. The party quarrel led to a trade union split.

The demonstration is clearer still with regard to the 1947 break. The discord between the two workers' parties resurfaced as early as October 1945, when the first legislative elections since the fall of the Third Republic were held, putting the PCF in the lead with 26 percent of the vote. It reached its height in May 1947 when Paul Ramadier revoked the mandate of Communist ministers. The November-December strike pitted the PCF against the socialist government incarnated by Interior Minister Jules Moch; at the CGT, the conflict between Léon Jouhaux's friends and Benoît Frachon's comrades, already visible at the 1946 congress, worsened during the November-December 1947 social crisis, and the Force Ouvrière (FO) picked up and left the CGT.

The 1947–1948 break did not, moreover, simply divide the organizations into two equal parts along the Communist/non-Communist dichotomy. To preserve their unity, teachers went for autonomy. The printing sector, although dominantly reformist, preferred to remain with the Communists. Civil servant unions with a Socialist bent made the same choice. To avoid a split, the Groupement Nationale des Cadres CGT (GNC) at Electricité de France (EDF) decided, with the PCF's benediction, not to condemn the Marshall Plan.[8]

The theme of trade union unity over the period from 1936 to 1968 mainly refers to the entente between leftist forces and, in the trade union sphere, between the two branches that grew out of the old CGT. The CFTC came into play only periodically; for example, in 1944, in the common call for the insurrectional strike augmented by a proposition of organic unity to which CFTC leaders Gaston Tessier and Paul Vignaud were opposed. The creation of the CFDT (the left-reform majority that broke with the CFTC in 1964) weakened the strategy of dialogue advocated (and constantly rejected) with the FO. On January 10, 1966, a CGT-CFDT accord was reached, the repercussions of which the CGT may not have recognized entirely. The Christian left wing of the CFDT, which was predominantly "new left" but did not identify with it, was the voice of social classes that felt somewhat remote from the secular Left; in any event, their values and practices differed.

A DUAL BASE: PUBLIC AND PRIVATE

In its early stages, the CGT united blue-collar and white-collar workers. Civil servants, first organized into associations and sanctioned if they transgressed the prohibition on using the 1884 law legalizing union organization, joined the reformist CGT in large numbers during the interwar period; they joined the CGTU to a far lesser degree.

The June 1936 movement affected industry and commerce. Léon Jouhaux saw to it that the banks, and mainly the Bank of France, did not get involved, so as to avoid any monetary or financial panic. Civil servants did not mobilize, nor did the railway workers.

The outlook changed after the Liberation with the building of a larger public sector and the enactment of a law regarding the status of the civil service, which recognized the right of state employees to form unions (except for prefects and the military) and to strike (except for the police and prison wardens). Henceforth CGT unionism stood on two equally solid pillars. With its capacity to jam the economy, the public sector occupied a strategic position in three industries: coal (the role of which was essential in the country's reconstruction and growth phase before facing competition from oil and nuclear power), transportation and postal services, and electricity. The SNCF (the nationalized railways), the Charbonnages de France (the nationalized coal industry), the EDF (the national electric company), and the PTT (post, telephone, and telegraph) were heavily involved in, if not at the heart of, all the major conflicts after 1936. The May-June 1968 movement undeniably warrants being called a general strike because the public and private sectors expressed their demands in unison through joint action.

The union movement did not attack the state simply in its capacity as the largest employer in the country, it contested its regulatory action on the entire economy. This observation leads to an acknowledgment that the confederation and its departmental structures indeed played a major role in political life. In a framework of real federalism tempered nonetheless by proportional representation, the CGT held much more power than its foreign counterparts, the DGB (the German national confederation) and the TUC (the British Trade Union Council). This interprofessional organization in fact counted three levels of action: problems common to the private sector (such as the SMIC—the minimum wage), problems relating to the entire civil service and public sector (such as retirement or the right to strike), and questions affecting all wage and salary earners (taxation). The far-reaching role of the confederation and its departmental units fostered a larger audience of workers liable to respond to calls for mobilization made necessary by a low number of card-carrying union members.

A Strategy for Political Power

What was accomplished in 1936 provided the Communists with a strategic model. The Resistance was a broader reality that was interpreted as a circumstantial factor. The PCF was part of the left spectrum, and in 1956, with the Republican Front, it hoped to rebuild an alliance similar to the Popular Front. The CGT naturally adhered to this viewpoint. Under the Fifth Republic, the bipolarization imposed by universal direct suffrage in the presidential election introduced into the constitution by the 1962 referendum stimulated a rapprochement between the SFIO and the PCF. In 1963 the CGT supported the idea of a common program. During the May 1968 events it stepped in so that the workers' parties could reach an agreement on the economic objectives that it considered fair and effective. Under pressure from the masses, the right granted social benefits, but was incapable of conducting an economic policy in favor of wage and salary earners; the CGT felt it advisable to work toward securing political power by creating a leftist front that was resolutely devoted to social progress.[9]

CONCLUSION

This analysis of how the CGT changed between 1936 and 1968, being both produced by and a producer of crucial events, should help readers understand the great crisis in trade unionism that appeared in 1976. The deterioration of the shape the CGT had established for itself affected its main structural elements: The image of the militant was eroded, difficulties developed within works councils and social security, the number of strikes was reduced, the PCF was weakened, the Parti Socialiste suffered a loss of identity that shook its dual foundation, and the left failed in the test of political power. The CGT, after having denied that its existence was in jeopardy, in 1991 set out to redefine itself. Its behavior in the events of autumn 1995 illustrate both a renewal in its practices and the persistence of old reflexes to such an extent that it is not yet possible to diagnose the emergence of a new union form.

NOTES

1. The thrust of 1918 to 1920 must not be forgotten. See René Mouriaux, "La Syndicalisation en France," *Historiens et Géographes,* no. 350 (October 1995): 363–376.
2. The Khrushchev report to the Soviet party congress in 1956 also shook the foundations of their Communist faith, of course.
3. The EDF-GDF's (Electric and Gas Company) own organization has a budget of 1 percent of the turnover, an exceptionally favorable situation that the CGT can rightly pride itself on.
4. The "Tourisme et Travail" organization is an important part of the union-worker committee interface. It went into a crisis in the second half of the 1970s.
5. The 1947 strikes escaped the theme of widespread action. Intrinsically linked to the Force Ouvrière split, they are, moreover, mainly analyzed from this perspective.
6. Danielle Tartakowsky "Les Evénements de Mai," in Claude Williard, *La France Ouvrière,* vol. 2, *De 1968 à nos jours* (Paris, Editions de l'Atalier, 1995), pp. 45–46.
7. Cited in Bernard Georges, Denise Tintant, and Marie-Anne Renaud, *Léon Jouhaux dans le Mouvement Syndical Français* (Paris: PUF, 1979), p. 29.
8. André Harris and Alain de Sedouy, *Voyage à l'Intérieur du PCF* (Paris: Seuil, 1974), p. 440.
9. George Ross, *Workers and Communists in France: From Popular Front to Eurocommunism* (Berkeley: University of California Press, 1982), p. 357.

CHAPTER THREE

Reconceptualizing the Relationship between Unions and Politics in France

Anthony Daley

Political involvement has been a contentious issue for trade unions in virtually all countries. Should unions attempt—either directly or through political parties—to influence public policy, or should they focus energies more narrowly on job concerns? While there can be an overlap between these "political" and "labor market" approaches, the debate involves core issues: organizational beliefs, the accurate and effective representation of member interests, and the allocation of limited resources.

Industrial relations in France have been shaped by the relations of trade unions to both political parties and the state. In the case of the former, the close nexus to the Communist Party (PCF) and the Socialist Party (PS) has provided many of the strategies as well as the identities of union organizations. French industrial relations also have been structured by public policy. As George Ross writes, "If there has been a 'web of rules' about industrial relations in France, then it has been predominantly spun by the state."[1] With several competing unions, these two forms of interaction have spawned a third form of politics—the unions' relations with each other.

This chapter examines the political trajectory of French labor since 1980. It suggests that weak French unions historically have had very strong incentives to seek recourse to the state and that such action discouraged the development of stronger organizations. By the mid-1990s, however, labor's dependence on the state had been challenged by forces external to the labor movement. Partisan allies have either become less pro-labor (in the case of the PS), or they have collapsed in electoral support (in the case of the PCF).

Likewise, governments of both center-left and center-right have introduced considerable labor market flexibility, thereby undermining some of the market pillars of French unionism. The state has been less willing to guarantee social peace and more inclined to force unions and companies to deal with each other directly. With a reinvigorated business world, organizationally weak unions have found themselves at a severe disadvantage. As a result, French unions have been forced to reassess their political strategies.

Redefining political strategies, however, has been taking place within the context of organizational depletion. After the early 1980s, the percentage of French employees belonging to unions declined to the lowest rate among rich countries—under 9 percent; as divisions in the major organizations created new ones, these few members belonged to more unions than ever before. While charismatic unions had never encouraged a large membership base, the decrease in members began to impair union ability to lead mobilizations, staff local sections, and bargain with employers. With less market muscle, French unions are even more attracted to state-led solutions to problems with employers. Thus any plan to rejuvenate French labor inevitably touched on tensions between political and labor market strategies.

Yet as French union organizations became anemic, they chose to maintain identities by perpetuating tensions with other unions. While partisanship has diminished in the 1990s, unions have redefined politics to increase the strategic importance of the French state and their relations to each other. Ironically, while anticommunism has become less compelling after the Cold War, French unions have become increasingly politicized.

THE POLITICAL TRADITION OF
FRENCH INDUSTRIAL RELATIONS

Observers have long noted that French unions were keenly political in both organization and practice. Georges Lefranc, a French union historian, thought that unions would survive only to the extent that they could overcome demagoguery and verbosity.[2] Val Lorwin, in his ground-breaking book on the post-war French labor movement, complained of the political subservience of the Confédération Générale du Travail (CGT) to the PCF.[3] Jean-Daniel Reynaud, the great French labor historian, found that party cleavages exacerbated destructive splits within the labor movement.[4] According to George Ross, French unions "have regularly sought state intervention in terms of regulation and legislation as a substitute for labor market victories which they have been unable to win on their own—a search that has contributed powerfully to the politicization of industrial conflict in France."[5] Common to these four authors is an observation about the balance in French union behavior between political and labor market approaches as well as an argument that the unions should bolster the latter at the expense of the former.

Partisanship has constituted the most visible expression of politics in the French labor movement, and it has been the most criticized by practitioners and observers. For a variety of reasons, working-class radicalism was stronger in France than in most northern European countries, adherence to the Third International dominated left politics, thereby influencing party development, and the Communists have been particularly strident in their critiques of French capitalism and French politics. The PCF became a lightning rod for the Left after 1920—attracting charges of disloyalty, illegitimacy, and sectarianism. In turn, the PCF's attempts to dominate the labor movement divided union loyalties.[6]

The ideological divisions among French unions have been exacerbated by the form of workplace representation. Elections every two years for works councils and annually for plant delegates measured the balance of union forces on a regular basis.[7] While electioneering tends to accentuate differences, the unions' monopoly on the presentation of candidates ensures that they receive votes regardless of their ability to sign up new members. (In the extreme, a union could win elections without any members in a given plant.) These divisions also had been intensified by French labor law, which allowed any union to sign on behalf of the bargaining unit, thereby making the tangible results of union membership less visible and deepening the importance of electoral competition to measure union strength.

Competition among both left parties and the unions further complicated partisan attachments. Since 1920 the PCF and the Socialists (both the SFIO and PS) have competed for shares of the working-class electorate. The self-defined Left was not alone in attempting to woo union members. Christian Democrats—organized in the Mouvement Républicain Populaire—sought to attract the loyalties of the Confédération Française des Travailleurs Chrétiens (CFTC) while Gaullists courted autonomous unions. Nonetheless, after 1945 union members favored the Communists disproportionately and otherwise spread their vote among other parties of the Left.

Until the 1970s the CGT dominated the labor movement, and it enjoyed an intimate relationship with the largest party on the Left, the PCF.[8] The CGT-PCF linkage was cemented organizationally by joint membership especially at the leadership level and culturally by the overt class conflict that characterized the French industrial landscape. In contrast, the relations between the Confédération Française Démocratique du Travail (CFDT), and Force Ouvrière (FO) on the one hand and the Socialists on the other were more informal and ambiguous. The CFDT had an ideological partiality for one faction of the PS, the progressive Catholic *courant* that joined from the Unified Socialist Party (PSU). The FO's fierce anticommunism (binding together its internal ideological mosaic) made it susceptible to loose affinity with the broad centrism of the SFIO, although its secretary-general, André Bergeron, managed warm relations with the governments of Valéry Giscard d'Estaing in the 1970s. Unlike the CGT, the CFDT and the FO forbade joint leadership positions in both union and party.[9]

For 25 years after World War II, union-party relations were used primarily to mobilize electorates and did not enjoy the give-and-take of social democratic counterparts in northern Europe. The strongest linkage was to the party least likely to govern. The more politically feasible linkages were unstable, affecting only a small fraction of the workforce, and did not provide a viable basis for a politywide system of political exchange.

French unions had a practical reason for focusing on the state. The capacity and willingness of governments to intervene in both industrial relations and industrial development had convinced labor that the state had the tools to determine the course of social and economic change.[10] Labor law determines who can bargain and over what issues, and it spells out in excruciating detail the legal relationship between employer and employee. Public policy sets the minimum standards for paid vacations, sick pay, working time, retirement pay-issues that frequently were the grist of collective bargaining in other countries. A network of labor inspectors developed the capacity to intervene in industrial disputes even to the point of prohibiting layoffs. Employment and training initiatives developed first in Parisian ministries. Finally, the public sector often had been the laboratory for innovations in industrial relations. (Witness the extent to which Renault set precedents for collective bargaining.) Unions looked to the state to counter the authoritarian reflex of employers.

The French state was even more influential in its capacity to direct investment. Until the 1980s the Ministry of Finance held the reins of credit allocation via control over the banking sector, price setting in securities markets, and foreign exchange controls. It made loans at below-market interest rates for investment projects it favored. It administered price controls, and through its policy of exceptions to those controls, it could influence company behavior. Finally, the ministry collected corporate income, value-added, and payroll taxes, and it could grant relief for favored firms. Political support for the interventionist state was constructed through the indicative planning process.[11]

Attempts by the unions to influence policy directly usually involved strike actions or threats of disruption, thereby perpetuating a long tradition in French politics of direct action against the state.[12] Political elites were susceptible. Politicians and civil servants shared a basic distrust of employers, believing them to be averse to risk-taking and unwilling to share power outside the family. Such incompetent capitalists needed to be pushed and prodded into modernity, which meant some accommodation between labor and capital. Thus the state pressured companies on labor issues.

For the unions, however, this type of power was hardly optimal. They could influence those industrial and labor market policies that affected the workforce directly—jobs and wages—but they had no influence over the broader investment strategies that ultimately determined labor market outcomes. A limited power to veto could not speak to the utopianism of radical ideologies. Threats to social stability required mobilization, which was not always possible for organizationally thin unions that frequently found themselves followers rather than leaders of popular protest. Most important, compromise with capital and the state left labor's broader goals unfulfilled.

The exclusion of labor and the Left from industrial governance after the 1940s had convinced the CGT and CFDT that economic growth could and would take place without their input unless they muted their own rivalries. An agreement between the CGT and CFDT in 1966 promised "unity in action," an attempt at the confederal level to coordinate action for the two largest unions and to end the destructive interunion competition. While there could be positive elements to trade union "pluralism," as it has come to be known, it was widely perceived to weaken the negotiating position of labor.[13]

Until the 1970s the CGT maintained its dominance in industrial relations despite serious splits, especially over the role of Communists within the confederation.[14] Smaller unions chafed at the dominance of their larger rival, but they necessarily acted in reaction. The alliance of the two largest unions gave the CGT potentially more leverage in bargaining and the CFDT more legitimacy. More important, it demonstrated that diverse interests could be subordinated to a common goal.

Partisan attachment, state focus, and partial union unity converged in the 1970s. The CGT and CFDT came to argue that political control was necessary to bring the full weight of the state to bear on economic decision making. The Common Program of Government signed in 1972 by the PCF, the PS, and the left Radicals promised to rebalance industrial relations and industrial development more in favor of labor: Sympathetic political elites would ensure access to policy making, and the promised reforms would wield the enormous resources of the French state in the interests of working people. Both the CGT and CFDT were strong supporters of the Common Program, while the FO based its opposition in large part on its distaste for the PCF.

However, the latter (along with other small unions) had too small a labor market presence to counterbalance the CGT-CFDT alliance. With unions speaking in the name of the vast majority of the workforce, trade union unity became an essential element in the viability of the Common Program reforms.

For over 30 years after World War II, French trade unions developed both a reliance on the state and a radical transformative discourse. This made sense given the policy tools of the French state, the ideological affinity to parties of the Left, and the unwillingness of employers to share power. Yet this political focus came at the expense of organizational development, as French unions never focused on membership or developed the services that linked members to union organizations. It assumed that left parties and unions would continue to share the same menu of ideas about French capitalism. It presumed a minimal level of membership to trigger local mobilization and force state involvement. Finally, it was premised on a belief that the state would continue to exert its influence over employers and attempt to "modernize" labor relations in ways that unions found at least tolerable if not entirely to their liking. These assumptions became problematic after 1980.

THE WEAKENING OF A POLITICAL TRADITION

Two pillars of labor's political strategy crumbled in the 1980s. The partisan linkage became less compelling for mobilization or governance, as party allies either collapsed in political support (the PCF) or distanced themselves from the unions (the PS). Likewise, under the presidency of the Socialist François Mitterrand, the French state converted from a sometimes passive, sometimes active ally of the unions to an adherent of market orthodoxy in economic policy. As a result, the assumptions supporting union political strategies were undermined.

The loosening of partisan linkages first began in the late 1970s, however, with the impetus coming from the unions. For factions within the CGT and the CFDT, the unexpected defeat of the Left in the 1978 elections for the National Assembly marked the failure of a partisan strategy. Political alignment failed to ensure a union-friendly government, and it had weakened organizations. With expanding unemployment, local unions spent more time on political campaigns than on creative ways to confront these labor market issues, and central offices censured local militancy to demonstrate responsibility to the broader electorate. Both confederations began to rethink the balance between political and labor market strategies. Both began to downplay political allegiances and experiment with bargaining strategies based on employment-generating investment trade-offs. The two unions set their staff and friendly economists to work developing "propositions"—medium-term plans to save employment by restoring competitiveness—for beleaguered companies.

"Proposition-force" unionism received considerable fanfare in 1978 and 1979. Its proponents claimed that it would avoid the demobilizing effects of heavy reliance on either party or state and would break with the "oppositionalism" that characterized French working-class culture. The CGT, and to a lesser extent the CFDT, had tended to stake out extreme positions designed as much for public consumption as for negotiating with management. In contrast, both unions sought to reorient industrial development and to extend the boundaries of collective bargaining from wages to employment.[15] The proposals for the industries in trouble—including steel, shipbuilding, and heavy engineering—were less original than the experiments in bargaining, the distancing of union from party, and the diminished reliance on the state.

After initial experimentation, the two confederations rejected propositionalism. Strategic change could not withstand other organizational forces. In the CGT, those wedded to confrontational strategies succeeded in marginalizing reformers, and the linkage to hard-liners in the PCF seemed to be critical. Meanwhile, partisans of a "collective bargaining" approach triumphed in the CFDT with the argument that unions should bargain only over wages and benefits and not attempt to plan the economy. From a similar starting point, the unions moved in different and conflicting directions, undoing in the process the interunion truce that had reigned for over a decade.[16]

The rejection of propositionalism combined with the victory of the Left in 1981 to create contradictory effects on partisanship and interunion relations, while strengthening the state focus of the unions. In the run-up to the presidential elections of 1981, the PCF's stridency had a polarizing effect for CGT-CFDT relations. Both unions had reverted to easy partnerships—the CGT endorsed the PCF, and the CFDT provided informal support for the PS. (Given its anticommunism, the FO could not be labeled nonpartisan throughout this period.) By 1980, with the Soviet intervention in Afghanistan and increasing East-West hostility being important contributors, the three French confederations were more separated by partisanship than they had been in a generation.

When the Left won the presidential and legislative elections in 1981, French unions could hardly present a united front to coordinate an agenda for what came to be the greatest opportunity for labor since 1945. The victory initially muted overt partisanship. With the Socialist landslide in the subsequent legislative elections and the inclusion of the Communists in junior positions in government, overt partisanship by the unions was overshadowed by the surprise at the outcome and the possibilities offered. The CGT and the CFDT sensed a friendlier environment in which to push their programs. Some union officials joined the government.

Likewise, the animosity between the CGT and the CFDT was put on hold after the electoral victory. Between 1981 and 1984 they worked hard to suppress public displays of rivalry, trying instead to influence (separately) the left reforms. The absence of overt conflict between the CGT and the CFDT signaled only that serious disagreements had been shelved, not resolved. Meanwhile, the FO lambasted the other two unions for supporting a government that included Communists.

In contrast, the rejection of propositionalism and the Left pledge to change society reinforced the belief within all three unions—for the FO shared the statism of its two major rivals—that the state could and should act as the impetus for social change. The CGT's move to oppositionalism perpetuated an industrial relations game premised on the state intervening to quell industrial unrest. The focus on collective bargaining—new for the CFDT and constant for the FO—was premised on the state's willingness to continue using its powerful policy tools to maintain employment. The electoral program of the PS and the policy initiatives of the first two years of government—demand stimulation, greater control of the public sector, and increased workplace rights—dovetailed with union demands for more purchasing power and greater public control of the economy.

Thus the window of opportunity for organizational change within French unions closed before the Left assumed power and remained shut during the activist period of left governance. While it remained open for little more than a year and can almost be labeled an aberration, that window constituted the best opportunity to adapt union strategies to the momentous changes taking place in the political system—the development of post-materialism as a rival political framework to class and religious cleavages and the search by labor-friendly political parties for new constituencies. French unions were crippled as they confronted economic change: the shift away from mass production, the development of information technologies, new forms of work organization, and the growth of a less blue-collar and male workforce.

The unions boxed themselves into a strategic corner. They neither developed a strategy of organizational renewal that might have permitted them to confront deunionization earlier nor translated the initial friendliness of the left government into a more permanent linkage. Political logics remained unchanged. Tensions between the two left parties simmered below the surface, as it was clear that the Socialists wanted to poach the Communist vote, the Communists were making only tactical concessions to share power, and no long-term doctrinal compromises had taken place. For cynics, the PCF was brought into government only to maintain social peace.

The left government received mixed reviews from labor even in the initial period. The CGT supported the Keynesian stimulation, although it pushed for more, and it applauded the increase in the public sector, but it was cautious about the industrial relations reforms (Auroux laws) and it had suspicions about the goals of Socialist ministries. Meanwhile, the CFDT helped write the Auroux laws, but it only tepidly supported macroeconomic policy, fearful of the inflationary effects. The FO attacked the nonunion aspects of the Auroux laws, but it welcomed the injection of purchasing power. Differences always arise between unions and a leftist government in power. Without strong organizational linkages, however, parties and unions cooperated with skepticism.

Not surprisingly, the years between 1979 and 1984 had a devastating impact on union organization. While membership data in French unions is notoriously unreliable, most accounts find net decreases to have started by 1977 in the CGT and the CFDT.[17] (Similar tendencies affected the FO after the mid-1980s.) The reasons for quitting were varied, but an uneasiness about interunion relations or perspectives on government policy played important roles. Conflicts separating union organizations were deemed petty, while the CFDT was perceived to be too soft on Socialist austerity and the CGT too knee-jerk on government policy.[18] During these years of rapid change, French unions acted as if the world had not changed. The opportunity to alter political strategies on their own terms was lost, and union organizations suffered as a result.

The U-turn in economic policy caused the greatest damage to a political strategy. The decision by the Socialists in 1983 to remain in the European Monetary System (EMS), the subsequent conditions imposed on the French economy to maintain the franc within it, and the shift from expansion to contractionary policy diminished state support for organized labor. Governments of both the Left (1984–1986 and 1988–1993) and the Right (1986–1988, 1993–1995, 1995 to the present) have altered the rescue role of the French state. Although there have been few adherents to American-style market openness, the concern to "modernize" labor relations and compensate for the social failings of French business has been replaced with a desire to promote new technologies, boost profits, and increase market share.

While the tolerance of high rates of unemployment hardly differentiated France from other European countries, the particular French approach to economic and labor policy was destructive to the unions. First, industrial policy abandoned wholesale subsidies. The Creusot-Loire bankruptcy of 1984 signaled that the French state would stop propping up lame ducks. This meant massive job loss in traditional industries—coal, steel, shipbuilding. Not surprisingly, these were bastions for the unions, and the bloodletting dramatically accelerated deunionization. Second, the policy of competitive disinflation—maintaining the value of the franc by aggressively reducing cost pressures to levels below those of trading partners—guaranteed that firms would look to reduce labor costs. This macroeconomic policy brought higher than normal interest rates to keep currency speculators interested in the franc, consequently depressing demand. Labor cost reductions were facilitated by the disindexation of public-sector wages in 1983 and the dampening of subsequent increases, an incomes policy copied in the private sector. Not surprisingly, wages as a percentage of national income fell after 1984. Third, governments after 1984 aggressively created workplace flexibility. Employment and training programs brought about the temporary hiring of hundreds of thousands of young people at low and frequently subsidized wages. The Auroux laws permitted derogations from agreements made at the sectoral or national levels.[19] The Socialist labor reforms strengthened employee participation outside the unions.

The U-turn transformed a nominal truce into a war between the two left parties. The PCF quit the government in 1984 and went into active opposition. Ensconced in ideological and strategic rigidity, the party opposed the Socialists to the point of its own unpopularity. To save its identity, it promoted strident policy perspectives and stifled internal dissent, almost choosing decline over adaptation.[20] Likewise, the unions tightened their partisan reflexes. The CGT took the policy shift as a betrayal and attempted to mobilize against consequent layoffs. Meanwhile, the CFDT praised the cautious policy making—much to the consternation of a membership that was being squeezed—and the FO applauded the exit of the Communists.

No new union-party bargains were created in the aftermath of the U-turn. While the Socialists sought to rely on friendly relations with the CFDT, they found an organization beset by inner turmoil. The leadership was attracted by the theme of "modernization," but the membership was affected by the increasing labor market precariousness. And the FO was no longer waiting in the wings to act as a responsible bargaining partner, as it too began to suffer the effects of deunionization. A decline in purchasing power and higher unemployment created restlessness within the confederation while the decline of communism encouraged FO leaders to pursue a more militant posture. Still, no other parties of the Left were waiting to replace the PS for the CFDT and the FO. Meanwhile, the CGT maintained strong support for the PCF right after the U-turn, but the latter was becoming politically less relevant.

The union hardest hit by this turbulence in political strategy—abortive intraunion reform, state focus, and the withdrawal of state support—was the CGT. Its membership was concentrated in industries that shed workers after the U-turn. And it tended to organize male production workers whose work was being radically transformed. Between 1977 and 1992 the CGT metalworkers federation, for instance, lost 80 percent of its members. By the late 1980s the CGT had shrunk to such a level that the three confederations could claim roughly equal memberships (500,000 each), and the CFDT scored roughly the same as the CGT (25 percent) in works council elections.

The decline of the CGT altered the French industrial and political landscape. The CGT had long offered the most credible opposition to employer unilateralism. In its absence, it was much easier for employers and the state to weaken labor market regulation and thereby make the renewal of union organizations all the more difficult. Likewise, the CGT's fall from dominance within the labor movement encouraged other unions to gain incremental advantages in works council governance and collective bargaining. This advanced game of competitive unionism alienated actual and potential members further.

French unions were grossly unprepared for the economic, social, and political changes of the 1980s. What began in the late 1970s as a union-inspired attempt to reflect critically on partisanship and state dependence developed into a fragmentation of the political sphere and an uncritical acceptance of the interventionist state. The weakening of individual labor organizations and the bickering among them diminished the capacity of all unions to confront business and the state. Industrial relations were changing rapidly, and union strategic creativity was at its lowest.

UNION ATTEMPTS TO RECONSTRUCT POLITICS

Attempts to reforge coherent political strategies have proven remarkably difficult for French unions. While it has been easier to lessen partisanship, given that the parties have become less reliable partners, the collapse of union organizations made the state focus even sharper. This coincided with state attempts to redirect, and in some cases reduce, its own influence. Meanwhile, interunion competition has heated up in the last decade even as the Communist lightening rod has fallen. The deepening of existing cleavages is taking place at the same time as employers are bent on aggressively reconfiguring industrial relations.

Developing coherent strategies has been complicated because the unions have long denied their crisis. Only in the late 1980s—fully a decade after problems were visible—did any of the three confederations publicly admit their organizational problems. A key example has been the controversy over membership. Because of the method of dues collection between union militants and members, only local organizations know real membership figures. And there are incentives to exaggerate the numbers. Local sections may want to retain funds. Industrial federations may want more power in confederal voting. Confederations look for bragging rights in interunion rivalry. An admission of cooked data was also an admission of weakness.

Yet understanding the depth of organizational bleeding was necessary to cure the patient. The CFDT was the first confederation to publish its real membership figures in 1988, as part of an organizational assessment. For the CGT, the truth was painful, since it confirmed how far it had fallen. Nevertheless, it began releasing figures that most analysts have found credible in 1992. Ironically, the FO has lagged behind its rivals, claiming a membership equivalent to levels in the late 1970s—and over twice those of its rivals—which, given its stagnation in workplace elections and impressions from case studies, is hardly believable. Yet the FO has a delicate balance of internal forces, many of which have an interest in either not knowing or not publishing figures. The delay in confronting the organizational anemia may come to be known as the lost decade for French labor.

Even as the scale of deunionization has been belatedly recognized, however, new strategies needed to be constructed. For the labor movement as a whole, altering partisan strategies really begins with the CGT, for its relationship with the PCF has set the standard for union-party linkages. By the early 1990s there were voices of dissent within leadership circles. As lame-duck secretary-general of the CGT, Henri Krasucki gave a scathing critique of the linkages and their effects on union mobilization.[21] A few members of the confederal bureau publicly pleaded for greater union independence, which would include prohibitions on leadership roles in political parties.[22] Struggles developed between the federations of metals, health care, and construction, which preferred both the discourse of class and the alliance with the party and less partisan leaders in the confederation, the white-collar union (the General Union of Engineers, Technicians, and Supervisory Personnel—UGICT), and several departmental unions that sought more political nuance and were uncomfortable with the party. Louis Viannet was promoted to secretary-general in 1992 at least partially because of his linkages to the PCF, but he had to tread a fine line between the different partisan strategies of the confederation. Beginning with the regional elections of 1992, the CGT refrained from offering a political endorsement, although this was nuanced by the endorsement of leaders *qua* individuals. Still, union leaders bickered with their party counterparts over the latter's attempts to reassert control. Even so-called hard-liners recognized that ideological rigidity did not play well to new categories of workers who did not see themselves as Communists.

Loosening the bonds between the CGT and the PCF has been hard for two reasons. First, CGT members were more loyal to the Communists after 1981 than were members from either the CFDT or the FO to the Socialists. In the 1981 presidential elections, 57 percent of CGT sympathizers voted Communist, a figure that dropped to 51 percent in the 1993 legislative elections. The corresponding figures for the CFDT were 50 percent and 41 percent for the Socialists, while FO sympathizers voted 33 percent and 22 percent for the Socialists.[23]

Second, and this is the real stumbling block for the CGT, overlapping leadership roles tie union and party. Rightly or wrongly, this has been seen as the test for union independence. The secretary-general of the CGT has sat on the PCF's political bureau, and numerous other leaders have been on the party's central committee. Even as the union leadership has refrained from overt electoral support, it has not attempted to bar joint leadership positions. CGT leaders who are Communist insist on constitutional rights and common working-class cultures in the face of rivals and commentators with long memories. The resistance to a clean break was evident in December 1996 when Viannet and another senior CGT leader resigned from the PCF's political bureau only to be replaced by leaders from three of the largest federations—railways, health, and energy.

The other unions had less difficulty distancing themselves from the Left. The CFDT leadership opted for electoral neutrality in the 1986 legislative elections and thereafter. Two years later it dropped all references to socialism in its union program. The FO refrained from overtly supporting individual parties, using that as the crucible for its opposition to the CGT. Ironically, given its combativeness in the early 1980s, the FO warmed to Mitterrand as he began to govern from the center with both Socialist and right governments, although it limited support to policy judgments rather than electoral calls.

Diminishing partisanship has taken place partially by choice, partially by force of circumstance. It has coincided with a strengthening of other political strategies. The greater vulnerability of union organizations simultaneously has brought a greater reliance on the French state. French unions have sought to influence public policy directly, unencumbered by party mediation. Likewise, interunion rivalry has been ratcheted upward.

Union participation in the French welfare state has become critical to political strategies. Designed in 1945 via government decree and 1958 through a collective bargaining agreement, French social security is unique because it is run by representatives of French unions and employers. Because the state has covered deficits in pensions, medical insurance, and unemployment compensation—necessitated in the 1990s because employers were unwilling to pay higher payroll taxes—it has had important leverage in directing policy. Still, the administration of French social security has been the mechanism by which the confederations could influence redistributive policies and maintain visibility, both particularly desirable in an era when unions had greater difficulty extracting wage increases.

Welfare policy brought the unions into policy conflict, accentuating their political differences. Until the 1980s the FO defended its responsible leadership while the CGT pressed for higher benefits and larger employer taxes. After the early 1980s the CFDT competed with the FO over responsibility. In 1992 it wrested the presidency of the unemployment compensation system from the FO, and in 1996 it did the same for the health care system.[24]

Welfare state policy became almost a litmus test for interunion politics. The attachment of French unions to this political role was evident in fall 1995, when the government of Alain Juppé sought to transfer control from the unions and employers by shifting funding from payroll to income taxes. The CGT and the FO, which saw this as a unilateral action taken on its terrain, helped extend the strike movement in the railroads to "defend" the welfare state, while the CFDT cautioned against the strikes and approved key provisions of the package.

The unions have sought to influence other public policies as well. In the mid-1980s the CFDT was behind many of the employment and training policies—creative use of unemployment funds, bridges to early retirement, training schemes—that were used to ease workers out of heavy industry. Part of this innovation came in the course of collective bargaining, but a significant portion came from negotiations with the Ministry of Labor. The CGT and the FO have been much less interested in policy innovation here largely because they are wary of assuming responsibility for job displacement and their organizations still adhere to adversarialism. In 1993 the CFDT was willing to bargain on key aspects of the Five-Year Employment law, a multifaceted piece of legislation that sought to lower employment costs through work flexibility, while the FO and the CGT were implacable in their opposition. Although most of the measures were passed into law, the unions' support for mobilization against the subminimum wage "vocational integration contracts" for youth encouraged the government of Edouard Balladur to withdraw the project.

The unions have learned to choose their political fights in a more judicious fashion. Even in the late 1980s the CGT wasted enormous political resources fighting battles it had little chance of winning. For instance, the confederation sought to martyrize those unionists who were fired and prosecuted (later to receive a presidential pardon) for assault against other union militants and vandalism during a demonstration to protest the partial (and eventual) closure of Billancourt—once the core plant of Renault and the bastion of the CGT.[25] This focal point for joint political mobilization by both the CGT and the PCF caused considerable internal dissent, provoked resignations, alienated potential members, and retarded the distancing between party and union. In contrast, the CGT toned down its stridency over the privatization campaign announced after March 1993. While all the unions held expected positions—principled opposition from the CGT, employment-based opposition from the FO, and cautious concern from the CFDT—union officials admitted privately that all-out strategies would be suicidal and they would not mount an offensive.[26] By virtue of their organizational decline, the confederations are expressing a more realistic perspective on their own capacities.

A renewed state focus has been given greater force by the way deunionization has taken place. By the 1990s private-sector union density was under 5 percent, making the public sector the only reserve left for dynamic unionism. The new dominance of public-sector unionism has had several consequences. First, the confederations are becoming more dependent on the state for organizational expenses. They draw an increasingly high percentage of full-time staff from the public sector, where employees can continue to draw salary while working for the union, thereby lowering personnel costs. The loss of income from dues has increased the importance of the other subsidies unions receive from the state—salaries (kicked back to the unions) for membership on tripartite committees, funds for training union members, subsidies for the union press, office space donated by municipalities. Second, while a public-sector incomes policy has been in place for over a decade, industrial relations remain easier than in the private sector because the state has not tried to circumvent union organizations. There is a danger that the obstacles to union development in the private sector will become increasingly foreboding in comparison. Third, confederal strategies are becoming increasingly unlike those feasible for the larger workforce. With few exceptions, for instance, the major strikes of the last decade have been in the public sector. Fourth, the higher proportion of public-sector unionists encourages their leaders to view strategy more in terms of political negotiation than the give-and-take of collective bargaining.

Over the longer term, the public sector will shrink in France, and that bodes poorly for the unions. Municipal governments have been subcontracting services for the last 15 years. The privatizations of 1986 and 1993 returned several hundred thousand workers to the private sector. The Juppé government announced the continuation and acceleration of privatization in 1995. France is not the United States or Britain, so it is unlikely that privatized companies will try to roll back industrial relations. Rather, the effects will be more subtle. Competitive pressures will give privatized companies even less room for bargaining over wages and employment. Those employees who remain in the public sector will be seen as increasingly privileged since they will tend to be congregated in sheltered sectors.

The unions have countered with a public relations campaign that emphasizes the importance of an efficient and sovereign *service public,* which has enjoyed some resonance. The massive transport strikes in November-December 1995 were widely supported in spite of the disruption. Similar pleas in favor of public service in the gas and electric utility as well as France Télécom, however, have fallen on deaf ears. While union activity is unlikely to delay privatizations, it may be able to influence the transformation. Perhaps the largest political battle for French labor is maintaining the integrity of labor law. The unions realize that they survive only because a legal framework forces employers to recognize them and bargain, and it maintains the integrity of representative institutions—especially works councils—that can compensate for organizational inadequacies. Since the U-turn, weighing in on such judicial issues has meant protesting attempts to inject flexibility at work and thereby weaken the Labor Code. While they lost the battle to ensure that labor inspectors authorize large-scale layoffs in 1986, the unions succeeded in strengthening legal requirements for layoffs.[27] What frequently comes across as caution and conservatism, especially by the FO and the CGT, is really the manifestation of an absence of trust.[28] A deep-seated adversarialism encourages these unions to hold desperately to existing law as a bulwark against possible encroachment.

The unions do not have the clout to alter political agendas on their own. When unions have worked with social movements, they tend to receive criticism either for deviating from traditional labor market concerns or for attempting to control smaller groups. For instance, the CGT has always worked with organizations, such as the peace movement, associated with the PCF, but those alliances had more to do with party than union concerns. Likewise, for the last 20 years, the CFDT has attempted to forge national and local alliances with new social movements involving gender and environmentalism, yet the creation of this "second left" had more of a political than an industrial relations goal.[29]

The most successful alliances with social movements have taken place when the unions have assumed secondary positions. When both unions attempted to work with student groups in the 1986 mobilization against university reforms, for instance, they were partially rebuffed because the students feared control from outside and because the unions were seen as out of touch with their concerns. Yet service work with the unemployed has taken place because it has occurred at the subconfederal levels. Cooperation with social movements has succeeded only when tied to specific issues. A good example was the work with student groups to mobilize against the vocational integration contracts of the Five-Year Employment Law in March 1994.

Poverty-stricken French unions have not forsaken their time-honored political resource of threatening social disruption. The CGT and the FO (more than the CFDT) have tried to ride the crest of public discontent, although strike actions have been difficult to mount and days lost to strikes continue to decline. Public-sector strikes—rail workers in 1986 and 1995; nurses, social workers, and postal employees in 1988; civil servants in 1989; and Air

France in 1993—enjoyed some resonance and brought pay and employment issues into open debate. While the unions did not necessarily initiate such actions, and sometimes were surprised by them, they could use them opportunistically to seek influence over public policy. Thus the unions could take advantage of the snowballing mobilization in the fall of 1995 over cost-cutting in the railroads and projected reforms in the social security system to bargain directly with the Juppé government.

Still, there are many more cases of failed mobilizations than successful ones. Strike rates dropped consistently through the 1980s and early 1990s, only to shoot upward with the 1995 mobilization. Given the increasingly crusading spirit of state officials in favor of market-conforming reforms, any strike victory promised to be temporary. Witness the delay only in the reorganization plans at Air France in 1993–1994. Likewise, while strikers in the fall of 1995 succeeded in shelving plans to harmonize public-service pensions, they failed to alter changes in the general fund for medical provisioning that further diminished union control.

Political strategies have a European dimension as well. The CGT historically has laid claims to being internationalist and thus necessarily pro-European, but its vision of Europe implied protection from employment-destabilizing imports tinged with French chauvinism.[30] In sharp contrast has been the CFDT, whose Europeanism rested on the faith that labor rights could be delivered on the European level, fortified by the presence of one-time member and then-president of the European Commission, Jacques Delors. The confederation was active in drafting the Social Charter. The FO historically has focused its international energies on developing free collective bargaining. The different policy positions taken by French unions betrayed an ambivalence about national identity and the European Community/European Union.

This ambivalence came to a head in the debates leading up to the referendum on the Maastricht Treaty in September 1992. The CFDT adopted an unambiguously positive position on the referendum, arguing that competitiveness and employment would increase with a common currency and that the social clause in the treaty would strengthen European collective bargaining. The CGT's opposition was based almost exclusively in the deflationary character of the convergence conditions. While the argument conflated with that of the PCF, it was also consistent with nearly half the electorate, and the confederation consistently emphasized the concrete economic effects and not vague notions of national sovereignty. Because of the referendum's divisiveness, the FO refrained from endorsing either position. The persistence of high unemployment has encouraged a more skeptical political vision of Europe among all the unions.

The unions have Europeanized their interorganizational conflicts. Through 1996, the CGT remained excluded from the European Trade

Union Confederation (ETUC) because of vetoes from the FO and CFDT. (Indeed, the CGT is the only major European labor union not in the ETUC.) The CFDT and the FO had long claimed that membership in the Communist-dominated World Federation of Trade Unions (WFTU) was incompatible with the free collective bargaining upheld by the ETUC. The WFTU disintegrated with the breakdown of Communist regimes, and the CGT distanced itself progressively until it finally quit in December 1995. Afterward, the veto was rationalized by the joint leadership positions between the CGT and the PCF. Both the CFDT and the FO claim that the CGT will be invited to join the ETUC when it ends that practice. It will be interesting to see if Viannet's resignation satisfies that condition.

The larger story is more tragic than the weakening of European unionism, for even with the CGT, the ETUC will not suddenly revive European industrial relations. Rather, the partisan cleavages of the Cold War have hardened into organizational ones. At least two generations of French union leaders now have known only competitive unionism. These are the barriers that are most difficult to tear down.

While there have been attempts to mend relations among the unions over the last 15 years, they have not produced less animosity. Confederal leaders occasionally will meet for a photo opportunity handshake at a public event, but it will elicit more criticism than praise in the federations. The example of the CFDT's attempts to forge a new union coalition revealed these organizational rigidities. Under the leadership of Jean Kaspar after 1988, the CFDT sought to bring together the moderate unions—the CFDT, the FO, the CFTC, the teachers' union (Fédération de l'Education Nationale, FEN), and the autonomous union for supervisory personnel (Confédération Générale des Cadres, or CGC)—into a "reformist" cartel that could coordinate activity and force the CGT to become more democratic. Yet the effort backfired. The FO refused to join what it termed "social Catholicism." The FEN, which had balanced Socialists and Communists for 40 years, expelled the unions where the latter dominated. Unfortunately for the FEN, those unions then formed a competitive confederation, the Fédération Syndicale Unitaire, that outpolled the FEN in subsequent workplace elections. The result of the reformist experiment was a proliferation, not consolidation, of unions. The labor movement is now more atomistic than at any other time this century.

CONCLUSION

For the last generation, trade unions in advanced industrial countries have been confronted with increasingly unreliable partisan allies and governments that have adopted promarket policies of economic adjustment. Likewise, the depth of economic change has forced them to rethink what they do and how they do it.

This new environment has been particularly difficult for French unions. Never capable of attracting mass membership in the first place, the unions relied on the power of ideas, the charisma of local militants, the capacity to jump-start militancy, the ideological affinities of left parties, and the willingness of the state to buy social peace. After 1980, however, membership sank to unacceptable levels, the old ideas could not solve the new challenges of globalization and localism, militancy declined, the left parties collapsed or moved to the center, and the state became aggressive in supporting business.

The drama has been particularly poignant for the CGT. Historically it had the tightest partisan linkages, for its oppositionalism meshed well with the PCF's outsider status. The CGT-PCF relationship was regularly reinforced by authoritarian workplace practices. Yet while its class base was compelling, the linkage became increasingly dysfunctional by the 1980s. It concealed changes the union and the Left needed to make to adapt to a new environment, and it became the symbol for a failure to do so. The costs of partisanship have been high. In the last 25 years, the CGT has lost its overwhelming dominance of the labor movement. In the process, French industrial relations have been changed.

While the legacy of partisanship has been mostly overcome, that of state focus has not. Neither economic transformation nor the shift in public policy altered the basic labor market capabilities of the state, although privatizations shrank its size and the structure of opportunities facing French unions. The drain on union organizations and the considerable influence that the French state maintained over market decisions militated in favor of seeking greater state help.

Yet while the pre-1980 political strategy made sense, it is not clear that the current state focus is healthy for the unions. Before 1980 French unions tied their fortunes to a state that could deliver goods and to parties that shared a radical transformative bias (whose promise was to deliver even more goods). Those latter two conditions have changed, and the unions have not found a coherent replacement. The political parties in power or likely to be in power in the foreseeable future will not expand the state's capacities. The state is likely to shrink further pending the completion of the current round of privatizations and European deregulation of such markets as telecommunications and air travel. The shrinking state poses an organizational challenge since membership in all three confederations is now overwhelmingly concentrated in the public sector.

Political strategies ultimately will depend on other organizational strategies—toward memberships and electorates, organizational maintenance, and bargaining. This short chapter has not been able to examine fully such an interplay. Yet it is evident that the membership, organizational, and bargaining demands on union organizations have played a role in the reexamination of partisanship. The membership outflow can be tied directly to the partisan vitriol that separated the unions. Likewise, the legacy of partisan competition still lives on in the profoundly different organizational cultures that now separate the confederations. And the state focus was desirable given those cultures and necessary given organizational deficiencies. For the future, the unions will need to appeal to new constituencies, especially white-collar employees and youth, to strengthen their organizations and permit the type of labor market bargaining that is now frequently relegated to state policy. A trade-off among different strategies is necessary.

Institutional stickiness undoubtedly will leave the peculiarities of French industrial relations in place for a considerable period, but we can expect a gradual erosion of protection for French unions, given the shrinkage of the public sector and the competitive pressures from other members of the European Union. French unions will need to leverage their reliance on labor law to strengthen their organizational positions. There are indications (organizing successes at McDonald's, for instance) that a potential exists for this type of maneuver. The point remains, however, that organizational renewal must be a top priority.

French unions are now innovating at an unprecedented rate. For the first time, those unions that once focused on ideas are now concentrating on membership, and the membership decline has been reversed in overall terms. (Here the CFDT and the FO have been more successful than the CGT.) They are developing a reliance on their own capacities with a special focus on constructing stronger local unions. Collective bargaining is burgeoning, although there has been considerable debate about the extent to which that bargaining has been on the employers' terms. Local unions have experimented with reducing working time to confront unemployment.[31] The decline of partisanship has made a limited rapprochement possible between the CGT and the FO, although it is far from achieved, and seems to have led to an increased distance between the CFDT and the FO. The CFDT has informal understandings with the CFTC, the smaller FEN, and the CGC. Movement toward a bifurcated labor movement would constitute a considerable step forward within the French context.

Changes in union behavior have altered the identity of the French labor movement. The culture of permanent conflict that characterized idea-based unions is now competing with a culture of permanent negotiation. It is even questionable if the term "labor movement" still can be used in France. While peripheral organizations involving specific facets of working-class life (youth, gender, consumption, retirement) still exist, there is little sense of common purpose and no collective political project within confederations, let alone among them. That may be both a strength and a weakness as French unions enter the next century.

NOTES

1. George Ross, "The Perils of Politics: French Unions and the Crisis of the 1970s," in Peter Lange, George Ross, and Maurizio Vanicelli, *Unions, Change and Crisis: French and Italian Union Strategy and the Political Economy, 1945–1980* (London: George Allen & Unwin, 1982), p. 71.
2. Georges Lefranc, *Le syndicalisme en France* (Paris: PUF/Que sais-je? 1953), p. 121.
3. Val Lorwin, *The French Labor Movement* (Cambridge, MA: Harvard University Press, 1954), p. 306.
4. Jean-Daniel Reynaud, "Trade Unions and Political Parties in France: Some Recent Trends," *Industrial and Labor Relations Review* 28, no. 2 (January 1975): 218.
5. Ross, "The Perils of Politics," p. 15.
6. George Ross, *Workers and Communists in France: From Popular Front to Eurocommunism* (Berkeley: University of California Press, 1982).
7. Other elections also pitted union against union. Civil servants elect representatives to administrative commissions every three years. Between 1947 and 1962 and again in 1983, the unions presented candidates for the employee representatives to the social security system. (Given the general apathy, both unions and governments have been reluctant to call for subsequent elections.) After 1979 elections have taken place every five years for employee representatives on the bipartite arbitrators councils (*conseils des prud'hommes*). Finally, after 1984, one-third of the board members of nationalized firms have been chosen through company-wide elections.
8. In 1970 the CGT organized half of all unionized workers and tallied 46 percent of all works council votes.
9. The problems of union linkages to political parties have been treated at length by a number of different authors. See Anthony Daley, "Remembrance of Things Past: The Union-Party Linkage in France," *International Journal of Political Economy* 23, no. 4 (Winter): 53–71; René Mouriaux, *Syndicalisme et politique* (Paris: Éditions Ouvrières, 1985); Jeff Bridgford, *The Politics of French Trade Unionism: Party-Union Relations at the Time of the Union of the Left* (Leicester: Leicester University Press, 1991).
10. For the relationship between industrial and labor policies, see Anthony Daley, *Steel, State, and Labor: Mobilization and Adjustment in France* (Pittsburgh: University of Pittsburgh Press, 1996), chap. 2.
11. Peter A. Hall, *Governing the Economy: The Politics of State Intervention in Britain and France* (New York: Oxford University Press, 1986), pp. 155–163.
12. Edward Shorter and Charles Tilly, *Strikes in France, 1830–1968* (Cambridge: Cambridge University Press, 1974).

13. At the conference, "A Century of Organized Labor in France," in February 1996, former Secretary-General of the CFDT Jean Kaspar distinguished between "positive" and "negative" pluralism. The positive variant guaranteed the articulation of different perspectives within the workforce. In other research I found that competitive unionism could put employers on the defensive under certain market conditions. (See *Steel, State, and Labor,* chap. 5 and 6.) In general, however, union pluralism has negative effects for unions because it drains their energies, diverts attention away from employers, and enables the latter to divide and conquer the labor movement.

14. The FO broke off in opposition in 1947 to the majority Communists while the teachers' union (Fédération de l'Education Nationale—FEN) broke off in 1948 to avoid an internal split and thereafter guarded its independence from all confederations.

15. Jean-Pierre Huiban, "The Industrial Counterproposal as an Element of Trade Union Strategy," in Mark Kesselman with Guy Groux, ed., *The French Workers' Movement: Economic Crisis and Political Change* (London: George Allen & Unwin, 1984).

16. Because French unions are so decentralized, there had been wide variations in the warmth of the CGT-CFDT alliance. Still, the confederal line in favor of close relations tended to dominate.

17. Guy Groux and René Mouriaux, "The Dilemma of Unions without Members," in Anthony Daley, ed., *The Mitterrand Era: Policy Alternatives and Political Mobilization in France* (London: Macmillan and NYU Press, 1996).

18. Both the CGT and the CFDT worked with outside research teams to uncover the cause of deunionization. The CGT discovered not only that 39 percent of all wage earners thought the union movement was in crisis for its politicization but that they criticized the confederation's politicization more than twice as often as they praised its combativeness. A plurality suggested that in order to regain influence the union needed to "cut itself off from all political influence." For the results of the CSA/CGT poll taken in July 1993, see *Le Peuple,* no. 1381, December 9, 1993, pp. 32–37.

    This message was consistent with the work of a Grenoble-based research team that received confederal endorsement to examine deunionization in the CFDT. Interviewing former members, it discovered that "political disagreement" was the single largest reason why members quit. Either the CFDT was perceived to be a "Socialist union" or it was seen to be overly aggressive in its "wars against the CGT." See Dominique Labbé, Maurice Croisat, and Antoine Bevort, "La désyndicalisation: Le cas de la CFDT," Institut d'Etudes Politiques-Grenoble/CERAT (October 1989).

19. According to French labor law, agreements made at one level must be consistent with those at higher ones.

20. George Ross, "Party Decline and Changing Party Systems: France and the French Communist Party," *Comparative Politics* 25, no. 1 (October 1992): 43–61.

21. *Politis,* January 30, 1992.

22. The case of Alain Obadia showed the difficulty of attempts to distance the confederation from the party. In the early 1990s he began to articulate positions in the mainstream press that were consistent with such a separation. As a member of the confederal bureau and widely touted as the "number 2" of the confederation, he became a symbol of the new openness of the union. He backed debates in the 1992 congress on union-party relations. In January 1994 he quit his position in the party to bolster his argument. Playing the outside press against the union, however, took its toll on Obadia, and he resigned from the union in October 1994, claiming that the union apparatus was too slow to change.

23. The 1981 data come from Gérard Adam, *Le pouvoir syndical* (Paris: Dunod, 1983). The 1993 source is Frédéric Lemaitre, "Législatives: Le vote selon la sympathie syndicale," *Liaisons sociales. Mensuel,* April 15, 1993. Both authors rely on SOFRES polling data.

24. Because the administration of social welfare programs is split between employer and employee representatives, a union seeking administrative leadership must gain some support from employers.

25. Virginie Linhart, "Les 'dix' de Renault-Billancourt: Les enjeux d'une mobilisation d'appareil, juillet 1986-décembre 1989," *Revue française de science politique* 42, no. 3 (June 1992): 375–401.

26. Interviews with confederal staff in September 1994.

27. Because of the state's willingness to codify or extend collective bargaining agreements, bargaining strategies can become legal strategies. For the 1986 legislation and bargaining agreements on layoffs, see Laurent Vilbœuf, "Le nouveau droit des licenciements pour motif économique," *Travail,* no. 14 (October 1987), and "Le licenciement économique: 2ème partie," *Travail,* no. 15 (March 1988).

28. For instance, all three retail-trade federations have publicly opposed derogations of a ban on Sunday work that dates from 1906. Likewise, the CGT and the FO have tried to restrict the night hours of women in manufacturing employment despite the decision of the European Court of Justice that such restrictions were discriminatory.

29. Hervé Hamon and Patrick Rotman, *La deuxième gauche: Histoire intellectuelle et politique de la CFDT* (Paris: Éditions Ramsay, 1982). See also René Mouriaux and Catherine Villanueva, "Les syndicats français face à l'écologie de 1972 à 1992," *Mots,* no. 39 (June 1994): 36–51.

30. Michael Rose, "Economic Nationalism and the Unions: The Decline of the *Solution Franco-Française,*" in Jolyon Howorth and George Ross, eds., *Contemporary France* (London: Pinter, 1988).

31. For an elaboration on these innovations and their limits, see Anthony Daley, "The Travail of Sisyphus: French Unions after 1981," in George Ross and Andrew Martin, eds., *Changing Place of Labor in European Society: The End of Labor's Century?* forthcoming.

Part II

Economic Restructuring and Technological Change

CHAPTER 4

The Restructuring of Capital and Employment

Jean Magniadas

THE TURNING POINT OF THE MID 1960S

The years 1966–1967 marked a turning point in the economic atmosphere in France and the beginning of a new phase of the Kondratieff long cycle.[1] This phase is far from finished and has some notable characteristics. The long cycle does not eliminate conjunctural movements (short cycles), even though it may affect them rather deeply. It is marked by difficulties for growth, strong pressure on labor costs, and intense and exacerbated competition. Few jobs are created and there is mass unemployment. This historic phase is far from coming to an end as it is a long-term structural crisis following from the phase of rapid economic growth, comparatively high real wages, and relative full employment, which one French economist called the "30 glorious years."

At the political level, this phase corresponded, roughly speaking, to the Fourth Republic and the Gaullist period. During this period there were major changes in economic structures, the most important being the concentration of capital. This process accelerated from 1965 on. Between 1965 and 1969 there were on average 50 percent more company mergers than during the period 1959 to 1964. The mergers were mainly self-financed and involved companies that were generally larger than those in the previous period. The "drive to concentration" was one of the aims of the so-called French style of indicative planning. One of the aims of the Fifth Plan (1966–1970) was the establishment of one or two world (global?)-scale companies in the major sectors of the French economy (aluminum, steel, engineering, automobiles, aeronautics, chemicals, pharmaceuticals, etc.). The Plan encouraged a high growth rate and the consolidation of the competitive capacities of the French economy. It also advocated an industrial policy—one of modernization—also favored by the party in power, especially in the de Gaulle-Pompidou period. Some scholars have described this period as "modernist." The social integration of workers was expected but did not materialize. On the contrary, major industrial strikes were promoted by unified trade union action and the agreement reached between the CGT and the CFDT that included demands for higher real wages, improved working and living conditions, more trade union rights in the workplace, and the guaranteed right to a job.

By the last quarter of 1966, household consumption fell, economic growth declined, and unemployment increased abruptly. At the time, very few observers saw anything other than a simple conjunctural movement in the development of the economic situation; whereas, in fact, it was a fundamental turning point. The CGT was, without doubt, the first trade union to have recognized and highlighted the concept of structural crisis.

The crisis continued to influence events throughout the decade. As far as economic factors were concerned (there were other dimensions as well), the May 1968 movement was born out of the worsening economic situation, government rulings concerning social provisions, and slow improvements in real wages made worse by the government's stabilization plan and restructuring related to mergers and company reorganization. Many books have been written about May 1968,[2] but few examine its economic impact. In my view, the social measures were beneficial in the sense that they partly delayed the effects of the structural crisis for a short period in spite of government measures that had the opposite effect.

The structural crisis is far from being a purely French phenomenon, even if it has certain characteristics related to France's national social formation and place in the hierarchy of capitalist countries. It is part of an overall process that concerns all capitalist countries.

THE DETERMINING FACTORS OF THE CRISIS

The structural crisis involves, in particular, a decline in the productivity of fixed assets. Many statistical studies demonstrate this problem,[3] even if they differ in analysis and choice of solutions. The crisis corresponds to a long phase of over-accumulation of capital and to difficulties in making capital profitable. Tables 4.1, 4.2, and 4.3 document the movements that characterize this period.

The data concerning labor productivity, capital efficiency, and jobs refer to a historical type of development of total labor productivity that is characteristic of the capitalist system. This productivity is based on the development of capital as opposed to the development of the labor force (that is,

Table 4.1 Labor Productivity, Productivity of Capital, and Total Factor Productivity

	Average Annual Rate of Variation (%)			
	1970–1974	1974–1979	1979–1987	1970–1987
Labor productivity				
All market sectors	4.3	2.9	2.6	3.1
including: industry*	4.3	4.2	2.4	3.4
services**	3.4	1.1	1.8	2.0
Productivity of capital				
All market sectors	−1.2	−1.5	−1.0	−1.2
including: industry*	−0.1	−0.6	−2.0	−1.1
services**	−0.9	−1.8	−0.3	−0.9
Total productivity				
All market sectors	2.7	1.7	1.6	1.9
including: industry*	3.2	3.0	1.2	2.3
services**	1.3	−0.3	0.8	0.6

*sectors U 04 to U 06
**sectors U 09 to U 011
Source: Comptes Nationaux

meeting its growing and diverse social needs), which would take into account changes in productive forces and the development of useful services (health, education, culture, community activities, etc.). The difficulties associated with achieving productivity are reflected in the crisis by a stark and lasting antagonism. This type of productivity leads only to a partial depreciation of capital. It can only cope with sporadic modernization, which leads to mass unemployment and counters any real solution to the structural crisis. Given the crisis in total labor productivity, counterattacks, aimed at defending capital's profitability, were developed.

RESPONSES OF ECONOMIC POLICIES AND COMPANY MANAGEMENT

Counterattacks were sought through exporting goods, services, and capital, through exchange-rate policies and through the organizational transformation of companies. Increased exploitation of the labor force was intensified in relation to organizational and structural changes of companies. There was also a series of attempts to integrate employees socially. The concentration and centralization of capital continued to develop. The developments were accompanied by successive economic policies and reflected in company management.

Table 4.2 Growth—Jobs and Capital (1950–1973)

	Annual Growth Rates (%)		
	1950–1957	1957–1964	1964–1973
Growth of value added (1959 constant prices)	5.5	6.0	5.9
Growth of employees	1.0	1.4	1.4
Growth of productive fixed assets (1959 constant prices)	3.4	5.3	7.0
Substitution of capital for labor (growth of per capita capital)	2.4	3.9	5.5
Apparent labor productivity (growth of per capita value added)	4.4	4.5	4.4
Apparent productivity of capital (value added per unity of capital)	2.0	0.7	−1.0
Total productivity of labor and capital	3.8	3.5	3.0

Source: Comptes Nationaux

As for the companies, the decisive role belonged to the large groups, simultaneously rivals and allies. Concurrently, small and medium-size companies were increasingly subjected to the large companies and faced a much more uncertain situation given their vulnerability stemming from the crisis. The big industrial and commercial companies and banks tried to impinge on the profits of the smaller businesses through subcontracting, pricing, and interest rates. In turn, the small and medium-size enterprises tried to transfer some of their difficulties to their employees through the unemployment crisis, which limits employees' ability to take action. These transformations led to weakened economic growth, lower real wages, almost constantly increasing unemployment, and the development of types of work (part-time, short-term contracts, and the like) can no longer be called atypical, given their recent proliferation. They also influenced the level and types of investment.

These measures led to the mass marginalization of the labor force and increased competition within it. These phenomena, which were the result of state policies and decisions made by major companies to stop declining profit rates, did not master the systemic contradictions but rather shifted them elsewhere and made them worse.

INSERTION IN FOREIGN TRADE

Attempts to make capital profitable led to foreign trade occupying an increasing proportion of French economic activity. Exports and imports of

Table 4.3   Development of National Wage-Earning Jobs by Major Sectors 1975/
1994 (thousands)

	1975	1990	1994	Variations 1975/90 (%)	Variations 1990/75 (%)
Agriculture	452	277	265	−38.7	41.4
Industry*	7,374	5,973	5,298	−19.0	39.2
Commerce	1,907	2,310	2,264	21.1	18.7
Transport	691	782	776	13.3	12.3
Telecommunications	365	443	427	21.1	17.0
Commercial services	2,012	3,530	3,758	75.4	86.8
Financial services	507	624	609	23.1	20.1
Non-commercial services	4,330	5,621	6,148	29.8	42.0
Total	17,638	19,560	19,545		

*Including agriculture industry, energy, manufacturing, building industry, and public works.
Source: Comptes Nationaux

goods corresponded to 14 and 15 percent of French gross national product in 1960; they represented 22.8 percent and 20.6 percent, respectively, in 1994. This led to a growing extroversion of its productive system in relation to people's needs and increased dependence on the conjuncture abroad.

This phenomenon is not uniquely French and concerns capitalist countries generally. It is influenced by technological developments and the beginning of the information revolution; but, in our view, one would be falling into technological determinism by ignoring that these transformations are dominated by the big companies and the dictates of profitability. The shift was stimulated in Europe by the creation of the European Economic Community (EEC). The Community's various stages of development, its enlargement, and the passage to Economic and Monetary Union are each said to be a solution to the structural crisis, which, in turn, is said to be a result of the "non-Europe." Trade deficits were not just the result of oil prices. They led to the search for corrective measures, including restraining real wages in an attempt to slow internal consumption and releasing a "surplus for export" rather than searching for a different kind of global productivity or developing production that would have replaced some imports and reduced the trade deficit.

The policy of "everything for export" did not prove effective, despite the state aid (subsidies, special loans) that private business firms received, nor did it lead to high growth levels and increased jobs as was projected. In fact, this policy often was accompanied by major companies reducing national production and increasing imports, whether from their own subsidiaries or elsewhere. High prices on the national market were used to facilitate exports at lower prices, in the auto industry, for example. Such a measure affects the balance of goods and services. France is the fourth major trading country in the world—far behind the United States, reunified Germany, and Japan—which creates strong pressure on the development of its economy and jobs.

DIRECT INVESTMENT ABROAD

France was late to join the trend of advanced capitalist countries directly investing abroad, which developed greatly in the second half of the 1980s. In the first half of the decade, the flight of capital through the balance of payments represented only 98 billion francs (compared with 58 billion throughout the 1970s), whereas in the second half of the 1980s it reached 430 billion. This movement corresponded to a worsening of the crisis, the concentration of capital, and intensified international competition. The announcement of the single European market led to a policy of French investment in the European "community" space. The EEC received 42 percent of French investment flows from 1976 to 1980 and only 28 percent from 1981 to 1985, but its share increased to 61 percent from 1986 to 1990. A recent study emphasizes that "French companies increasingly super-imposed onto its goods and services export strategy, a strategy of establishing international productive structures, either by creating subsidiaries and/or by taking shares in existing companies abroad."[4]

The distinguishing characteristic of the international companies financed by French capital is that they are more profitable and more capital-intensive, they use a wages/profit distribution that is less favorable to labor, and, in equivalent industries, they show high apparent labor productivity. The structure of the transnational firm, which often is dominated by a holding company, facilitates the implementation of tactics leading to a globalization of development strategies and, frequently, a division of labor between subsidiaries. "Given the difficulties faced by some of its subsidiaries, the group can choose to impose the constraints experienced on all or some of the other subsidiaries, especially as the group is integrated."[5] This statement shows how difficult it is for trade unions to obtain information regarding the international group, whose high-level management considers that such information is strategic and therefore should be restricted. Hence, trade unions recognize that they need to develop a joint strategy at the level of the transnational firm.

FROM NATIONALIZATION TO PRIVATIZATION

Throughout its history, the CGT always has considered nationalization to be an important issue. Such concern sometimes has led to passionate debate within the union. Nationalization continues to be one of its economic demands. It was also part of the Left's Common Program—albeit not without debate. The Left came to power in 1981 and significantly increased the public and nationalized sector,[6] especially in the financial sector and among the large industrial groups. Along with democratic planning, the nationalized companies, which were meant to be an important pillar of support for planning, were a great disappointment. Despite a few personnel changes (individuals called "pink elites" by some sociologists), the boards of directors of the nationalized companies, to which employee representatives were added, remained dominated by the company's managing directors. They were dominated by the relevant ministry and were subjected to a so-called modernization policy that continued and reinforced the strategies that existed before nationalization.

The situation is more than symbolic if one remembers that the president of the Republic himself was against the newly nationalized companies resigning from the employers' association, as the CGT proposed. The nationalized companies' disappointing performance was for many well beyond the frontiers of the Left. They did not break with the classic criteria of capitalist profitability. The CGT did not think that the nationalized companies could represent an "island of socialism," but demanded new criteria based on social efficiency that would be different from those of financial profitability and that would include economic and social efficiency. Thus they would promote economizing on material and financial costs by cooperating with small and medium-size companies, as well as possibly with foreign partners, provided the agreements allowed a fair sharing of costs and were based on strict reciprocity.

Employees and the CGT insisted that changes in legal ownership—the passage of private ownership to public ownership—should not be confused with *social* ownership and were not sufficient to impose new goals of economic and social progress on nationalized companies. They held the same position regarding planning. In both cases, experience demonstrates that the issues of the criteria on which management decisions are based and the extent of employees' real power are vital.

Nationalized companies were subjected to a program of denationalization during "cohabitation" governments, when a president of the Left (François Mitterrand) coexisted with prime ministers of the Right (Jacques Chirac and Eduard Baladur).[7] These privatizations, which were extended by the Juppé government, encountered several obstacles, including the poor state of the financial market. Although their aim was to provide the state with finances to make up the deficit, the privatizations were, in fact, a fundamental part of a restructuring of French capitalism around two dominant centers constituted through cross-holdings by financial and industrial groups, around the Union des Assurances de Paris (UAP) on the one hand and the Société Général and Paribas on the other.[8] This process of restructuring is far from finished. It opens up the way to strategic alliances and even to new concentrations and configurations of capital with "foreign" groups.

This is part of a movement of deep changes that tends to ensure the position of some "French" groups in a larger process of creating—at the European and world level—a space dominated by a small number of oligopolies. Public services and nationalized companies are without doubt an obstacle to this process because of their very nature (legal status, type of company, staff guarantees and types of employment, consumer interests, equality), because of the way they function, and because of the conditions of their profitability. This process is inseparable from sharp competition between groups and its new forms, which lead them and states toward the destructive competitiveness characteristic of the current economic war.

COMPETITIVENESS AND ECONOMIC WAR

The globalization of finance, industry, markets, infrastructure, and services linked to information and communication[9] leads to increased competition between transnational companies and also extends to states (competitive devaluation, strong currency policies, high interest rates, increased "economic intelligence" concerning companies' and states' activities).

Competitiveness is the current creed, although some differing views can be heard now. Competitiveness even has become an ideology, claiming to be the answer to global challenges. It is directly related to the "neoliberal" orthodoxy that favors deregulation in its different forms and is contemporary with the so-called policies of competitive deflation adopted by the conservative governments of the United States and Britain and that will become established in other countries. One can see this influence behind the European approach, even if the continent adds some "social" promises with Keynesian overtones, as when, for example, there are questions of "major public works." However, the dominant criteria included in the Maastricht Treaty aim at reinforcing constraints and removing states' control over essential instruments of economic sovereignty. As far as ordinary people are concerned, they lead to austerity policies.

Open neoliberalism, in its near obsession with the dogma of competitiveness, serves to legitimize destructuring in the field of international financial regulations and national public services and puts their privatization on the agenda. It also leads to mass unemployment and job insecurity as well as an attack (unprecedented since the end of World War II) on social systems that were won through trade union action and that ensure a certain degree of job and wage security and relatively developed social protection schemes. Competitiveness, under whose cover powerful world oligopolies develop, represents above all a war against people. It would be wrong to say that the satisfaction of people results from the dominance of the market, even if the collapse of the Eastern European countries highlighted the inefficiency of bureaucratic and centralized planning.

HIGH LONG-TERM UNEMPLOYMENT AND WIDE-SCALE JOB INSECURITY

The crisis, combined with employers' strategies, gradually changed completely the situation of wage-earning employees. The rate of net job creation (wage-earning and others) dropped significantly (see table 4.3.). The sharp decline in industrial jobs varied from sector to sector, and there was an increase in commercial services and trade, due partly to the restructuring of industrial companies' activities and the contracting-out of some of their services. There was also a large increase in noncommercial services. These changes were not unique to France. In our view, they are one of the causes of the drop in trade union membership, particularly if one takes into account trade union pluralism. The most important phenomenon was the existence of mass unemployment, which increased from 912,000 in 1975 to 3,164,700 in 1994 and now represents 12.4 percent of the active population. Added to this are mass forms of job insecurity that affects millions of people (women and young people), primarily in the form of downgraded jobs (part-time work, short-term contracts, training programs that do not lead to useful jobs). Employers are actively replacing permanent work contracts with short-term ones which, in some cases, are renewable. Management also has introduced a strategy of flexible working hours. In France, all in all, 5 million people are either unemployed or in downgraded types of work. These developments cannot be separated from a major deterioration of working conditions as documented in official studies. They are directly related to the "competitiveness" priority and are based on increased competition between employees themselves, instigated by the crisis and employers' tactics.

WORSENING OF EMPLOYEES' SITUATION

Increasing job insecurity, which affects all levels to varying degrees, worsened as a result of wage policies and attacks on social protection. On average, wages increased very little in the past several decades. They were reduced by increased national insurance contributions and national and local taxes. Companies developed practices of individualizing wages—a practice that some employers think is counterproductive.

Management policies—along with the policy of wage restraint introduced in 1982 by a Socialist-led government and the deindexing of wages and prices—led to an almost constant drop in the share of wages in the companies' value added: on average, from 68.1 percent in 1983 to 60.2 percent in 1995. During the same period, companies' profit rates increased from 26.1 to 31.5 percent and their gross savings grew from 11.1 to 18.1 percent. This represented a major shift in the structure of value added to the benefit of companies and to the detriment of employees.

Attacks on social protection have continued since the beginning of the crisis.[10] They involve higher taxes on households, a decline in health care, pensions, and family benefits, and increased national insurance contributions. They also aim at changing the pension system from one based on redistribution to one including capitalization, which will open the door to private pension schemes, as lobbied for by insurance companies and some other major companies. Prime Minister Juppé's plan was based on these principles and led to the powerful strike movement at the end of 1995. Public-sector employees' rights and working conditions were also at stake, especially those working for the French railroad system.

NEW SOCIAL CONFLICT

The various changes in companies' economic and social policies led to employee responses that the media often presented as old-fashioned or reflecting "corporate egoism." Employers' policies were accompanied by numerous attempts to integrate employees, in order to ensure social peace and employee motivation, within the framework of a strategy dominated by competitiveness. We will not analyze these policies here[11] but mention only a few examples: quality circles, company projects, company cultural initiatives, communication and information activities, and participatory management. The policies were accompanied by repression, which, as far as trade union activists were concerned, could be extreme in nature (firing) or more subtle (change of work station, lack of promotion). The annual report of ISERES, the CGT's Trade Union and Social Research Institute, which is devoted to the economic and social situation, endeavors to analyze the potential for conflict.[12] In the edition covering 1993, the report noted "the diversity of struggles, a change in employees' state of mind, divorce from the company," "demotivation," employees tending more than in the past to "take over the struggle" concerning its form, aims, and organization. The same document found a qualitatively different aspect in united action. It emphasized that "[united action] was based on the stronger desire among employees to defend their demands together." I am not asserting that ISERES forecast the big strike movement at the end of 1995, but it is certain that the movement did reflect many of these characteristics.

This movement reflected a huge and profound process of employee resistance to a new and particular stage of the structural crisis linked to the government's policies and its European ambitions. As the *International Herald Tribune* noted on December 15, 1995: "French people are not docile."

NOTES

1. Our analysis is in line with the problematic of long cycles studied in economic history by N. V. Kondratieff and currently developed in France by Paul Boccara, Louis Fonvielle, and other economists.

2. Georges Séguy, *le Mai de la CGT* (Paris: Julliard, 1972, new ed., 1988); Adrian Dansette, *Mai 1968* (Paris: Le Seuil); Roger Martelli, *Mai 1968* (Paris: Messidor/Editions Sociales); Danièle Tartakowski, *Les événements de mai 1968,* vol. 7, éditions sociales (Livre Club Diderot, 1981).

3. Paul Boccara, "Travaux statistiques sur le 'système productif' français et théorie des facteurs de la crise de structure," *Issues,* no. 1 and no. 2 (1978, 1979).

4. Marie-Christine Parent, "Stratégie d'implantation régionale, nationale ou internationale: Quelle influence sur le développement des entreprises français," *Economie et Statistique,* no. 290 (1985): 10.

5. Ibid.

6. If we take employees in the public sector (excluding civil servants), their numbers increased from 1,638,000 at the beginning of 1980 (11.8 percent of all nonagricultural employees), to 2,379,000 (17.6 percent) in 1986.

7. An assessment made in the beginning of 1989 shows that the scope of nationalized companies had declined because the percentage of employees had dropped to 13.

8. These groups included the following companies: the first—UAP, Suez, Elf, Saint-Gobain and the Lyonnaise des Eaux; the second—the Société Générale, AGF, Alcatel-Alsthom, Générale des Eaux, Paribas, according to F. Morin, *Le Monde,* November 7, 1995.

9. It does not exclude the creation of polarized regional entities: Triadization is not discussed here because it would require a long explanation.

10. Catherine Mills, *Economie de la protection sociale* (Paris: Sirey, 1994).

11. See Jean Magniadas, *Le patronat* (Paris: Éditions Messidor, 1991).

12. CGT's annual report on the economic and social situation, under the title of "Affrontements" (March 1994).

CHAPTER FIVE

Technology and the Labor Movement: Constraint or Opportunity for the CGT?

Mark Kesselman

The massive strikes and demonstrations that immobilized France in 1995 and 1996 reminded many who had fondly bid farewell to the proletariat that the working class was alive, well, and angry. But it would be premature to reject the many analyses of the past several years documenting how the French trade union movement, and particularly its most influential segment, the Confédération Générale du Travail (CGT), confronts what is probably the most severe crisis in its century-old history. Although the labor movement has periodically experienced crisis throughout its existence, an indication of the gravity of the current situation is that some scholars, not hostile to organized labor, have seriously discussed the possible demise of the trade union movement.[1]

The topic of this chapter—the relation of the labor movement to technological change—is central to the current crisis of the CGT. The vast technological changes of the past several decades, that is, the microelectronic revolution—including numerically controlled machine tools, computer-assisted design and manufacturing systems, and new means of telecommunications—have wreaked havoc with the stable systems of mass production that prevailed for well over half a century as well as with the regulatory institutions and understandings linked to Fordism.[2]

FORDISM AND THE LEGACY OF THE POSTWAR BOOM

In the postwar period, labor unions displaying diverse organizational forms and sharply opposed ideological persuasions were able to reach a relatively secure position. As countless studies of neocorporatism in Western Europe in the postwar period have described, organized labor was a key participant in and beneficiary of the regulatory arrangements of the postwar settlement.[3] Peak-level union confederations, organizing relatively homogeneous blocs of semiskilled industrial workers, were able to defend labor's organizational interests as well as to achieve significant benefits for their members—notably, higher wages, improved working conditions, and more ample state-secured social benefits—through collective bargaining with peak-level employer associations and the state. The process has been termed one of political exchange, in which organized labor lengthened the time horizon for pursuing its goals by shifting from the use of direct confrontation to pursue demands for sweeping economic and political change to seeking moderate concessions and reforms from employers and the state within existing institutions.[4]

Labor movements varied widely, of course, in their capacities, strategies, and internal organization. The CGT, for example, continued to espouse a rhetoric of class confrontation and to mount strikes and demonstrations to press radical political and economic demands throughout the postwar period (at the same time that it played an important role in regulating workplace relations and fostering economic modernization). But differences among different national labor movements were less significant than the fact that for decades the escalator of economic expansion proved beneficial for all labor movements.

Until the early 1970s, trade unions did not focus on issues relating to technological change, including the design and use of equipment, skill levels, and occupational health and safety. They generally granted management a free hand to sponsor technological innovations on condition that workers share in the expansion that resulted from productivity increases. In the short run, technological change should not jeopardize (but rather should positively promote) steady wage gains. In the medium run, technological change should not jeopardize (but rather should positively promote) secure and relatively full employment. Given the steady economic expansion of *les trentes glorieuses,* it appeared that these aims were feasible. (American political sociologists were not the only ones to believe that the basic problems of an industrial order had been solved.) Given the fact that technological change would improve productivity and economic competitivity, all that was needed were mechanisms to ensure that an equitable share of the resulting benefits would be redistributed to the working class through higher wages and job creation. This was the goal of collective bargaining arrangements in the economic sphere and pro-growth (often social democratic) coalitions in the political sphere.[5]

In the brave new world following the second industrial divide, labor has been forced to confront acute challenges involving the globalization of production, capital flows, and finance; fundamental changes in the organization of work and processes of production, in which unions becomes less useful to employers as managers of discontent; technological changes that marginalize the semiskilled industrial workers who formed the core of the labor movement; ideological reversals in which, rather than being regarded as an engine of progress and the bearer of universalistic interests, a secure, organized, and well-paid labor force has come to be seen as particularistic and selfish as well as a constraint on economic efficiency; and political shifts that have excluded labor from governing coalitions.[6]

Organized labor need not be marginalized as a result of technological change. Some features of the new technology potentially constitute an opportunity for the labor movement—for example, the need for worker involvement, team-based production, flatter hierarchy, and polyvalent, skilled workers. Furthermore, one should beware of technological determinism, which suggests that the microelectronic revolution inevitably dictates a given outcome. Technology can be designed and programmed to intensify hierarchy and routine. Or it can be used to promote rich possibilities of worker participation. For example, as one study of the impact of technological change suggests (in what may be an overly sanguine analysis): "To the extent that technology is used only to intensify the automaticity of work, it can reduce skill levels and dampen the urge toward more participatory and decentralized forms of management. . . . [H]owever, this approach cannot exploit the unique power of an informating technology."[7]

How have labor movements confronted the dramatic technological changes of recent decades? Whereas some unions, notably those in Scandinavia and Germany, demonstrated a keen capacity to seize opportunities and gain new responsibilities, other union movements—including the French— have been seriously destabilized by technological change.[8] A key feature of those labor movements that were quite successful in confronting the technological challenge was that they *entered* the recent era in a more powerful position. Thus their secure position enabled them to grasp the nature of the challenge and to react effectively.[9] Early in the 1970s, soon after shop-floor revolts erupted against the fashion in which technological change was occurring, the Swedish and German labor movements successfully sought expansion of collective bargaining, codetermination, and works council legislation. By contrast, the French and American labor movements, among the weakest of the advanced capitalist world, were slow to grasp the gravity of the potential danger posed by technological change and were quite ineffective in meeting the challenge. In France, the CGT reacted to worker mobilization erupting in 1968 by seeking to increase workers' material benefits rather than attempting to gain a voice in decisions about economic and technological change. During the critical decade of the 1970s, when, as a result of the creation of consultative mechanisms, organized labor was helping to shape the process of technological change in northern Europe, the French labor movement began to experience an accelerating crisis. Although the Socialist government elected in 1981 sponsored reforms aimed at reversing this decline, in part by broadening labor's role in economic and technological decisions, the trajectory of decline continued through the 1980s.

THE CGT CONFRONTS TECHNOLOGICAL CHANGE

Although there are many causes of the deep-rooted crisis of the French labor movement, the unions' failure to enhance their position by exploiting the possibilities offered by the vast technological changes of the past two decades ranks high in importance. My explanation for this failure focuses on features associated with the political framework of regulation in France and major characteristics of the CGT's organizational identity.

THE POLITICAL AND REGULATORY CONTEXT

The French political framework represents a major obstacle to effective union initiatives in the area of technological change. While hardly of the CGT's making, France's statist political culture heavily influenced the union's strategy.

France's Characteristic Mode of Regulation
The typical French *dirigiste* style regulation, in which the state plays an active role as organizer, participant, and guarantor, contrasts with voluntarist self-regulation by private actors. In France, legislation and administrative regulations have accomplished what occurred elsewhere as a result of private negotiations, notably, determination of wages, retirement, paid vacations, health and safety measures, skill classifications, and maximum working hours. Although France's statist pattern produced significant achievements in the postwar period, it has proven much less effective since the 1970s; many speak of a crisis of state regulation. The problem is especially evident regarding the issue of recent technological change, in that centralized statist regulation is apparently less effective than the more flexible, decentralized networks of firms, unions, and local governments that successfully have promoted technological innovation elsewhere in the current era.[10]

Paradoxically, at the same time that the CGT bitterly contested the legitimacy of the French state, it eagerly sought to extend the state's reach. There were two important reasons for this statist orientation. One cluster of reasons involves the weakness of the labor movement, the predominance of small firms (with a resulting tendency for employers to be antiunion), and a characteristic pattern in France by which social gains traditionally have been achieved as a result of state mandate. (The most dramatic occasions were the Popular Front/Liberation period—when a Communist was minister of labor, May 1968—and the period of Socialist-Communist governance following 1981.) Second, in the postwar period the CGT's organizational culture was heavily influenced by the union's close relations with the Communist Party (PCF) and support for the Soviet model of state-organized socialism. The result was to orient the CGT toward a focus on political change rather than on becoming involved in the attempt to shape technological change.

Conservative Ruling Coalitions

Given the important role that the state played in regulating economic and technological change in France, organized labor has been at a great disadvantage because the state typically has been in unfriendly hands. Whereas in northern Europe, ruling coalitions closely linked to the labor movement were sympathetic to labor's reform proposals, the French union movement—and especially its dominant constituent, the CGT—was a political outsider.

The Institutional Framework

The framework regulating the organization of work and production has further discouraged union participation in the process of technological decision making. In order to understand why, it is useful to describe the larger context in which consultation between management and works councils over technological change, which has been mandated since 1982, occurs in France.[11]

There is a paradox at the heart of the legal framework of French industrial relations. On one hand, the French labor code is a thick volume of incredibly detailed regulations, dutifully enforced by a corps of inspectors in the Ministry of Labor. Yet, on the other hand, even after the passage of the Socialist government's far-reaching labor reforms of 1982 (the Auroux laws), French labor law has left enormous areas unregulated. One key example is strikes, about which little is said in French labor law.

The Auroux reforms sought, with substantial success, to strengthen unions' representational rights. Employer associations at sectoral levels were required to bargain collectively with unions at least once every five years in order to establish or review sectoral framework agreements regarding minimum wages, hours, working conditions, and skill classifications in the industry. (However, employer associations were not required to conclude agreements during these negotiations.) Following the passage of the Auroux laws, the number of employees not covered by a sectoral framework agreement dropped from 3 million to 1 million.[12]

Another important provision of the Auroux reforms that both empowered unions yet placed a heavy burden on them aimed at providing local unions with a role in the plant and firm. For the first time employers were required to bargain collectively with local unions over wages, hours, and working conditions. (As with sectoral bargaining, employers were not required to conclude agreements.) Although legislation passed after the May 1968 general strike recognized the legal existence of local unions, the unions were given no rights and responsibilities. The requirement that employers bargain collectively at the local level effected a minor revolution. Along with other provisions, which granted local unions new rights and privileges, the reform in effect represented the French equivalent of the Wagner act (passed nearly 50 years earlier!). A government-appointed commission charged with evaluating the impact of the Auroux laws reported in 1993 that, in the decade since the laws had been passed, there occurred "the most extensive wave of negotiations in the history of French professional [labor] relations."[13] This was not mere hyperbole: The number of firms and/or plants in France that negotiated local bargaining agreements soared from 1,477 in 1981, just prior to passage of the laws, to 6,750 in 1991, the high point of firm-level bargaining.[14] However, most of these agreements regulate wages, hours, and working conditions, the traditional stuff of industrial relations; there is little union involvement in the area of technological choices.

Closer analysis, moreover, suggests that the impact of the Auroux reforms was more limited and contradictory than its supporters claim. The reforms not only failed to guarantee legal representation for all workers but in part served to divide workers. For example, nearly half of all private-sector workers continue to be employed in plants that lack any representative institution, including local union organization, works committee, or *délégués du personnel* (elected grievance committee representatives).[15] Despite the fact that employers in firms with over 10 employees are legally obliged to organize elections in which workers select *délégués du personnel,* only one-quarter of plants with 10 to 49 employees actually have one. Similarly, well over a decade since the passage of the Auroux laws, only one-quarter of all private-sector workers are covered by a firm-level collective bargaining agreement. Workers not covered have jobs in firms whose small size exempts them from the requirement to bargain collectively, in firms where collective bargaining failed to produce an agreement, and in firms where, despite the legal injunction, employers violate the law by refusing to bargain collectively.

With respect to technological change, the Auroux laws provided unions and works councils with a role in the domain of technological change. Employers were required to consult works councils before introducing technological changes that promised to have a significant impact on employment levels, working conditions, and skill levels. Unions were empowered to negotiate collective bargaining agreements to specify the procedures by which works councils would be consulted over proposed technological changes in the firm.

In the past decade, several national-level agreements, as well as lower-level agreements in a variety of industrial sectors (including chemicals, banking, and metalworking), were negotiated between unions and employers associations that codified the role of unions in regulating technological change. But these agreements merely organized the framework for local-level bargaining and consultation over the organization of work and technology. They specify procedures, not outcomes. Only some large bellwether firms, such as Péchiney and Rhône-Poulenc, have negotiated agreements at the plant or firm level. Moreover, the issue of union participation in shaping technological change does not rank high among the concerns of most rank-and-file workers compared to issues of more immediate concern, notably, wages and job protection.

Although the Auroux laws mandate works councils to be consulted over technological matters, remarkably few cases of consultation under the law's procedures actually have occurred, and works councils have generally been unable to influence managerial decisions.[16] Two provisions of the Auroux law on technological change limit the scope of consultation. First, works councils are granted only one month to investigate and evaluate management's proposals—a period patently insufficient to review a complex project. Second, technical provisions of the law and restrictive court rulings have facilitated employers' obstructionist tactics. Perhaps the most important example is the scope of the legislation. When proposed changes in technology have a significant impact on the firm's operations (including employment levels and workers' skill classifications), a firm's works council is legally authorized to hire an outside expert, at company expense, to assist in the consultation process. Employers claim that this procedure is costly and potentially damaging to the firm because outsiders can gain access to sensitive proprietary information. The law provides that an employer may challenge the designation of an expert, in which case the works council must bring suit in order to compel compliance. Employers frequently have vetoed the designation of an expert on the grounds that the proposed technological changes are not sufficiently innovative and/or that their impact is limited, and judges usually have sided with employers. The result has been to narrow considerably the potential scope for prescribed consultation.

Because consultation over technological change has been so infrequent, we have little evidence of how works councils would exercise their responsibilities. However, employers are required by law to consult works councils in a related domain—when a firm plans layoffs for economic reasons. In these quite frequent cases, consultation occurs on a routine basis. Yet such consultation has a ritualistic aspect. Rather than consultation producing labor-management cooperation in seeking a mutually satisfactory outcome, works councils nearly invariably oppose such layoffs on the grounds that they are not warranted. Consultation over the terms of layoffs may improve the severance package for workers scheduled for dismissal, but it does not involve a genuine dialogue about the firm's operations.

Recent Trends: State Retrenchment, Decentralization of Regulation, Deregulation, and Crisis of Organized Labor

After a brief period following the Socialist government's election in 1981, when it substantially extended the state's reach by its nationalization reforms and passage of the Auroux laws, the trend since 1983 has been toward state disengagement. It is not that the state has adopted a hands-off stance toward the economy; rather, it actively has sought to promote flexibility and private initiative.[17] Yet the decline of state involvement in industrial relations and a shift toward firm-level regulation has not promoted greater CGT participation in the process of regulating technological change.[18]

A major reason for union inactivity in this domain is the unprecedentedly severe crisis of French unions, and especially the CGT, in the past decade. Given the blow after blow that they have suffered, unions have responded to the restructuring and recession of the French economy by seeking to defend past gains rather than venturing into new areas by seizing the opportunity offered by the enlarged space for private negotiations. At the same time, unions have been overburdened by the new responsibilities delegated to them by the Auroux laws.[19]

As Guy Groux points out, in order to benefit from the opportunity for autonomous activity afforded by state retrenchment (as well as the state directive for management to engage in collective bargaining), unions would need to be strongly organized at the enterprise level. Yet the dwindling number of union militants and leaders have less contact with workers and weaker organizational capacity because they are involved in negotiating and participating in a welter of representative and consultative bodies. Given the fragility of local unions, combined with high unemployment and pressure by employers to increase labor market flexibility, local-level bargaining often produces not the advance of unions into new domains such as technological change but the erosion of past gains codified in sectoral and national bargaining agreements.[20]

Plural Unionism

The CGT's reluctance to place high priority on contesting managerial choices in the domain of technological change derives in part from the plural character of the French union movement. Competition among unions complicates the possibility of intervening in the area of technological change.[21]

The CGT's reluctance to champion participation in the area of technological innovation derives in part from the fact that its principal rival, the CFDT, got there first. The CFDT historically has been more active in scrutinizing the substance of managerial decisions in areas like technology: initially (from the 1960s through the 1970s) by highlighting *les dégâts du progrès;* more recently (from the late 1970s to the present) by seeking to play a "constructive" role in regulating technological and other changes.[22] In part to maintain its distinctive identity, and consistent with its traditional ideological orientation, the CGT defended a hands-off policy, on the grounds that it wanted to avoid the evils of cogestion and social democracy.

For a brief period in the late 1970s, as it became apparent that industrial restructuring threatened to devastate the CGT's core constituency, it struck out in a new direction, by promoting proposals to counter employer initiatives to downsize basic industries. This approach—known as "proposition-force" unionism—represented an about-face for the CGT. Rather than simply opposing planned layoffs, it (and the CFDT, which developed its own counterproposals) developed new alternatives to maintain production levels, identify new markets, and safeguard employment.[23] Granted, as Anthony Daley observes, "The specific proposals for the troubled industries—steel, ship-building, and heavy engineering—were less original than the methods employed."[24] However, if the strategy of union counterproposals had succeeded at least partially, it might have encouraged the CGT to widen its involvement beyond the areas included within the counterproposals to embrace the design and use of technology. This was not to occur, both because the union movement was unable to persuade management to accept its proposals and because the new orientation was soon abandoned.[25] By the end of the decade, the CGT and CFDT had ended their strategic alliance, the Union of the Left between the PCF and Socialist Party was shattered, CGT autonomy shrunk, and it again espoused the rhetoric of class confrontation that paralleled that of the PCF as it moved away from the Socialist Party.

CGT STRATEGY, IDENTITY, AND TACTICS

Although the wider context did not predispose the CGT to place priority on playing a role in shaping technological change, an equally important set of factors involving its organizational identity further diminished the possibility of effective efforts to influence technological change.

Organizational Culture: The CGT's Tradition of Ouvrièrisme

Long after important ideological changes in French society and the composition of the working class dictated the need for a rethinking of the French class map, the CGT continued to remain faithful to a traditional workerist mentality. This political/cultural legacy limited the CGT's ability to develop a proactive capacity to deal with technological change. The archetypal CGT militant has been a native-born, white, male semiskilled worker in basic industry: metalworking (the *métallo*), mining, and transportation. Groux points out, "For the union movement [especially the CGT], the primary reference is not a vague and undifferentiated proletarian, but the skilled worker, a member of the labor aristocracy, such as the printer or construction worker, who embodies the involvement and contestatory discourse found in the first great strikes."[26] Women, office workers, technicians, and teachers do not figure prominently in this cognitive space. In the postwar period, Groux asserts, engineers were elevated to a vanguard role as part of the rising "new working class," both by social theorists and within the labor movement. However, he observes, "The notion of 'the new working class' challenged the hegemony of the PCF and the CGT within the political left and union movement."[27] In analyses of the 1960s and 1970s describing economic changes and changes in class structure, "The primacy of technological development and the hegemony of the new middling classes or strata in the field of conflicts appeared inextricably linked."[28] Thus the CGT was in the uncomfortable position of championing scientific and technological progress yet finding its hegemony within the labor movement threatened because these same developments threatened to marginalize the basic industries where its support was centered. However, the dilemma was resolved in practice from the 1950s until massive and destabilizing deindustrialization began in the 1970s by the fact that although the numbers of "technicians, managers and engineers increased rapidly . . ., [the CGT came] to be dominated by industrial workers."[29]

The CGT's workerist culture helps explain its opposition to the complex negotiations involved in seeking to influence technological change. This emphasis can be seen in the marginal position within the CGT's organizational structure both of the Union Général des Ingénieurs, Cadres, et Techniciens (UGICT, the "lateral union" of technicians, engineers, and other skilled categories) and the CGT's confederal economic sector. Is it purely fortuitous that the most influential advocates of CGT involvement in the area of technological change were often technicians and economists themselves—who themselves eventually were marginalized and ostracized within the CGT? Two significant examples: When Jean-Louis Moynot, director of the CGT's economic research sector in the 1970s, sought to promote a counterproposal approach to planned retrenchment of the steel industry, he was soon forced from the CGT. Similarly, Gérard Alezard, his successor as director of the CGT's confederal economic sector, was isolated and dropped from the *bureau confédéral* in 1995 because he advocated more vigorous efforts to democratize the CGT's internal organization.[30]

Ideological Orientation and Partisan Ties

The CGT's somewhat traditional "old left" brand of Marxism helps account for its faith in the blessings of science and technology—and has rendered it less sensitive to the complexities of technological change. The CGT has tended to support such change—which it implicitly equates with an expansion of productive capacity (the forces of production, in Marxist terminology)—and to focus its efforts on altering the balance of forces controlling technology (the relations of production). In practice, this means that it focuses on the impact of technological change on wages, employment and skill levels, and job classifications.[31] However, whether such a neat distinction actually exists between forces and relations of production is questionable: The basic design of technology (the "forces of production") is influenced by the prevailing balance of social forces (the "relations of production"). Thus the design and control of technology are closely intertwined.[32]

Historically, the CGT has been most enthusiastic about technological innovation in the large public-sector firms that constituted its major "bastions"— Renault, EDF (the electricity supplier), SNCF (the railway sector), Elf-Aquitaine, and the like. Within these firms, the CGT typically dominated the union movement and works councils. Thus, especially during the economic boom years during the 1950s and 1960s when it was at the height of its power, the CGT lost an important opportunity to redistribute power to shop-floor workers, upgrade workers' skills, and promote safer and less environmentally damaging production. Rather than participate in a debate about the design and ends of technological change wedded to large-scale industrialization, the CGT championed France's massive state-organized nuclear power, aerospace, and transportation projects, and proved highly successful in obtaining handsome material benefits for workers in these industries. Indeed, its relatively uncritical acceptance of science and technology meant that it often downplayed the risks of environmental and social damage that might result from industrial production. In collective bargaining, the CGT typically pressed for monetary gains rather than a role in shaping technological development. It was an enthusiastic member of the coalition supporting France's pro-growth, modernizing, forced-march industrialization.[33] For years the CGT mocked France's antinuclear movement, dismissing its position as tantamount to a preference for nineteenth-century candlepower.

The CGT's quite orthodox Marxist outlook in the postwar period was strengthened by its close links to the Communist Party, for decades among the most Stalinist Communist parties in Western Europe.[34] The intimate ties between the CGT and PCF had a vital impact on French labor history for 40 years. The result was to prevent the CGT from forging an autonomous attempt to convert its "negative" labor market power—the power to disrupt production—into a positive role in shaping economic and technological decision making. Although the CGT became quite autonomous in the 1980s, the shift has coincided with the end of its commanding position within the labor movement.

Strategy and Vision

The CGT's conception of "class-struggle unionism" (*lutte de classe*) typically consisted of two broad goals: On the one hand, it sought radical political change, which would involve ending capitalist control, regulation by market forces, and the system of wage labor in which workers are treated as a commodity. On the other hand, the CGT prided itself on its militant defense of workers' immediate interests. The union was most comfortable and effective when it sought to check proposed austerity measures, as in the mid-1990s retrenchment at Air France and cutbacks in benefits for railway workers.

The CGT traditionally accepted an ideological division of labor in which management manages and the labor movement contests in the name of a radiant future. Correlatively, the realm of the economy (and technology) are management's domain; the CGT is responsible for the social sphere, that is, improving workers' benefits as wage labor. But the CGT has been viscerally opposed to close involvement in managerial and political decisions, as reflected in its rejection of such concepts as cogestion, participatory management, and social democracy. As Jean Lojkine, an industrial sociologist sympathetic to the CGT, has observed, "Victory can be achieved by vanquishing management in naked [and limited] combat. Or it may mean achieving a transition from a capitalist system to one governed by entirely new criteria of decision making. But there is a range of intermediary possibilities [between these extremes]. However, the CGT has difficulty operating within this intermediate zone. It is wedded to a tradition of denunciation and defense of past gains rather than a 'culture of propositions.' . . ."[35]

The CGT's traditional mode of action in the postwar period was to pressure the state for benefits via national demonstrations (*journées d'action*) that enunciated political demands.[36] This pattern is at the antipodes from negotiations at the local level over the design and operation of technology. As Pierre-Eric Tixier points out, "Although the CGT has apparently preserved an organizational *savoir-faire* vis-à-vis wage earners, its strategic renewal has been limited by its opposition to the current trend toward firm-level restructuring and the absence of alternative proposals capable of mobilizing workers."[37]

Tactics

The CGT's major tactical weapon has been the strike: direct protest by mobilizing workers in the workplace and community. This approach typically was directed toward maximizing quantitative benefits, especially wage gains. In the recent period, strikes have opposed corporate downsizing, plant closings, and cutbacks in state benefits. In order to apply the strike/negotiations approach to shaping technological change, it is necessary both to have a project or counterproposal around which to mobilize *and* to convince workers that the demand is feasible and worth struggling to attain. It also helps if the possibility exists that the union might persuade—or pressure—management to grant concessions. Identifying what is needed illuminates why the CGT has placed such a low priority on the attempt to shape technological change.

The CGT's Weak Technical Capacity

Although the CGT has created consulting firms with the economic and technical expertise to conduct analyses of technological change, its technical resources are dwarfed by those of any large firm. As a result, the CGT is poorly equipped to develop viable proposals on technical matters. Even if it wished to strengthen its technical capacity, the perilous state of its finances makes this difficult.

The CGT's Internal Structure

Despite decisions made by two CGT congresses in the 1990s to pursue internal reform and democratization, the union has been quite timid in encouraging democratic debate; those who dare to challenge its orientation or structure risk being castigated. Indeed, two leading students of the West German labor movement have characterized the CGT as an "antimodel" and cite its refusal to reform as the reason why the CGT has "declined precipitously." They claim that the CGT has "thus far responded conservatively to the most recent wave of social and economic challenges buffeting labour movements the world over, adopting policies of isolation and protectionism rather than taking a progressive approach that 'dares more democracy.'"[38] Stephen Silvia and Andrei Markovits urge union strategists to "recognise the immense democratising potential of new technologies and cultural innovations and harness these developments to improve the lives of employees instead of clinging to an allegedly 'authentic' conceptualisation of working-class culture. . . . This fanciful depiction, firmly rooted in the past, has made it all the more difficult for many union officials actually to come to grips with the essential task of carving out a central place for unions within the complex and cross-cutting series of social networks that constitute the substance of wage earners' lives today."[39]

In brief, CGT intervention in a more effective manner within the field of technological change would require the confederation to undergo a veritable organizational, ideological, and culture revolution. Given the relatively unfavorable external environment, including plural unionism, hostile employers, and a difficult economic situation, there is little likelihood of this occurring in the foreseeable future.

CONCLUSION?

What has been the consequence of the massive end-of-year strikes in 1995 and others since then? While the strikes dramatically signify the resurgence of labor militance, they do not appear to presage a basic change in the CGT's orientation, since they were primarily defensive in nature, seeking to prevent benefit reductions, layoffs, and the privatization of public-sector firms. Further, they were concentrated in the public sector (especially postal and transportation workers) and did not spread to private firms. The strikes were highly influential in terms of France's wider political climate: They doubtless contributed to delegitimating the conservative government of Alain Juppé and thereby helped produce the extraordinary defeat of the conservative coalition in the 1997 parliamentary elections. However, contrary to many analyses appearing in the United States, in important respects the strikes were quite unsuccessful.[40] Stephen Bornstein and Pierre-Eric Tixier, for example, point to "the stunning contrast between the lengthy and extensive nature of the 1995 movement and its extremely limited outcome."[41] Although the Juppé government postponed some elements of its planned restructuring of the welfare state, it speedily adopted others (including the weakening of union control over the social security system); the Socialist government elected in 1997 took pains to limit expectations that it would alter the basic social and economic policy orientation of its conservative predecessor.

The 1995 strikes and others since then have had virtually no effect in stimulating greater CGT efforts to shape technological change. In contrast to the previous nationwide strike wave of May 1968, there were no demands in 1995 for a voice in decisions concerning control of production and technology.

Another catalyst for change might derive from the process of European integration, especially the implementation of the Social Charter of the European Union, which mandates works council consultation among firms with operations in multiple member countries of the European Union. However, the CGT is not a member of the European Confederation of Trade Unions, which means that the latter's impact on the CGT will be limited.

And yet we have learned in the present momentous and tumultuous epoch to beware of all predictions, especially those that proclaim that the future will resemble the past. History, including that of the CGT as it has entered its second century, is surely not yet at an end.

NOTES

1. The most provocative statement of this position is Dominique Labbé and Maurice Croisat, *La fin des syndicats* (Paris: L'Harmattan, 1992). Their position is more nuanced than the quite unequivocal title of the book. Alain Touraine et al., *Le Mouvement ouvrier* (Paris: Fayard, 1984), had earlier argued that the historic mission of the labor movement may have been exhausted. For a review essay analyzing alternative approaches to the crisis of French trade unions, see René Mouriaux and Françoise Subileau, "La Crise syndicale en France entre 1981 et 1990: Analyses et interprétations globales," paper presented to the Twelfth World Congress of Sociology, Madrid, 1990. The crisis of French unions has considerably worsened since their paper was completed. Also see Geneviève Bibes and René Mouriaux, eds., *Les Syndicats européens à l'épreuve* (Paris: Presses de la FNSP, 1990). The best treatment of crisis in the CGT is Guy Groux and René Mouriaux, *La C.G.T., Crises et alternatives* (Paris: Economica, 1992). Also see their *La C.F.D.T.* (Paris: Economica, 1989), and "The Dilemma of Unions Without Members," in Anthony Daley, *The Mitterrand Era: Policy Alternatives and Political Mobilization in France* (London: Macmillan, 1995), pp. 172–185. For other analyses of the recent trajectory of the French labor movement, see Mark Kesselman, "The New Shape of French Labor and Industrial Relations: Ce n'est plus la même chose," in Paul Godt, ed., *Policymaking in France: From de Gaulle to Mitterrand* (London: Pinter Publishers, 1989), pp. 165–175; Kesselman, "Where It Stops, Nobody Knows: The Troubled Trajectory of the French Labor Movement," in John T. S. Keeler and Martin A. Schain, eds., *Chirac's Challenge: Liberalization, Europeanization, and Malaise in France* (New York: St. Martin's Press, 1996), pp. 143–165; René Mouriaux, *Le Syndicalisme face à la crise* (Paris: La Découverte, 1986); Pierre Rosanvallon, *La Question syndicale* (Paris: Calmann-Lévy, 1988); and Pierre-Eric Tixier, *Mutation ou déclin du syndicalisme? Le cas de la CFDT* (Paris: Presses Universitaires de France, 1992).

2. For some data on the diffusion of technological innovations in France in the last two decades, see Jean Magniadas, "La vie difficile des travailleurs en cette fin de siècle," in Claude Willard, ed., *La France Ouvrière*, vol. 3, *De 1968 à nos jours* (Paris: Les Editions de l'Atelier, 1995), pp. 186–187. For analyses of changes in the character of production in France, see Benjamin Coriat, *L'Atelier et le Robot. Essai sur le Fordisme et la Production de Masse à l'Age de l'Electronique* (Paris: Bourgois, 1990); Jean Lojkine, *La révolution informationnelle* (Paris: PUF, 1992); Jacques Bidet and Jacques Texier, eds., *La Crise du travail* (Paris: PUF, 1995); Philippe Zarifian, *Quels modèles d'or-*

ganisation pour l'industrie européenne? L'Emergence de la Firme coopératrice (Paris: L'Harmattan, 1993); and Zarifian, *Le Travail et l'Evénement. Essai sur le travail industriel à l'époque actuelle* (Paris: l'Harmattan, 1995). As Michael Hanagan observed, commenting on an earlier draft of this chapter, one should beware, when using a concept like "fordism," of obscuring how complex and variegated is production, distribution, and regulation in any large economy. Different techniques of production coexist and, when technological changes occur, they neither begin from a blank historical slate nor wipe that slate clean.

3. For a few examples of a vast literature, see Stephen A. Marglin and Juliet R. Schor, *The Golden Age of Capitalism: Reinterpreting the Postwar Experience* (New York: Oxford University Press, 1990); Philip Armstrong, Andrew Glyn, and John Harrison, *Capitalism since 1945* (Oxford: Oxford University Press, 1991); and Andrew Glyn, "Social Democracy and Full Employment," *New Left Review,* no. 211 (May/June 1995): 33–55.

4. See Alessandro Pizzorno, "Political Exchange and Collective Identity in Industrial Conflict," in Colin Crouch and Alessandro Pizzorno, eds., *The Resurgence of Class Conflict in Western Europe since 1968,* vol. 2, *Comparative Analyses* (New York: Holmes & Meier, 1978), pp. 277–298; Adam Przeworski, *Capitalism and Social Democracy* (New York: Cambridge University Press, 1985), chaps. 1, 4, 6; Claus Offe, *Disorganized Capitalism: Contemporary Transformations of Work and Politics* (Cambridge, MA: MIT Press, 1984), chap. 7; and Samuel Bowles and Herbert Gintis, "The Crisis of Liberal Democratic Capitalism: The Case of the United States," *Politics and Society* 11, no. 1 (1982): 51–94.

5. Again, the literature is vast. See Walter Korpi, *The Working Class in Welfare Capitalism* (London: Routledge and Kegan Paul, 1978); Przeworski, *Capitalism and Social Democracy;* Gosta Esping-Andersen, *Politics Against Markets: The Social-Democratic Road to Power* (Princeton, NJ: Princeton University Press, 1985); and Jonas Pontusson, *The Limits of Social Democracy: Investment Politics in Sweden* (Ithaca, NY: Cornell University Press, 1992).

6. The foundational statement is Michael J. Piore and Charles F. Sabel, *The Second Industrial Divide: Possibilities for Prosperity* (New York: Basic Books, 1984). Also see literature cited in earlier footnotes.

7. Shoshana Zuboff, *In the Age of the Smart Machine: The Future of Work and Power* (New York: Basic Books, 1986), p. 243.

8. For descriptions of some relatively successful efforts, see Kathleen Thelen, *Union of Parts: Labor Politics in Postwar Germany* (Ithaca, NY: Cornell University Press, 1991); Lowell Turner, *Democracy at Work: Changing World Markets and the Future of Labor Unions* (Ithaca, NY: Cornell University Press, 1991); Christian Berggren, *Alternatives to Lean Production: Work Organization in the Swedish Auto Industry* (Ithaca, NY: ILR Press, 1992); and Miriam Golden and Jonas Pontusson, eds., *Bargaining for Change: Union Politics in North America and Europe* (Ithaca, NY: Cornell University Press,

1992). The fact that in other countries labor movements have been quite successful in helping shape the process of technological change belies claims that unions necessarily lack the necessary technical competence or vision to be effective in this domain. (Commenting on an earlier draft of this chapter, Bernard E. Brown questioned the implicit premise that there was potential latitude for any labor movement to play a constructive role in regulating technological innovation.) And of course, on a broader level, northern European labor movements played a key role in the social democratic "success stories" in these countries in the postwar period that involved promoting economic and technological modernization. However, in the current period, all labor movements have come under severe stress.

9. From the vantage point of the late 1990s, however, it appears that the disparity between the capacity of national labor movements to safeguard benefits is a matter of degree, not a difference in kind; alternatively, there may be a time lag between ability of the more and less favorably situated labor movements in this respect—but an increasing convergence as the decade advanced. For a study that stresses the importance of institutional factors in explaining why labor unions respond in different ways to large-scale layoffs (a related but quite different matter from technological change), see Miriam A. Golden, *Heroic Defeat: The Politics of Job Loss* (New York: Cambridge University Press, 1997). Golden does not include the powerful labor movements of northern Europe in her study.

10. For a study of France's characteristic style of organizing the political economy, see Peter A. Hall, *Governing the Economy: The Politics of State Intervention in Britain and France* (New York: Oxford University Press, 1986). Hall and others demonstrate that the statist pattern was very successful in certain situations and for certain purposes. It was able to help France overcome economic backwardness and achieve a commanding position in some key industrial sectors. But this pattern appears to be ill-equipped to promote rapid innovation, decentralized initiative, and lateral cooperation among a variety of actors—the requisites for success in the current era. For a study of how decentralized, self-organized networks have been effective in Italy, see Richard M. Locke, *Remaking the Italian Economy* (Ithaca, NY: Cornell University Press, 1995).

11. For analyses in English of the Auroux reforms, see Bernard E. Brown, "Worker Democracy in Socialist France," New York: Center for Labor-Management Studies, The Graduate School and University Center of the City University of New York. Occasional Papers, no. 7, 1989; Brown, "The Rise and Fall of *Autogestion* in France," in M. Donald Hancock et al., eds., *Managing Modern Capitalism: Industrial Renewal and Workplace Democracy in the United States and Western Europe* (New York: Praeger, 1991), pp. 195–214; Duncan Gallie, "*Les lois Auroux:* The Reform of French Industrial Relations?" in Howard Machin and Vincent Wright, eds., *Economic Policy and Policy-making under the Mitterrand Presidency, 1981–1984* (New York: St. Martin's Press, 1984), pp. 205–221; Chris Howell, "The Dilemmas of

Post-Fordism: Socialists, Flexibility, and Labor-Market Deregulation in France," *Politics & Society* 20, no. 1 (1992); Howell, *Regulating Labor: The State and Industrial Relations Reform in Postwar France* (Princeton, NJ: Princeton University Press, 1992); Bernard Moss, "After the Auroux Laws: Employers, Industrial Relations and the Right in France," *West European Politics* 11, no. 1 (January 1988): 68–80; W. Rand Smith, "Towards *Autogestion* in Socialist France? The Impact of Industrial Relations Reform," *West European Politics* 10, no. 1 (January 1987): 46–62; and Frank L. Wilson, "Democracy in the Workplace: The French Experience," *Politics & Society* 19, no. 4 (1991): 439–462.

12. Michel Coffineau, *Les Lois Auroux, dix ans après, Rapport au premier ministre* (Paris: La Documentation Française, 1993), p. 48.

13. Ibid., p. 23.

14. However, the number has declined since then as a result of the recession of the early 1990s. For example, according to figures from the Ministère du Travail, *La Négociation collective en 1993*, vol. 1 (Paris: La Documentation française, 1993), p. 12, the number of enterprise-level agreements declined by 12 percent between 1992 and 1993.

15. Coffineau, *Les Lois Auroux*, p. 77. Other figures in this paragraph are from the Coffineau report.

16. For analyses of this question, see Mark Kesselman, "French Labour Confronts Technological Change: Reform that Never Was?" in Anthony Daley, ed., *The Mitterrand Era: Policy Alternatives and Political Mobilization in France* (London: Macmillan, 1995), pp. 161–171; Tiennot Grumbach, "Nouvelles technologies et relations collectives du travail, syndicat et comité d'enterprise: une nouvelle répartition des rôles," *Droit social*, no. 6 (June 1992): 544–555; Pierre Cam and Patrick Chaumette, "Expertise technologique du comité d'enterprise," *Droit social*, no. 3 (March 1989): 220–228; François Cochet, "L'expertise en nouvelles technologies: le point du vue du praticien," *Droit social*, no. 6 (June 1992): 556–562; Danièle Linhart, *Le Torticolis de l'autruche. L'éternelle modernisation des enterprises françaises* (Paris: Le Seuil, 1991); and Véronique Sandoval, "La 'négociation' de l'introduction des nouvelles technologies dans l'enterprise," *La Note de l'IRES* 20, 2nd semester, 1989: 11–24. It is significant that a more than 40-page review of the functioning of works councils barely mentions their consultative role regarding technological change: Robert Tchobanian, "France: From Conflict to Social Dialogue?" in Joel Rogers and Wolfgang Streeck, eds., *Works Councils: Consultation, Representation and Cooperation in Industrial Relations* (Chicago: University of Chicago Press, 1995), chap. 5.

17. See Vivien A. Schmidt, *From State to Market? The Transformation of French Business and Government* (New York: Cambridge University Press, 1996), chaps. 5, 6. Schmidt aptly characterizes the shift in the key period following 1986 as "*dirigiste* disengagement," in order to underline that the state continued to play an activist role, albeit toward quite the opposite end than that of direct management.

18. Howell, in *Regulating Labor,* stresses the importance of the coincidence between the decentralization and deregulation of French industrial relations beginning in the 1980s.

19. See Guy Groux, "Le Syndicalisme d'enterprise: Lieu commun ou notion ambigue?" *Raison Présente,* no. 111 (third quarter, 1994): 61–80; Groux and Mouriaux, "The Dilemma of Unions without Members"; chapter 12 in this volume; and Kesselman, "French Labour Confronts Technological Change." An early analysis of this conundrum is Gérard Adam, "L'Institutionalisation des syndicats: esquisse d'une problématique," *Droit Social* 46, no. 11 (November 1983): 597–600; cited in Anthony Daley, "The Travail of Sisyphus: French Unions After 1981," in George Ross and Andrew Martin, eds., *The Changing Place of Labor in European Society: The End of Labor's Century?* (forthcoming).

20. Groux, "Le Syndicalisme d'enterprise;" Howell, *Regulating Labor;* and Daley, "The Travail of Sisyphus." The Auroux laws provided the legal opening for such retrenchment by authorizing local unions to bargain away gains that were enshrined in higher-level agreements. This practice had hitherto been prohibited.

21. See Martin A. Schain, "Relations between the CGT and the CFDT: Politics and Mass Mobilization," in Mark Kesselman and Guy Groux, eds., *The French Workers' Movement: Economic Crisis and Political Change* (Boston: Allen & Unwin, 1984), chap. 16. Plural unionism need not necessarily weaken unions, as the Italian case suggests and as is evident in certain periods of French labor mobilization. However, for plural unionism not to occur, it seems essential for unions to be autonomous vis-à-vis political parties. The PCF's intimate ties to the PCF and, to a lesser extent, other French unions' politicization have been key factors in limiting unions' unity and popular support. As chapter 10 in this volume documents, there is strong popular opposition to unions having close ties to political parties. In a poll of wage earners commissioned by the CGT, when asked what the CGT should do to regain its former standing, one of the two most frequently given responses was that it should distance itself from political [i.e., political party] influence. CGT, *Analyses et Documents Economiques,* no. 67 (December 1995): 15. Yet the matter is not so simple: Recall that the CGT enjoyed its greatest popular support when its ties to the PCF were closest (in the immediate postwar decade). See George Ross, *Workers and Communists in France: From Popular Front to Eurocommunism* (Berkeley: University of California Press, 1982).

22. The title of what is arguably the most famous union publication in the postwar period: CFDT, *Les dégâts du progrès: Les travailleurs face au changement technique* (Paris: Editions du Seuil, 1977). This study—which relied on information supplied by CFDT federations in sectors experiencing rapid technological change—was heavily influenced by a "new-left" orientation critical of the then-dominant technocratic discourse championing "the benefits of technological progress" (p. 20). The CFDT's stance was in part a reaction to the

CGT's orientation. The CGT in turn tended to react defensively to the CFDT's position. In the late 1970s, in its centrist turn (*recentrage*), the CFDT abandoned the attempt to play a leading role in shaping technological change. It continued to seek a role in negotiating the process of change, but it now proclaimed that it should focus on representing workers' interests in minimizing the social costs of technological and economic change. For the views of CFDT leaders defending the new approach, see Edmond Maire, "Interrogation sur l'enterprise et l'anticapitalisme, l'individu, et l'action syndical," *CFDT Aujourd'hui* (March-April 1986): 43–60; and Jean-Paul Jacquier, *Les cow-boys ne meurent jamais: L'aventure syndicale continue* (Paris: Syros, 1986).

23. See Jean-Pierre Huiban, "The Industrial Counterproposal as an Element of Trade Union Strategy," in Kesselman and Groux, eds., *The French Workers' Movement*, pp. 224–237; and Anthony Daley, *Steel, State, and Labor: Mobilization and Adjustment in France* (Pittsburgh: University of Pittsburgh Press, 1996), chap. 6. Also see Jean-Louis Moynot, *Au milieu du gué: CGT, syndicalisme et démocratie de masse* (Paris: PUF, 1982) and Ross, *Workers and Communists in France*.

24. Anthony Daley, "The Travail of Sisyphus."

25. As described by Daley, *Steel, State, and Labor,* and Smith, chap. 11 in this volume, the labor movement did succeed, both by its counterproposals and its militant opposition to layoffs, in improving the severance packages that workers received.

26. Guy Groux, *Le conflit en mouvement* (Paris: Hachette, 1996), p. 39.

27. Ibid., p. 43.

28. Ibid., p. 45

29. Dominique Labbé, "Trade Unionism in France since the Second World War," *West European Politics* 17, no. 1 (January 1994): 151. Labbé claims that a similar shift occurred within the CFDT, although I would imagine to a lesser extent. He characterizes the general trend as "the tendency of the union to become concentrated in social categories in relative decline and to become less interested in those sectors which have, quantitatively and qualitatively, increased in importance in French society."

30. He develops his position in Gérard Alezard et al., *Faut-il réinventer le syndicalisme?* (Paris: L'Archipel, 1995).

31. For example, in a fine study of organized labor's attempt to influence the evolution of the French steel industry, Anthony Daley notes that the CGT "mimicked the productivist rhetoric articulated by industry managers." Daley, *Steel, State, and Labor,* p. 83. Although Daley is referring here to the 1950s, the CGT displayed this stance through most of the postwar period. Daley notes that, in the 1960s, "the CGT viewed industrial policy toward steel in terms of its impact on employment . . ." (ibid., p. 111). The CGT pressed for higher wages and job protection, as well as nationalization of the steel industry, but not control over the design of technology. Even at the height of the CGT's attempt to shape investment and technological decisions, what Daley calls propositional unionism in the late 1970s, the union

paid little attention to technological design. Instead, it focused on increasing the demand for steel, improving working conditions, and maintaining employment levels.

32. See Michael Burawoy, *The Politics of Production: Factory Regimes Under Capitalism and Socialism* (London: Verso, 1985), chap. 1. Burawoy challenges a conception of technological change (implicit in Harry Braverman's magisterial *Labor and Monopoly Capital: The Degradation of Work in the Twentieth Century* [New York: Monthly Review Press, 1974]) that is quite similar to that of the CGT.

33. This is evident in the collective bargaining agreements negotiated in the 1960s and 1970s. I owe this point to Jean Kaspar. The most dramatic example of the way that the CGT tended to convert "qualitative" grievances into demands for wage hikes occurred during the general strike of May-June 1968. There was an embarrassingly wide chasm between the varied goals of the movement and the major gain proposed in the Grenelle accords negotiated by CGT leaders—an increase in the minimum wage—as Georges Séguy learned when he was hooted down by workers at the CGT's "fortress" of Renault-Billancourt after proudly visiting striking workers there to announce the proposed agreement. (It should be noted that the negotiations also resulted in local unions later gaining legal protection.) As Bernard E. Brown observed in comments on an earlier draft of this chapter, given its hegemonic role in the labor movement until the 1960s (the CGT received as many votes in shopfloor elections as all other confederations combined), the union bears a heavy responsibility for the labor movement's failure to confront the issue of technological change for so long.

34. Ross, *Workers and Communists in France.*

35. Jean Lojkine, contribution to a round table with CGT officials, as reported in *Analyses & Documents Economiques* (Cahier du Centre Confédéral d'Etudes Economiques et Sociales de la CGT), no. 71 (March 1997): 21. Lojkine develops the argument more fully in *Le Tabou de la gestion* (Paris: Editions de l'Atelier, 1996), based on case studies of attempts by CGT unions to influence firm policies.

36. I noted earlier that one exception was the brief period of proposition-force unionism. In the 1980s the CGT followed the lead of the PCF in advocating that *nouveaux critères de gestion* replace capitalist calculations of profit and loss. But the CGT did not sufficiently demonstrate what this meant or how it would occur, and the new approach failed to mobilize local union activity.

37. Pierre-Eric Tixier, "La Représentation des salariés au quotidien: Perspectives comparatives européennes," *La Revue de l'IRES,* no. 14 (Winter 1994): 38.

38. Stephen J. Silvia and Andrei S. Markovits, "An Ounce of Prevention? The Reform of the German Trade Union Federation," *German Politics* 4, no. 1 (April 1995): 75.

39. Ibid., p. 76. They observe that there has been no counterpart in the CGT to the thoroughgoing debate, review of union structure, and reform efforts that recently occurred in the German labor movement.

40. For "triumphalist" analyses of the strikes appearing in the United States, see Miz Butzbaugh, "Impressions from the French Strike: A Glimpse of Labor's Power," *Against the Current* 11, no. 1 (March/April; 1996): 11; and Bob Fitch, "Dead Men Leading: Our City Labor Union Leaders Need French Lessons," *Village Voice,* April 11, 1996. This contrasts with the tone of most French accounts, including some by those who ardently supported the strike movement.

41. Stephen Bornstein and Pierre-Eric Tixier, "The Strikes of 1995: A Crisis of the French Model?" Working Paper 5.46 (Berkeley: Center for German and European Studies, 1996), p. 4. I believe, however, that they overstate the case. (Their position parallels that of CFDT leader Nicole Notat, who provided qualified support for the Juppé plan and distanced herself from the strike.) For example, they claim that "the strikes never really moved beyond the point at which they started—groups of public employees striking to defend their working conditions and their particularistic benefits packages . . ." (p. 16). Granted that private-sector workers, fearful for their jobs in an era of retrenchment and downsizing, did not actively strike. But emphasizing the particularistic character of the strikers' demands obscures that, despite the hardships caused by the strikes, they enjoyed enormous public support. Why? Doubtless because it was commonly believed (doubtless accurately) that the Juppé plan presaged a more comprehensive effort to scale back the welfare state, introduce further flexibility in labor markets, and weaken the labor movement. Their interpretation also makes it difficult to explain the 1997 electoral turnaround.

Part III

Unions, Society, and Worker Mobilization

CHAPTER SIX

Immigration and Trade Unions in France: A Problem and an Opportunity

Martin A. Schain

During the past century, unions have had little, if any, influence over the influx of immigrant workers. Policy over entry has been decided by the state either directly or in cooperation with selected business interests, without the participation of union representatives. Policy over incorporation of immigrant workers already in the country, on the other hand, has deeply involved union organizations, sometimes in collaboration with political parties.

In this chapter I analyze attempts by unions to deal with the challenge posed by immigrant workers during the period of European immigration between the two world wars and compare union action to the parallel period of Third World immigration during the Fifth Republic. Clearly the patterns of union action are different—but why? The answer, I would argue, lies in part in the difference in the challenge, but also in differences in the environment within which trade union organizations have functioned during these two periods as well as differences in the structure of trade union organizations themselves.

For trade unions in France, immigration has provided both a problem and an opportunity. As in other countries, the problem has been that immigrant workers, often recruited by employers and the state over the opposition of trade unions, have competed economically with native workers for scarce resources, including jobs, housing, and community services—especially in localities and industrial sectors where they have been specifically recruited by employers. Socially, immigrants also have presented a challenge to community identity, particularly in working-class communities in the suburbs of cities in which there has been industrial expansion.

Nevertheless, for a trade union movement, able to organize and *encadrer* this new labor, immigration could offer a real possibility for worker mobilization and organizational expansion. Organization also could foreclose the possible challenge of the mobilization of immigrant workers by associations outside of the trade union movement. In this sense the marketplace challenge also presented—under certain conditions—an opportunity for greater strength. Given these possibilities, what has been the reaction of French trade unions to immigration? How have unions reacted to the influx of immigrant workers? And how have they dealt with the concentrations of immigrant workers in specific industrial sectors?

EUROPEAN IMMIGRATION

The Post–World War I Wave of Immigration

In this century, three overlapping waves of immigrants were recruited into France from neighboring European countries. The early part of the century was dominated by Italian and Belgian immigration, followed by a period of Polish immigration (and significant "internal migration" from Algeria), and then (after World War II) by a wave of immigration from Portugal.

Each wave of immigration was directed in various ways into specific industries in specific areas of the country, and within a generation of their arrival, each wave, as a part of the French working class, formed a potential constituency (and problem) for the French trade unions. With a stagnant native population, the number of resident immigrants increased from just over 1 million at the turn of the century to 2.7 million in 1931. About 60 percent of this population was active in the labor force in that year (about the same percentage as in 1901), and 63 percent of immigrants in the labor force worked in industry and transport (also about the same as in 1901).

A great deal has been written recently of the high concentrations of immigrant labor in specific industries and at specific skill levels in the 1980s. However, the pattern of that decade was not substantially different from the one that developed after World War I. In 1901 only 6 percent of workers in industry and transport were immigrants, compared with 17 percent (of a larger industrial workforce) in 1931. By the 1930s trade unions claiming to represent workers could not avoid dealing with immigrants in some way. This is particularly evident if we note the higher concentrations of immigrants in industries that were important to trade unions (see table 6.1). In particular geographic areas, concentrations were even greater. In the coal mines of the department of the Nord, 62 percent of the workers (and 75 percent of un-

Table 6.1   Percentage of Foreigners in Specific Industries

Occupation	1906 (%)	1931 (%)	% Change
Mining	6.2	40.1	548
Steel mills	17.8	34.8	96
Quarrying	8.7	26.1	200
Construction	10.2	24.1	132
Rubber/paper	3.6	10.7	197
Chemicals	10	14.7	47
Metalwork	4.5	10.5	133

Source: *Résultants statistiques de recensement général de la population* I, no. 5 (1936): 51, as reprinted in Gary S. Cross, *Immigrant Workers in Industrial France* (Philadelphia: Temple University Press, 1983), p. 160.

dergound workers) were immigrants in 1931, as were 70 percent of the iron miners and 90 percent of the workers in certain factories in Lorraine.[1]

These concentrations have been attributed largely to a pattern of state intervention that had begun before World War I. The loss of manpower during the war accentuated the need for immigrant labor, and both public and private means were set into place to recruit workers and to direct them into specific areas. In 1919 and 1920 the French government concluded bilateral agreements with a number of countries (most notably, Poland, Italy, and Czechoslovakia) for labor recruitment, and in the years that followed commercial agencies organized by employers were authorized to recruit immigrants directly for particular work sites. Polish workers from the same regions of Poland, for example, were sent to the same areas of France. This way of organizing immigration assured that there would be high concentrations of immigrants with similar backgrounds installed throughout the country, in places where labor was in short supply and in occupations that native French workers were less willing to fill. Of course, the dynamics of the process also modified the occupational and geographic structure of the French working class.[2]

Indeed, each wave of immigration altered the structure of the working class, and each reacted politically in a somewhat different way.[3] Moreover, because they were a large proportion of workers in several sectors in which strike activity exploded during the postwar period, immigrant workers rapidly posed an unexpected challenge to the French trade union movement.

STRIKES AND STRATEGY

Two waves of strikes particularly challenged the authority of organized labor at critical moments: the strike wave of 1919–1920 and the better-known sitdown strikes of 1936 that followed the election of the Popular Front government. In each case the challenge of immigration was part of the larger challenge to the relationship between the trade union movement and the emerging industrial working class. The most dynamic strikes were in areas in which the CGT had few members and where many workers had come from elsewhere. In many cases they were in plants and areas where there were high concentrations of immigrant workers.

The 1919 strike wave began as an uprising in May/June in the Paris region against the first national agreement that had ever been reached between the employers association and the national federation of metals workers. "Day after day the committee rooms of the various syndical organizations were invaded by the excited mob of workers, who treated the leaders to all manner of abuse, and even on one occasion, carried them off bodily to be exposed in public to the insults of an infuriated crowd."[4] The strike movement soon spread to other industrial areas and rapidly involved more than 200,000 workers, mostly in areas of more recent industrialization. In the new industrial areas of Paris, Lyons, and Marseilles, the population doubled and quadrupled between the prewar period and 1931. The largest share of this increase can be attributed to migration from the countryside, but perhaps 8 to 10 percent consisted of immigrants from Poland, Italy, and Spain.[5]

In the end, the challenge posed by this postwar strike wave contributed to the split of the CGT in 1922. Shortly after the end of the strikes, the CGT National Confederal Committee had voted to exclude the minority factions created throughout the organization during the strikes. The dissident factions accused the confederation of having lost touch with the masses of industrial workers. Many of the dissidents were soon integrated into the CGTU, which had split from the CGT, but within a few years it was clear that neither the CGT nor the CGTU could successfully *encadrer* these new workers. Membership in the industrial federations first rose dramatically and then declined just as rapidly a few years later.

Despite imaginative attempts to organize a mass membership, CGTU leaders generally failed, and often found that they were informed of strike movements in the morning editions of the bourgeois press.[6] At the 1927 CGTU congress, the rapporteur Gaillard indicated his frustration about the failure to organize the new industrial workers in a way that is reminiscent of many of his counterparts in the American Federation of Labor during the same period: "Let us continue to organize the skilled workers, above all in the small and middle sized industries. As for the others, when they have decided they will come to us."[7] By 1927 two-thirds of the vastly reduced membership of both confederations were employed by either the government or by public utilities.[8]

In this context, the CGT supported government efforts in the 1920s to import labor but sought to influence the placement of workers in ways that would protect the interests of French workers. The confederation supported legislation in 1926 and 1932 that would limit the right of immigrant workers to change jobs and that permitted unions to petition for a quota on immigrants working in a particular sector. With the onset of the Depression, the CGT construction and garment unions petitioned the government to limit the percentage of immigrants employed and to shorten the duration of work permits. In general, they tended to see immigrant workers as a problem, not as an opportunity.[9]

In contrast, after a series of confusing policies, the CGTU in 1926 developed a position that tilted strongly toward the integration of immigrant workers. In his report to the 1925 congress of the CGTU, the national secretary declared that "If you do not support the foreign workers they will be formed in the hands of the capitalists as a mass of labor which can be used to beat you in all the demands which you make."[10] By 1926, 16 percent of the confederation's budget was devoted to propaganda among immigrants, mostly to publication of foreign-language newspapers. The CGTU organized separate language groups and, at the departmental and national levels, put into place immigrant manpower commissions. Finally, it supported ethnic organizations and demonstrations among immigrant groups.[11]

How successful were these efforts? In one sense, the numbers are not impressive. By 1930 the confederation had recruited about 17,000 members who had been born outside of France, 5 percent of its total claimed membership. This represented less than 2 percent of immigrants working in industry. Nevertheless, in context the effort was relatively successful. Union organization was not impressive during this period; the total CGTU membership in industry comprised no more than 4.3 percent of all industrial workers.[12] If we assume that immigrant workers were far more difficult to mobilize than native French workers because they were more vulnerable to management and state pressure, this effort seems more impressive. Finally, the effort to incorporate immigrant industrial labor was undertaken in the context of an ambivalent attitude toward the organization of industrial labor in general.

The context of the challenge had changed by 1936. The CGT and the CGTU had reunited in 1935. Five days after the Popular Front victory, a wave of strikes broke out that eventually involved almost 2 million workers. Although the better-organized public services did participate, once again it was the poorly organized industrial workers who took the lead. Once again the strike movements posed both an opportunity and a challenge for the now newly reunited CGT, and once again the challenge involved, although it was not dominated by, immigrant workers.

The opportunity was particularly important in the mining areas of the Nord/Pas de Calais, where whole communities of Polish miners had been moved after the war. Until 1936 the tight organization of the company towns, combined with the activities of the antiunion and anti-Communist Polish Workers' Association, made union activity difficult. However, the sit-in strikes of 1936 marked a sharp break with the past in this region. By the end of the strike wave, it was estimated that 80 percent of the Polish miners were members of the united CGT.[13]

In the Nord and Lorraine (particularly Meurthe-et-Moselle), CGT membership grew rapidly in the mining areas of high Polish and Italian immigration. Pierre Belleville, a French sociologist, explains the difference between implantation in Meurthe-et-Moselle and Moselle after the war by the preponderance of Italian militants in the *cités minières* and by their impact on both the Communist Party and the CGT. Exploiting the opportunity created by the great strike movement, they first established a CGT presence and mobilized new CGT and Communist militants. "The PCF benefitted when, after 1945, a second period of naturalization began. It gained in one single blow active militants, members and [an] audience. . . . The consequences are still being felt. As a general rule, the dynamism of the militants of Italian origin is considerable. After having largely contributed to the orientation of the CGT, to the elimination of the SFIO in the working class community, they continue to make their mark on the CGT and the PCF."[14]

There is no way to isolate the proportion of membership contributed by immigrants, but available analyses indicate that in the Nord and the Meurthe-et-Moselle union presence was dynamic and rapidly expanding. Analyses also indicate that these were not areas of conversion but new territory. Thus, with their integration into the newly united CGT, immigrant communities contributed to the establishment and expansion of the CGT and the Communist Party in industrial areas where their strength was either relatively stagnant or even diminishing. Unlike other industrial sectors, union membership in these *cités minières* (and in the Mining Federation) remained stable after 1936.

Although the confederation continued to oppose new immigration until World War II, the 1936 strike mobilization of immigrant workers stimulated greater integrative efforts and more effective organization for those immigrants who were already in France.

THIRD WORLD IMMIGRATION

THE NEW IMMIGRATION

The ultimate effort of the CGT to integrate Italian and Polish (as well as Spanish and Jewish) workers into unions, and ultimately—through the

PCF—into the French political system strengthened the position of organized labor and was related to the acceptance of these workers as a potential clientele. By contrast, from the earliest years—even before World War II—North African immigrants were seen as temporary workers, who would—indeed should—return to their countries of origin.[15] In fact, during the period of the Fourth Republic, fewer than 20 percent of North Africans who arrived in France each year remained in the country.[16]

The larger context for this position was a growing opposition by all unions to the increased immigration (and the pattern of regularization of undocumented immigrant workers) that was being supported by the government and employers through the Office Nationale d'Immigration (ONI) after World War II. In 1948 the CGT passed a resolution opposing all new immigration; it continued to pass similar resolutions through 1961. The Force Ouvrière (FO) was somewhat less hostile (it linked immigration to a policy of full employment), and the CFTC remained open to immigration in specific sectors.

During the 1960s, however, the positions of all three unions (the CFDT more or less replaced the CFTC in 1964) grew increasingly similar and more sympathetic to immigration. On the one hand, the unions dropped their strident opposition to labor market immigration; on the other hand, they tended to accentuate the need to integrate immigrant workers into the working class individually rather than collectively.[17] Unions represented the individual interests of immigrant workers in various ways but were reluctant to co-opt them collectively as they had in the interwar period. This was particularly true regarding the new immigrants from the Maghreb.

Nevertheless, because North Africans accounted for a large number of workers in key sectors of industry, union organizations were not able to ignore them. By the early 1980s almost 25 percent of French miners, 25 percent of construction workers, 30 percent of sanitation workers, 5.4 percent of workers in merchandise services, and 15 percent of workers in auto construction were immigrants.[18] By the late 1980s the old working-class suburbs were overwhelmingly concentrations of new working-class immigration. "In neighborhoods [in the Paris region] where more than 40% of the active population are workers, we find only 15% of the native French [population], 18% of the Spanish, 21% of the Portuguese, as opposed to 46% of the Moroccan population and 43% of the Algerians."[19]

Immigrant workers also were difficult to ignore because of labor law changes. After 1968 immigrant workers gained more or less full access to trade union rights. Legislation passed by governments of the right in 1972 and 1975 granted immigrants the right to vote in "social" elections for shop stewards, union representatives, and plant committees. The 1975 legislation, moreover, permitted them to stand for election and to hold office in trade unions themselves, provided that they were able to "express themselves" in French and had worked in France for at least five years.[20] Paul Dijoud (Giscard's secretary of state for immigration) referred to the new legislation as a "confirmation of the government's dedication to assuring the equality of social rights between foreign and French workers."[21]

Finally, immigrant workers were difficult to ignore because, like their counterparts in 1936, they have refused to remain passive and periodically have been at the core of major strike movements.

STRIKES AND STRATEGY

Beginning in the 1960s, immigrant workers (particularly assembly-line workers) began to emerge as initiators of strike movements, often against the wishes of union militants and union organizations. By the 1970s the CGT and the CFDT, and the PCF, as a result of a series of important strikes that followed the crisis of May–June 1968, began to give considerably more attention to demands made by these workers and were more sympathetic than they had been in the past to expressions of "the right to difference."[22] The challenge that such strikes consistently posed, however, was an evident resistance on the part of immigrant workers from North Africa to simple, individual integration into the trade union movement.

The most concerted series of strikes through which this challenge was expressed occurred after the victory of the Left in May and June, 1981. While there had been a general decline in strike activity up until that time, these strikes tended to break out in sectors and in plants in which there were large numbers of immigrant workers.

The immigrant workers who struck between the fall of 1981 and the spring of 1983 were, for the most part, the most endangered workers in an endangered sector: assembly-line workers in a shrinking auto industry. Like many intense strikes in France, this movement that lasted a year and a half began with mostly nonunionized assembly-line workers in two Renault plants, Billancourt and Flins. In both of these plants, immigrant workers constituted over 50 percent of the blue-collar workforce, concentrated on the most repetitive assembly-line work.

The combination of job cutbacks and assembly-line speedups provoked a three-week walkout in Renault-Billancourt in October 1981, a precursor, as it turned out, to a larger strike wave in the spring and fall of 1982 and then the winter and spring of 1983. The press reports sometimes referred to these strikes as "the May–68 of the immigrants."

What made these strikes most notable, perhaps, was the fact that they were almost the only large strikes that lasted for long periods at this time. In fact, at a time when union membership was in sharp decline, when union influence among French workers also was declining, when unions were increasingly viewed as "too powerful," and when the frequency and amplitude of strike action was diminishing, commentators on the left viewed these immigrant strikes as a (hopeful) sign of mobilization.[23] They were also notable because generally standard demands were posed in terms of "dignity," leading commentators to refer to the most bitter of these strikes (at Citroën and Talbot) as "the springtime of dignity."[24] Although speedups and changes in work rules provoked the strikes, most of the demands that were finally negotiated involved financial settlements of some kind.[25]

The strikes themselves generally followed a well-known pattern of French strike movements. First, they were initiated "at the base" by small groups of nonunionized workers, then they gained the support of others. Thus, the conflict at Citroën-Aulnay began with a remark by a foreman to an assembly-line worker on April 22, 1982, reported as: "I don't discuss things with slaves, with *bougnoules* [a pejorative name for North Africans]." An hour later several hundred workers had walked out.[26] The strike lasted until June. At Renault-Flins, the strike was initiated on January 6, 1983 (the second strike in less than a year) by a few hundred mostly immigrant workers in the paint shop with the support of CFDT, the leading union in the plant. The movement soon spread to other shops in that plant, in part because production was halted.

Second, the strikes caught the unions by surprise, particularly at Citroën, which was dominated by a company union and where the established unions were particularly weak. The unions then attempted to "canalize" the movement, to act as intermediaries with management (and state authorities), and competed with one another in this role. Nevertheless, in no case did the unions seem to dominate the strike process. "But the conflicts in Flins and Billancourt show that the unions are not the masters of the game. The strikers have imposed their own will: 'It is the workers who have set off the strike who must decide about return to work' affirmed a spokesman for the strikers in Flins, the majority of whom are immigrants."[27] In this context, the role of the union delegates from the different centrals varied. The CGT tended to be more open to negotiation in Flins, while the CFDT tended to "stick" closer to the striking immigrant militants.

Finally, the movements lost steam, and settlements were reached with at least short-term gains for the striking workers.[28] Less obvious, however, were the changes that had broader implications for the immigrant workers as a group and for their relationship with the trade unions, which were increasingly dependent on their support in declining industries.

Thus these strikes seemed to mark the integration of North African workers into the more general working-class conflict, but with conditions specific to who they were. Research conducted during this strike period shows a permanent tension between two goals for the unions: "On one hand the recognition of worker individuality, and thus of foreign identity, without which the union cannot be firmly entrenched in its 'base' . . . ; on the other hand, the elimination of ethnicity, age, and sex in the search for a broader legitimacy and representativeness."[29] The result was a compromise, both in the process of canalizing the strikes and in the settlements that were reached.

In each of the auto industry strikes, the force behind the organization and definition of the movement was a committee of striking workers themselves, a committee that remained more or less apart from the union delegates. In each case these committees, which had the confidence of the strikers, performed intermediary roles that ranged from language interpretation to bargaining interpretation and intermediation. In some earlier cases (such as Usinor-Dunkerque in the spring of 1981), these committees had presented themselves as alternatives to the established unions, but during the strike wave of 1982–83, their actions were canalized, if not controlled by the unions. In the end many of their members were integrated into the CGT (most frequently) and the CFDT.

In this sense, the strike movement was an organizational success for the unions, particularly the CGT, but at the cost of recognizing and dealing with collective immigrant representation. It was also an organizational success for the immigrants, many of whom, sponsored by the unions, became shop stewards and members of plant committees after the strike movements.[30]

This pattern was part of a more general struggle by unions to come to terms with the "different," specifically Islamic, aspects of North African workers. In some plants (particularly Renault), the CGT was a more active supporter than the CFDT of specifically religious demands of Muslim workers. During the 1970s, in response to what they perceived as attempts by the government and by management to use Muslim workers to weaken the bargaining strength of the unions, the CGT attempted to mobilize and integrate them by supporting demands for religious practice in the workplace.[31] However, the union was wary of such an approach, and in 1983, during the strike wave, it complained to the government of the dangers of "Iranian influence" in the workplace and in social conflicts. The CGT was also wary of the independent strike committees organized by immigrant workers; the 1982–1983 strike wave marked the first time that it was successful in both working with them and, ultimately, bringing their leaders into the union. In fact, the CGT generally has seen the organization of workers around Islam as a direct challenge to union organization rather than simply a means of union mobilization of Islamic workers.[32]

These strikes also were marked by an element of bitterness that both solidified them as an immigrant movement and that set immigrant workers apart from native French workers. During the run-up to the 1983 local elections, the prime minister, the minister of the interior, and the minister of labor all found occasions to interpret the movement as a challenge of foreign-directed Islamic fundamentalism. Prime Minister Pierre Mauroy noted that this was not a "normal" strike and that "the main difficulties are posed by some immigrant workers who, without disregarding the problems . . . are agitated by religious and political groups that are guided by criteria having little to do with the realities of French society."[33]

Two weeks later, as the strikes gained in intensity (and the elections were closer), Minister of Labor Jean Auroux echoed the same sentiments more directly: "There is evidence of a religious and fundamentalist element in the conflicts which we have encountered, which gives them a slant not entirely confined to trade unionism. Having said that, we live in a secular state and we expect things to remain as they are. I am against the institutionalization of any religion inside the workplace, just as I am against politics in the workplace."[34] Minister of the Interior, Gaston Defferre, also spoke darkly of "fundamentalists" and of "shiites."

In fact, Islamic demands were not important in the 1982–1983 strike movement, and there was no evidence of "outside agitators." Nevertheless, this movement stimulated deep fears within the government and the trade union movement about collective, as opposed to individual, integration of immigrant workers into the trade union movement and into the national community.

THE NEW CONTEXT: LE SYSTÈME AUROUX

Superficially the strike movement of 1982–1983 could be seen as an important step in forging a relationship with immigrant workers and the trade union movement, much as the movements of 1919 to 1929 and 1936 proved to be, even if some of the material gains proved to be temporary (all of the plants concerned continued to reduce employment, particularly among the workers who spearheaded the movement) and the penetration of the union organizations was slow and marginal. In fact, the comparison between the periods serves to reveal a very different trend.

The strikes of the early 1980s were not a watershed for the mobilization of immigrant workers. Despite the presence and periodic activism of immigrants, they have become increasingly easy to ignore, or at least marginalize. During the early period striking immigrant workers posed a challenge in sectors that were areas of growth for the trade union movement. This is no longer true. The "normal" strike level has declined to a third of what it was before 1981, and many of the longest strikes have been in the public sector, where there are relatively few, if any, immigrants.[35] Thus, compared with the earlier period (or even with the years 1981 to 1983), strike mobilization has not provided a context for the integration of immigration workers into the trade union movement. Despite the effective and dramatic strikes in the public services of November and December 1995, this movement served only to reemphasize the relative marginalization of the private sector.

If the traditional proletariat is increasingly dominated by new immigrant labor, it also is shrinking and is less important for the growth and influence of the trade union movement than ever before. The CGT no longer claims a membership of more than 4 to 5 percent of the workforce, and far less among traditional blue-collar workers; however, in the private sector, where the vast majority of immigrant workers are employed, it claims a membership rate of barely 2 percent, a third that of the public sector.[36] Indeed, while the balance of CGT membership has almost always been in favor of the public sector, this balance has changed dramatically against the private sector since the 1970s.

Although union membership has dropped by two-thirds in 20 years, little effort has been made to recruit immigrants from the declining sectors of the economy into organizations whose representational structures have been changing in ways that do not favor immigrant representation. Indeed, the new model of industrial relations that emerged during the Mitterrand period—*le système Auroux*—was one of "trade unionism without members," in which unions negotiated record levels of collective agreements while their memberships rapidly declined.[37]

During the past 20 years, the number of immigrants among the delegates at the national congress of the CGT has fallen considerably. In 1982 they represented just over 8 percent of those present; this percentage fell to 6 percent in 1985.[38] In 1992 there were only 20 immigrant delegates at the Forty-fourth Congress, little more than 2 percent of those present. A comparison of the immigrant delegates with native French delegates reflects the new representational structure.

Fewer than a third of the total delegates identified themselves as *ouvriers,* or "workers," but among this group the proportion of immigrants was more than double (4.7 percent) their proportion at the congress. Therefore, it is possible that at least part of the decreased representation of immigrants can be accounted for by the more general decrease of worker representation. Moreover, the structure of representation reflects the growing gap between the native and immigrant working-class communities: Three-quarters of the immigrants identified themselves as either *ouvriers* (65 percent) or *employés* (10 percent), compared to only 42 percent of the native French delegates (30 percent *ouvriers* and 12 percent *employés*).[39]

The special problems presented by the new immigration accentuate the diminished structural importance of immigrant workers. During the early period, the trade union movement engaged in considerable efforts in experiments that would—at least provisionally—incorporate immigrant workers collectively, rather than simply individually. More recent efforts have been much less important. Both the CGT and the CFDT supported the amnesty program initiated by the new Socialist government in 1981, and since then union militants from both confederations have devoted considerable time to efforts to help undocumented domestic workers gain legal status. In addition, the CGT Construction Federation has developed programs for language and literacy training for the large number of immigrant workers in the construction trades.[40] However, these efforts have been limited by the fact that the responsibilities of union militants have increased substantially under the Auroux laws, while the number of militants has declined. They also have been limited to only a few federations (above all the Construction Federation in the CGT) and some regions (such as the Regional Union of the Ile de France of the CFDT).[41] In any case, unions have had very limited success in attracting immigrant workers into their ranks.

Part of the problem is certainly that unions in general have had a difficult time in attracting young workers. However, their problems with immigrants is more complex. Unions have a special problem with the Islamic component of the collective identity of the new generation of immigrant workers. Although sometimes they have been able to make some concessions to this collective identity in the context of strike movements, it is now perceived as more of a challenge to mobilization (indeed, sometimes a danger) than an opportunity. It is interesting to note that unions seem to have had a far more difficult time with this religious difference than they had with the language differences (but not religious differences) of earlier immigrant groups. This problem with religious difference makes it far more difficult for unions to develop collective modes for immigrant organization as they had during the earlier period.

In addition, younger immigrant workers have organizational alternatives to trade unions. Several scholars have argued that three generations of organizational militants have been analyzed among immigrant workers. The first generation was generated largely within the trade union movement, the second during a period of immigrant activism during the 1980s, and the third seems more and more rooted in community action in the 1990s.[42] It is this third generation, born in France and better integrated in most respects,[43] that appears to be largely beyond the reach of the trade union movement. Therefore, it is not surprising that a survey of delegates to the 1992 CGT congress indicates that only four of the small number of immigrant delegates were below the age of 36, a far smaller number and a smaller percentage than among the native-French delegates.[44]

Table 6.2 Union Supporters and Immigrants: Feelings and Evaluations

	CGT (%)	CFDT (%)	FO (%)	No Union (%)	Total Pop. (%)
Negative personal feelings about:					
• "Beurs" (second generation)	39	27	28	37	35
• Maghrébins (North Africans)	43	37	38	44	42
• Black Africans	18	12	18	19	18
• Asians	18	13	13	17	17
Feels there are too many:					
• Muslims	52	53	66	62	59
• Arabs	60	61	68	63	62
• Blacks	31	18	37	38	35
• Asians	23	15	44	29	27
Policy judgments:					
Immigrants are costly for the French economy.	63	49	54	60	59
Agree that "a democracy is judged by its capacity to integrate foreigners."	70	71	58	59	62
Unions fulfill their integrative roles well or well enough.	55	63	47	34	40
Associations fulfill their integrative roles well or well enough.	71	88	72	63	67
It would be useful to send home "irregular" immigrants.	71	69	76	71	71
It would be useful to send home those immigrants guilty of a crime.	80	73	84	80	79

Source: CSA survey, "Les français et la lutte contre le racisme," November 1994.

Finally, although union militants generally allude to such matters only indirectly, they are certainly aware of the negative sentiments among their own members and sympathizers about immigrants. This is a special problem for the CGT and the FO. Workers who are close to these unions appear to have more negative feelings about immigrants, are more likely to feel that they are costly (rather than beneficial) for the French economy, and are more supportive of policies that would restrict immigration, particularly undocumented migrants, than are workers who are close the CFDT.

On the other hand, all union sympathizers are more likely to approve of the present integrative role of unions, although far more of them attribute greater importance to other associations as agents of integration (see table 6.2). In this environment, the ability of unions to develop programs that would mobilize and incorporate immigrant workers more effectively appears to be limited. The strong support that the National Front has attracted among workers in recent years (25 percent or more) accentuates these limits.

Thus, all of the dynamics of current industrial relations seem to give unions little incentive to incorporate immigrant workers forcefully. Immigrants are now on the defensive edge of expiring smokestack industry and construction. Even outside of these sectors, in merchandise services, for example, where the proportion of immigrant workers has increased by almost 40 percent since 1982, only limited attempts have been made to organize these workers.[45]

In a trade union system in which massive strike movements generally have been the source of increased membership, the current pattern of diminished strike activity (particularly in sectors in which immigrant labor is strong) poses little challenge—and little opportunity—for union organizations. In addition, in an industrial relations system in which institutionalized trade union presence seems to be more important than membership mobilization, there seems to be little reason to seek ways to mobilize these most marginal workers. Finally, high levels of negative feelings about immigrant workers among workers and union sympathizers appear to place limits on the efforts of union leaders to mobilize immigrant workers.

NOTES

1. Catherine Wihtol de Wenden, *Les Immigrés et la politique* (Paris: Presses de la FNSP, 1988), p. 54.
2. The organization of immigration in the 1920s is described by Gérard Noiriel in *Le Creuset Français: Histoire de l'immigration XIX–XX siècles* (Paris: Seuil, 1988), pp. 306–312, and Gary Cross, *Immigrant Workers in Industrial France* (Philadelphia: Temple University Press, 1983), pp. 52–63.
3. See Noiriel, *Le creuset Français,* chap. 6.

4. David Saposs, *The Labor Movement in Post-war France* (New York: Columbia University Press, 1931), p. 95. For an excellent account of the 1919 metals strikes, see Edouard Dolléans, *Histoire du movement ouvrier,* vol. 2 (Paris: Armand Colin, 1939), pp. 303–309.

5. Raymond Pronier, *Les municipalités communistes* (Paris: Ballard, 1983), pp. 261–262.

6. Saposs, *The Labor Movement,* p. 95.

7. Cited in Michel Collinet, *Esprit du syndicalisme* (Paris: Les Editions Ouvrière), p. 56.

8. Saposs, *The Labor Movement,* p.138. In fact, Saposs's figures indicate that a higher proportion of the CGTU membership consisted of industrial workers but that the CGTU had a far lower total membership than the CGT. During the late 1920s, the *total* membership of the industrial federations of all of the confederations combined was no more than 130,000.

9. See Leah Haus, "Opposing Restrictionism: Labor Unions and Immigration Policy in France," ms. 1998.

10. Cited in Cross, *Immigrant Workers in Industrial France,* pp. 147–148.

11. Wenden, *Les Immigrés et la politique,* p. 50.

12. The number of immigrants in the CGTU is reported by Wenden, *Les Immigrés et la politique,* p. 52. The best comprehensive source for union membership for this period is Antoine Prost, *La C.G.T. à l'époque du front populaire* (Paris: Armand Colin, 1964), Annex I, pp. 177–194.

13. See Janine Ponty, *Polonais méconnus: histoire des travailleurs immigrés en France dans l'entre-deux-guerres* (Paris: Publications de la Sorbonne, 1988), pp. 327–328.

14. On the other hand, success certainly was not guaranteed by the integration of immigrant militants into the CGT. In Moselle, many industrial areas were dominated by PCF militants of German origin, who were, argues Belleville, "isolated and sectarian," and far less successful in mobilizing both members and voters. Pierre Belleville, *Une Nouvelle classe ouvrière* (Paris: Julliard, 1963), pp. 91–92.

15. See Rémy Leveau, "Les paris et l'intégration des 'beurs'," in Yves Mény, ed., *Idéologies, partis politiques et groupes sociaux, études réunies pour Georges Lavau* (Paris: Presses de la FNSP, 1989), p. 229.

16. George Tapinos, *L'Immigration étrangère en France,* Travaux et documents de INED (Paris: PUF, 1975), cited by Ralph Schor, *Histoire de l'immigration en France* (Paris: Armand Colin, 1996), p. 198

17. Wenden, *Les Immigrés et la politique,* pp. 122, 128–130, 152–155.

18. The best estimates of immigrant employment during this period have been made by Jeanne Singer-Kérel, *La Population active étrangère au recensement de 1982* (Paris: Presses de la FNSP, Service d'étude de l'activité économique, 1985); some of these figures (derived from the census of 1982) were taken from Maryse Tripier, "Français et immigrés dans l'entreprise," paper presented at a Colloquium on U.S.-French Immigration Policy, Royaumont, October 12–14, 1989.

19. Guy Desplanques and Nicole Tabard, "La localisation de la population étrangère," *Economie et Statistique,* no. 242 (April 1991): 57–58.

20. There were some other restrictions as well, such as a limit of one-third on the proportion of trade union administrators. See Patrick Ireland, *The Political Challenge of Ethnic Diversity* (Cambridge, MA: Harvard University Press, 1994), pp. 76–77.

21. *Journal Officiel de l'Assemblée Nationale,* June 16, 1975, p. 4241. In fact, Dijoud's reforms were part of a larger package that included increased spending for housing, special classes for immigrants in primary and secondary schools, and special scholarships for universities. See Douglas Ashford, *Politics and Policy in France* (Philadelphia: Temple University Press, 1982), p. 280.

22. Wenden, *Les Immigrés et la politique,* pp. 152.

23. In 1982, 2.3 million work-days were lost to strikes, most of them attributable to the immigrant workers' strikes, a record for the decade of the 1980s. I have explored the decline of the trade union movement in "Relations between the CGT and the CFDT: Politics and Mass Mobilization," in Mark Kesselman, ed., *The French Workers' Movement* (London: George Allen and Unwin, 1984), p. 257. The reports in *Le Monde* by Jean Benoit were particularly insightful during this period and particularly upbeat both about the positive impact of these conflicts on the trade union movement and the ability of the immigrant workers to make significant gains through the trade union movement. In particular, see *Le Monde,* December 3 and 4, 1982, and January 29, 1983.

24. See Floriane Benoit, *Citroën: le printemps de la dignité* (Paris: Ed. Sociales, 1982).

25. See Wenden, *Les Immigrés et la politique,* pp. 711–714.

26. See Benoit's article in *Le Monde,* December 4, 1982, p. 35.

27. See the lengthy report by Michael Noblecourt, "Les syndicats et la direction de Renault tentent de débloquer la situation," *Le Monde,* January 27, 1983, p. 1.

28. I have explored this pattern in "Corporatism and Industrial Relations in France," in Philip Cerny and Martin Schain, eds., *French Politics and Public Policy* (New York: St. Martin's Press, 1980), p. 191.

29. Maryse Tripier, "French Citizens and Immigrants in the Workplace: Marginality of the Subject, Marginality of the Research?" in Donald Horowitz and Gérard Noiriel, *Immigrants in Two Democracies French and American Experience* (New York: New York University Press, 1992), p. 297.

30. See Floriane Benoit, "Les Nouveaux immigrés," *Le Monde,* December 4, 1982, p. 35.

31. The link between organization and religion did not begin with Muslims. See Ralph Schor, "Le Facteur religieux et l'intégration des étrangers en France 1919–1939," *Vigntième siecle,* no. 7 (July-September 1985): 103–115.

32. See René Mouriaux and Catherine Wihtol de Wenden, "Syndicalisme français et Islam," and Stéphane Courtois and Gilles Képel, "Muselmans et

prolétaires," in Rémy Leveau and Gilles Képel, eds., *Les Muselmans dans la société française* (Paris: Presses de la FNSP, 1988), p. 39.

33. *Le Monde,* January 29, 1983.

34. *Le Monde,* February 11, 1983.

35. Strike levels are reported by the Ministry of Labor in "Les conflits de travail," *Premières synthèses* (Paris: Dares). An interesting trade union perspective on the decline of strike activity can be found in the annual report of ISERES, *Rapport sur la situation économique et sociale, 1994–95* (Paris: VO Editions, 1995), pp. 24–28.

36. See CGT, *Connaissance des syndiqués C.G.T.,* paper prepared for the Forty-fifth Congress of the CGT, December, 1995.

37. See Guy Groux and René Mouriaux, "Syndicalisme sans syndiqués," in Pascal Perrineau, *l'Engagement politique: déclin ou mutation* (Paris: PFNSP, 1994), p. 67.

38. Mouriaux and Wihtol de Wenden, "Syndicalisme français et islam," p. 44.

39. René Mouriaux, *Enquête sociologique sur les délégués du 44e congrès confédéral* (Paris: Etudes et recherches d'ISERES, 1992), pp. 67, 114.

40. Haus, "Opposing Restrictionism."

41. Ibid.

42. Catherine Wihtol de Wenden, "Les associations 'beur' et immigrées, leurs leaders, leurs stratégies," *Regards sur l'actualité,* no. 178 (February, 1992): 40.

43. See Michèle Tribalat, *De l'immigration à l'assimilation: Enquête sur les populations d'origine étrangère en France* (Paris: La Découverte/INED, 1996).

44. Mouriaux, *Enquête sociologique,* p. 22.

45. For changing employment patterns of immigrant workers, see: *Les étrangers en France* (Paris: INSEE, 1994), pp. 72–73; and *Economie et Statistique,* INSEE, no. 242 (April 1991): 36. The CFDT in the Ile de France region has been successful in greatly increasing its membership in this sector, but it is not clear if this is related to an increase in the mobilization of immigrant workers (Haus, "Opposing Restrictionism").

CHAPTER SEVEN

Trade Unions and the Diversification of Class Structure: Technical Culture and Criticism of Power

Guy Groux

"White-collar workers," the "world of office workers," the "new petty bourgeoisie," the "new class," the "new middle classes," and so on. The profusion of terms and notions that have cropped up in scholarly research to describe societal changes in the 1960s and 1970s indicates how much restructuring and diversification have affected the labor market, the significance of skills and statuses, and the new relationships being established in the context of collective action between "intellectual" and "manual" or "productive" labor. Over the past three decades, marked simultaneously by a phase of Fordist development and the emergence of trends that prefigure what some have called "postindustrial society" and economic crisis, all of which have radically transformed the production process, we have witnessed an exponential growth of the "middle class."

The impact of these trends on the union movement can be viewed in counterpoint. According to much of the literature published 15 years ago, the motivating forces that infused collective mobilization among the "new classes" were not rooted in the more traditional forms of union culture nor in the labor sphere; although bearers of a radical and critical culture, members of the alternative class more or less abandoned the production sphere and turned their attention to areas such as culture, the environment, the city, lifestyles, and consumer rights.[1] Although some of these trends are observable, the approach toward the middle classes from the 1960s to the 1980s often was based on questionable assumptions that distorted historical and theoretical points. The operative postulate suggested a cultural (and social) breach between "the white-collar world" and the "union movement" when in fact the problem was quite different.[2]

The forms of social reorganization that have accompanied the modernization of the French economy have, with respect to collective action, redefined new practical and cultural issues. New paradigms and symbolic images, breaking with former dogmas that grew out of a traditional economistic vision based on ownership of the means of production, have contributed to renewing the unions' ways of thinking (and doing). This has been more significant than a split between "new classes" and "trade unions."

Of course, relations between the two have not been entirely smooth. The 1960s and 1970s nevertheless can be characterized by closely interwoven processes of social reorganization, changes in protest practices, involvement of theoretical and political debates, and transformations that affect the symbolism of militancy. As a result, the "highly material" blends intimately with the "symbolic," as illustrated by the issue of technology and the role taken on by white-collar workers in collective action.

HISTORICAL BACKGROUND: THE BIRTH OF THE "MASS ENGINEER"

In the early days of unionism, admitting certain professions as members into the "first" CGT was far from a foregone conclusion. Those who shared a "fragment of the boss's or the states' authority, either directly or by delegation," were denied the opportunity to organize.[3] As to engineers, they were classified as "bourgeois."

Between the two world wars, a new situation took shape. The USTICA (Union Syndicale des Techniciens de l'Industrie, du Commerce et de l'Agriculture), informally allied with the CGT, was created in 1919. Other more professionally oriented organizations of engineers, such as the Union des Syndicats d'Ingénieurs Français, also were founded.[4]

With the end of World War II, change occurred at a much faster pace. After the Liberation, a new social compromise was implemented that was based on two broad principles: the development of the welfare state and especially the expansion of the middle classes. In organized labor, and particularly the CGT, views quickly changed regarding the white-collar group. An engineer was no longer necessarily a bourgeois nor even a wholesale collaborator with the employer. The title "engineer" became more widespread, and the very "popularization of the title"[5] related it to other employees not only from the standpoint of subordination but also from an economic standpoint.

This was highly significant for a worker-oriented unionism thoroughly permeated by Marxist culture: Roger Pascré, a CGT leader, observed in 1946 that, "A growing number of increasingly specialized engineers and managers, in an economy run less by technicians than by financiers, has led the latter to view the engineer as part of the 'mass' and no longer as an individual and to regard him as a potential target for cutting costs rather than as an essential agent of prosperity."[6]

After the "mass worker" dear to Antonio Gramsci, we have seen the advent of the "mass engineer," the emergence of which evokes the conflicts and contradictions that have come to oppose "knowledge" to a form of economic power essentially oriented toward the financial sphere. In fact, after the war, certain signs indicating a boom in the managers' union movement in the midst of workers' organizations became increasingly apparent. But the process developed on a broader scale in the early 1960s.

On June 8, 1962, Benot Frachon, secretary-general of the CGT, organized a meeting of federal secretaries to enable the CGT to handle the organization of managers. The Thirty-fourth confederal congress held in Saint-Denis in 1963 displayed two features: an overture to other union organizations to consolidate the trade union unity that had been forged during the recent large-scale miners' strike, and an overture to white-collar workers. Overall, that congress was defined by a coalition-building strategy that sought trade union unity[7] and a convergence among occupational groups.[8]

"CORPORATISM" AND POLITICS: A DIALECTIC AT WORK

Obviously, the context in which the CGT performed a major policy redefinition with respect to white-collar workers is highly significant. The year 1963 was marked by the return of the workers' movement with the miners' strike that put an end to the lull in collective action during the Algerian war. It began, however, with one of the longest conflicts involving managers and technicians that France has ever known, which continued for several months in Neyrpic-Grenoble.

Strike action was complemented by new discussions in the academic sphere that structured the theoretical debate. Serge Mallet argued that changes in the nature of work in the course of industrial modernization were characterized by the increased importance of tasks that preceded (studies, research) and followed (market and consumer analyses) the material production process. Economic changes thus produced social reorganization, which, extending beyond the "material work process alone," involved the entire cycle(s) of production in the broadest sense. Those who possessed cultural capital based on mastery of technical knowledge and know-how—technicians, engineers, and the like—were to play as important a role as the workers actually toiling away on the shop floor. A "new working class" was being formed, consisting of technicians working in automated sectors and more traditional skilled workers.[9]

Outside academe, the debate rapidly reached the political and union spheres. Theories about the "new working class" were conveyed by powerful networks that brought together activists, unionists, politicians, journalists, notables, and other elites. The PSU (Parti Socialiste Unifié), the Nouvel Observateur, and Témoinage Chrétien contributed aid and support to various degrees. Among trade unions, it was in the CFDT that Serge Mallet's ideas struck the deepest chord. In 1964 Eugène Descamps predicted that "the working class of 1975 will be an educated working class, counting in its ranks . . . 20 percent of unskilled workers and a large proportion of middle managers and technicians."[10] At the Fédération de la Chimie, Edmond Maire and Jacques Moreau championed the theme of the "new working class" and amplified it using the notoriety they enjoyed at the time. Later Pierre Rosanvallon warned against confusing white-collar managers with the real power structures in industry.[11]

Theoretically, politically and socially, the debate spread through the various sectors of French society, and for good reason. The notion of "new working class" challenges the PCF's and the CGT's hegemony over the Left and the trade union movement. The "new working class" was not defined solely with respect to the modernization of the economy. Due precisely to their role in industrial progress, its various factions were attributed a central position on the political as well as the historical level.[12] On the basis of the main postulates of Marxism—particularly the primacy of the economic infrastructure and the influence that social groups within it exercise over ideological, cultural, and political superstructures—the concept of the "new working class" radically challenged the traditional meaning of "working class." In other words, the "old working class" appeared to have lost its historical role; it no longer exercised cultural and political hegemony.

In the face of what appeared as a frontal political offensive, the CGT adopted a position distinct both from CFDT modernism as well as the pure corporatism of the Confédération Général des Cadres (CGC).[13] It opted for an alliance strategy between the "new classes" and workers. The growth of the white-collar group required revising the Leninist model that advocated an alliance of workers and peasants.[14]

But to claim that those who occupy an intellectual function henceforth constitute the major pole of union (and political) alliances with the traditional working class is not only to reject any principle of organic fusion between white-collar workers and blue-collar workers.[15] It is equivalent to saying that the former demonstrate social, occupational, cultural, and ideological particularities and that, as such, they possess a *specificity* that must be incorporated into union practices.

Within the CGT, the specificity of white-collar workers was first recognized in its statutes, as reflected in the very structures of the UGICT that operates at the confederal level, with the support of the Unions Fédérales des Ingénieurs, Cadres et Techniciens (UFICT), which in turn coordinate and direct the action of (specific) union sections at the grass-roots level, in industry.

The principle of specificity was never challenged; quite the contrary. After May 1981 the CGT was the only organized trade union movement to negotiate with the public authorities to gain for its affiliated Union des Cadres the status of national representation enjoyed until then only by the CGC.

The specific status of the white-collar group within the CGT naturally is not only a matter of administrative or organizational logic. It is rooted in an analysis of the evolution of intellectual labor. As Jean-Louis Moynot, a leader (at the time he propounded the view) suggested, the specificity of white-collar workers does not arise only from the notion of hierarchy. Authority (in its more disciplinary form) is disappearing. The tendency is basically due to the fact that "many white-collar workers are specialized mainly in one technique"; according to Moynot, that technique can be construed as part of the standard production processes or come under administrative and commercial activities. They put their knowledge to practical use in their work.[16]

A specific status and a specific function in the evolution of production systems obviously must lead to the formation of specific demands. For the CGT, white-collar workers are confronted with closely intertwined concerns, which include "job security, in-service training, career advancement, job classification" and consequently "salaries."[17]

The claim of white-collar specificity thus leads to a specificity of demands. And, as a result, the CGT did not hesitate to make overtures to the CGC and defend *"hierarchical pay structures,"* which the CFDT opposed. The notion of theses hierarchical pay structures was legitimated at the Second Congress of the UGIC in 1967. In 1970 René Le Guen—UGIC secretary-general—opposed certain government plans that dealt with a definition of the notion of wage pool involving redistribution to low-wage workers.

On the contrary, the CFDT rallied to the principle of "social solidarity."[18] For Le Guen, the issue of wages was merely a technical means of redistributing income ("within a total wage amount that can be allocated to the workers"). And the "solidarity" invoked at the time most certainly did not lead to "a new mystification."[19] The position of CGT white-collar workers was echoed at the highest confederal level. During the same period, Henri

Krasucki declared: "Giving an anti-hierarchical character to demands . . . would mean pitting categories [of workers] against one another."[20]

Of course, the importance that the salary issue took on in the specific strategy of the white-collar group cannot be divorced from the surrounding context of development that was marked by a period of wage regulation resulting from a Fordist-style compromise. But above all, it cannot be dissociated from that broader spectrum of alliances that was taking place during the social reorganization of the 1960s and 1970s in the nation as a whole as well as within the CGT itself.

As a result, the specificity of the UGICT—its statutes, analyses, and claims—cannot be reduced to pure occupational corporatism. For one thing, it was part of a system of alliances (and convergences) among different social groups; in the CGT's symbolic representations, the notion of specificity thus appears as one of the constitutive traits of the theory of (class) alliances. Second, it implies a greater efficacy that aims to mobilize the cultural resources of the white-collar workers and thereby redefine certain aspects of union culture as well as the way demands are formulated. Naturally, the process of cultural change that accompanied the process of social restructuring did not occur without occasional tensions, even clashes between confederal authorities, workers' unions active at the grass-roots level, and the white-collar workers.

TECHNOLOGY AND INDUSTRIAL PROPOSALS: FROM A CRITIQUE OF PROPERTY TO A CRITIQUE OF ECONOMIC CONTROL

The inclusion of white-collar technicians, managers, and engineers as a specific group in the political realm of class alliances was not the only major change that the CGT underwent in reaction to the evolution of the 1960s and 1970s. Outside the political field one can identify changes in union practices and ideas, based on presuppositions relating to technical culture. A discussion of technology in relation to white-collar workers brings up two obvious facts: Group identity often was legitimated by the existence of a cultural capital that gained recognition by way of scientific experimentation or technological advances; furthermore, the processes of social reorganization that bestowed on the group an eminent role grew out of an economic context marked by the computerization, robotization, and automation of productive tasks.

But the means by which technical culture took hold in French organized labor do not affect merely the identity of the new class or the processes linked to the social reorganization of the labor market. In the CGT, there were important implications for the political heritage linked to Marxism as well as for general analyses in the 1960s that attempted to comprehend industrial change. In other words, the influence of technical culture on the confederation involved theoretical-political procedures of "legitimation"[21] that, at the symbolic and practical level, lead to a convergence between "unionism" and "new class."

When the *Communist Manifesto* was published, the notion of the development of productive forces, science, and technology stood out, for Marx, as a central historical paradigm that structured the succession of various production methods and social relationships. With time, the notion took on greater importance. It marked the work of the "adult Marx" as opposed to that of the "young Marx."[22] In the twentieth century, the notion then expanded by the very nature of industrial development to cover the whole of symbolic images specific to the worker movement and the "technical-productive" culture it long stood for.[23]

In the 1960s Radovan Richta's neo-Marxist contribution regarding the "Scientific and Technical Revolution" further confirmed the presence of the manager group in the field of organized labor. The theories of the Prague School not only concluded that the most traditional forms of manual labor would decline with automation, they foresaw a central role for the new strata in the political project of socialism. For them, "going beyond capitalism to build new social relationships" depended on a prerequisite: that the development of productive forces would not be hindered by the "financial logic of profit."[24]

With regard to practice, the way white-collar workers in the CGT viewed the changes in the 1960s and 1970s and their cultural effects assumed a variety of forms. In 1975 the UGICT organized a major symposium on industrial automation.[25] Together with the British Trade Union Congress (TUC), it created an international liaison committee of engineers, managers, and technicians uniting over 80 organizations and registered with the International Labor Organization (ILO). It also participated in a world federation of scientific workers.

Of course, mobilization of white-collar intellectual resources, the creation of international networks for professional cooperation,[26] and the declaration of general principles is only a part of the CGT's activity. "We must lead the battle so that science and technology work toward social and economic progress," Alain Obadia, leader of the UGICGT, wrote in 1981.[27] And the "battle" here was incarnated in innovative practices in the labor movement that concretely involved a "strategy of industrial proposals and demands" that took root in the late 1960s and aimed to endure.

When the Neyrpic-Grenoble strike broke out, it became clear that demands did not concern salaries alone but also pertained to management of the firm. For supporters of the "reconstruction" current in the CFDT, these were demands for control that henceforth should be officially integrated into the social movement. The CGT was at first reticent, not to say hostile. It felt that control was not the central issue of social conflicts; rather, private property was basically at the root of capitalist exploitation and alienation. In 1968 white-collar workers joined in strikes at a number of plants, including Sud-Aviation, Renault, Snecma, Bull, Berliet, and Radiotechnique. And it was in this context that demands concerning management appeared. At the Snecma-Suresnes factory, the UGIC demanded that workers' committees be elected to participate directly in the firm's financial management. At CGE, ONERA, and Compagnie des Compteurs, similar demands were formulated.

At the Renault-Rueil plant white-collar workers demanded a "real union counter power" to act in certain areas of management such as wage policy, investments, and work hours.[28] "The relations between white-collar workers and blue-collar workers will never be the same. . . . White-collar workers have become aware that they no longer have to be second-class citizens in the firm, but can act and express their claims and have their say in the direction that management is taking."[29] Over time, the movement asserted itself to a much greater extent, although within the CGT it ran into staunch opposition and provoked numerous debates, polemics, and even obstacles.[30]

At Manufrance, a firm threatened by closure, CGT white-collar workers participated as early as the late 1970s in drawing up a schedule of priorities and produced a set of proposals aiming to ensure the firm's viability; at a number of plants elsewhere, including Chaix, Destival, La Chapelle-Darblay, Dufour, and Technip, the CGT adopted the same approach throughout the 1980s. Besides focusing on local production sites (factories, services), union industrial schemes targeted certain industrial sectors (energy, automobiles, etc.). As UGICT leader Gérard Juquel explained in the foreword to the *Rapport d'Orientation* presented at the eighth UGICT congress in May 1982, the managers' organization is above all "a genuine force with proposals that are capable of involving engineers, managers, technicians not only with regard to their immediate demands but also the entire range of fields in which they can play an important role . . . : employment, industrial policy, production costs and costing, task organization . . . , scientific and technological innovation."[31]

To better implement new union practices, the UGICT used the notion of "new management criteria" that defines management (of the firm) as one of the grounds of "class struggle."[32] New management criteria imply a new vision of the organic composition of capital. The UGICT rejected the notion of economic crisis as inevitable as well as the desirability of industrial modernization based on massive job cuts, and embodied these criteria in concrete applications.

To support their demands regarding work hours and staffing, the UGICT took into account how long equipment would last, and thus its depreciation; it demanded real control over computerization of work methods and its effects on task organization and employment[33]; and it proposed certain types of savings plans and investments linked to industrial development.

The new management criteria opposed employment practices that, in the context of economic crisis and increased market competition, tended to reduce expenses on variable capital (jobs, wages, payroll) in favor of fixed capital (investments, new technology). The new criteria ran counter to capitalist logic; they inspired industrial schemes that were based not solely on decisions driven by short-term "profitability" (or on purely financial considerations).

TECHNICAL CULTURE AND NEW GROUNDS OF STRUGGLE

Beyond the CGT alone, the effect of the emergence of new salaried classes on organized labor and the symbolic images that they conjure up has affected the entire union movement. Thus issues concerning the relationship of the labor movement to technology or developing industrial projects that take into account management constraints without submitting to the dominant logic that governs them suggest not only new grounds for struggle but also and especially a new culture for organized labor.

In the past, unionism was basically, and with rare exceptions,[34] characterized by a protest culture that was founded on purely economic struggle. Focusing exclusively on ownership of the means of production and the resultant exploitation of workers, unions asked how to globally transform economic management in the face of future political change. Union culture was thus doubly dependent and submissive: Locked into the straitjacket of the economic constraints of capitalism, it remained a prisoner of the game of political alternation.

The virulence of protest discourse barely disguised the mechanisms of cultural submission that typified traditional—and current—unionism. With the convergences that began to occur in the 1960s between the new classes and unionism, new cultural postulates were defined.

Coexistent with the old forms of protest culture is a newly emerging *economic culture* that, *in its practical effects,* implies various characteristics. Reaching beyond the realm of property relations, the struggle occurs at the level of exercising control and economic decision making; oriented toward the most direct forms of business management, it becomes more autonomous with regard to the various political influences that in many ways mark union battles; refusing to consider engineers as "a reducible element of the cost price," the struggle takes into account the variety of knowledge that structures production and the inherent contradictions that take shape in duplications of expertise; finally, in work methods it promotes new relationships between "knowledge" and "power," the former no longer—nor necessarily, nor always—reinforcing the latter.

On the contrary, knowledge (and union expertise) now shapes economic decisions (and no longer property alone). For a long time economic management and decision making were part of "what unions hadn't considered" and were ignored in both union symbolism and practice. Today, in the militant culture, both have acquired genuine legitimacy.

White-collar unionism slackened considerably during the 1980s. Employer mobilization of senior management in industries where new forms of management were tried, the economic crisis and its effects on the climate of opinion, and unemployment have all left traces. In French society, white-collar workers, along with youth and women, are one of the social segments that constitute the "union deserts" that Louis Viannet spoke of in Limoges in September 1995, during the centennial celebration of the CGT's constitutive congress. But more than youth or women, white-collar workers, and generally those with advanced degrees, legitimate the broad trends that characterize the evolution of capitalism on a global scale as well as on the firm level. (Examples include the question of the market emerging as a universal category, job-sharing practices, the acceptance of wage controls, and so on.[35])

The fact remains that the legacy of the convergence between what some have named the alternative class and the trade union movement endures. Beyond forms and statutes, the social recomposition of labor thus has promoted changes in militant cultures, some elements of which still persist today. And they are being reproduced through symbolic and practical issues, the existence of which will produce their effects tomorrow as organized labor evolves further; in other words, on union struggles in the future.

NOTES

1. In the wake of Alwin Gouldner's works, other research to be consulted includes Monique Dagnaud, "La Classe d'Alternative. Réflexions sur les Acteurs du Changement Social dans les Sociétés Modernes," *Sociologie du Travail*, no. 4 (1981): 384–405.

2. The same postulate starts from a vision of unionism defined only in terms of its relationship to the workers. But in reality, the history of the collective movement in France has involved support not only from industrial workers, but from white-collar employees, particularly civil servants, in other words what I term elsewhere the "state foundation."

3. Maxime Leroy, *La Coutume Ouvrière* (Paris: Giard et Brière, 1913).

4. On this period, see Jean-Louis Robert, "1914–1935: L'Organisation," in Marc Descotes and Jean-Louis Robert, eds. *Clefs pour une Histoire du Syndicalisme Cadre* (Paris: Editions Ouvrières, 1984), pp. 57–109.

5. Luc Boltanski speaks of its *vulgarization.* See *Les Cadres. La Formation d'un Groupe Social* (Paris: Minuit, 1982), pp. 406 ff.

6. *Travail et Technique,* Organe du Cartel Confédéral des Ingénieurs et des Cadres Supérieurs, CGT, no. 3 (August-September 1946).

7. A pact for unity of action was signed by the CGT and the CFDT in 1966.

8. A specific managers' union—the UGIC—was founded within the CGT in 1963. It became the UGICT (Union Général des Ingénieurs, Cadres et Techniciens) in 1969.

9. Serge Mallet, *La Nouvelle Classe Ouvrière* (Paris: Seuil, 1963); see also Pierre Belleville, *Une Nouvelle Classe Ouvrière* (Paris: Julliard, 1963). For a Marxist and more recent version of the evolution of productive tasks, see Jean Lojkine, *La Classe Ouvrière en Mutations* (Paris: Messidor, 1986).

10. Eugène Descamps, *Evolution et Perspectives de la CFTC* (Paris: CFTC, 1964), pp. 26–27.

11. Pierre Rosanvallon, "Les Cadres, la Hiérarchie et la Division du Travail," *CFDT-Aujourd'hui,* no. 23 (January-February 1977), esp. p. 63. Let us recall that Pierre Rosanvallon had previously, under the pseudonym of Pierre Ranval, devoted a work to hierarchical pay structures entitled *Hiérarchie des Salaires et Lutte des Classes* (Paris: Cerf, 1972).

12. See Jean-Daniel Reynaud's critical article "La Nouvelle Classe Ouvrière. La Technologie et l'Histoire," *Revue Française de Science Politique* 12, no. 3 (June 1972): 529–542.

13. We will explore below the influence of Radovan Richta's theories on the evolution of the CGT's positions.

14. Robert Linhart, *Lénine, les Paysans, Taylor* (Paris: Seuil, 1976).

15. Regarding the political aspect of the matter of new alliances for the working class, see Collectif, *Traité Marxiste d'Economie Politique. Le Capitalisme Monopoliste d'Etat* (Paris: Editions sociales, 1971), esp. vol. 1, p. 252. See also "Manifeste de Champigny" (Paris: PCF, 1968).

16. Jean-Louis Moynot, "Le Mouvement Syndical. Les Cadres et les Techniciens," *L'Humanité,* January 18, 1971. Let us note that with regard to the evolution of the notion of hierarchy, Moynot advanced arguments that were similar to those used later by Pierre Rosanvallon.

17. Ibid.

18. It should be noted that at the time, Jacques Delors, former national CFDT leader, was one of Prime Minister Jacques Chaban-Delmas's key advisors.

19. *Options,* no. 47 (May 1970), Editorial.

20. *La Vie Ouvrière,* June 17, 1970.

21. "Legitimation" in the sense that the presence of a phenomenon, in this case a cultural one, is considered legitimate (and relevant) or on the contrary illegitimate and unfounded.

22. On the relationships between the "young Marx" and the "old Marx," see the well-known works of Pierre Naville, Maximillien Rubel, Henri Lefebvre, Kostas Axelos, and Louis Althusser, among others. In Germany, see also the work of the Frankfurt School.

23. "Productivism" in the organized labor movement was the subject of long debates between the CGT and the CFDT throughout the 1970s, thus typifying the "conflictual unity" that linked the two organizations.

24. Radovan Richta, et al., *La Civilisation au Carrefour* (Paris: Seuil, 1974, new ed.).

25. *Options,* no. 102 (June 1975).

26. This sort of task was already in place after Liberation with the Cartel des cadres—CGT.

27. *Le Peuple,* no. 1121 (December 1981): 10.

28. *Options,* no. 28, Spécial Evénements (June 1968): 18–20, among others.

29. Ibid., Editorial, p. 5.

30. For greater detail on this matter, see George Ross, "La CGT: Crise Economic et Changement Politique," in Mark Kesselman and Guy Groux, eds., *The French Workers' Movement* (London: George Allen and Unwin, 1984), pp. 51–74.

31. Report of the Eighty-seventh UGICT Congress, May 1982, p. 21.

32. At the same time, the notion filtered into the PCF economists' approach. See, among others, Paul Boccara, "Pour de Nouveaux Critère de Gestion," *Issues,* no. 11 (February 1982): 70–128; Philippe Herzog, *L'Economie Nouvelle à Bras-le-corps* (Paris: Editions Sociales-Messidor, 1982).

33. See *Le Peuple,* no. 1121. It should be noted that the CFDT was developing a far-reaching approach to technological innovation: see, for example, Yves Lasfargues, "De la Défensive à l'Offensive," in Pierre Dommergues, ed., *Les Syndicats Français et Américains face aux Mutations Technologiques* (Paris: Anthropos-Encrages, 1984), pp. 305–319.

34. For instance, the Liberation was a brief exception, with direct worker management of a number of factories. Or the proposals that aimed to create the future works councils, real instruments for worker control, and even economic co-decision making.

35. See on this subject the results of a survey conducted by the CEVIPOF and the Institut CSA in the framework of a study entitled "Work, Regions and Politics." See also Jacques Capdevielle et al., *Crise de l'Emploi et Fractures Politiques* (Paris: Presses de la Fondation Nationale des Sciences Politiques, 1996).

CHAPTER EIGHT

The French Strike and Social Divide: The End of Consensus Politics?

Bernard H. Moss

The strike that paralyzed public transport in France from November 24 to December 15, 1995, was both an ordinary and an extraordinary event. On the one hand, what could have been more common, banal, and "archaic" than a rail strike led by the Communist-dominated CGT in defense of early retirement? Sparked off by the announcement of a reform of the social security system, the strike, strongly backed by the union rank-and-file, nevertheless ended once the government of Alain Juppé yielded on issues of immediate concern, chiefly that of early retirement. Yet at the same time this was a strike of historic proportions rivaling in importance, it can be argued, the generalized strike of May-June 1968.[1] In defending their own interests, the rail and transport workers called up a truly national movement of strikes, demonstrations, and sympathy that challenged more than ten years of official consensus built around monetarist policies and the justice of the free market. The strike thus raised questions about many assumptions that have underlain studies of contemporary France and indeed other Western societies.[2]

These assumptions were set by the experience of the Mitterrand years. During these years France, which had appeared to present an exception to the "end of ideology," was normalized, its working-class and Socialist movements broken for good, it seemed. François Mitterrand had been elected president in 1981 on a program of nationalization and social reform that promised to reduce unemployment, diminish inequalities, and revitalize French industry. Despite improvisation and lack of cohesion, the government had succeeded in maintaining growth and stabilizing employment for two years. But faced with a weakening franc and a trade deficit, Mitterrand had to choose in 1983 between an industrial policy involving protection and departure from the Exchange Rate Mechanism (ERM) and monetary alignment with the Germans accompanied by austerity measures. The government chose to reverse direction, to cut back subsidies to industry and reduce social expenditures in order to win the confidence of markets and opinion. From a movement that had vaunted its break with capitalism, Mitterrand and the Socialists were transformed into the modern managers of a market-led economy in which wage incomes stagnated and unemployment rose but returns to capital soared—an extra 7.5 percent per year between 1987 and 1990.[3]

Mitterrand, as the *Wall Street Journal* exulted, had proven the impossibility of socialism. He could now take credit for restoring faith in profits and free enterprise and destroying the power of the Communists. The party, which had lost one-quarter of its vote to Mitterrand in 1981, went from defeat to decline as socialism disappeared from public discourse. Trade unions, which had known a brief upsurge during Mitterand's first two years, proved incapable of responding to the restructuring of industry and plumbed record lows for rates of unionization and strikes.[4]

Intellectuals whose mystique had vanished into *économique*—incremental technical problems of inflation and interest rates—fell silent. As conservatives alternated with Socialists in power, revealing marginal differences between them, France remained tied to the franc fort and domestic deflation. Faced with rising unemployment at the end of his tenure, Mitterrand could only throw up his hands and say "We tried everything." The working class and the Left seemed headed for a terminal decline.[5]

Historians might object that the Left had been defeated before by Napoleon I and III, by Adolphe Thiers, by Vichy, by Charles de Gaulle, and had always stormed back, but this time was different for it was linked with the disappearance of the working class, which had lost 2 million jobs since 1975. France, most commentators agreed, was becoming a middle-class society of competing individuals freed from the ideological demons of the past that had to contend with but a minority of *exclus,* or unemployed.[6]

By 1989, the year of the bicentennial of the Revolution, were there any reasons not to conclude that France had reached the end of a certain kind of history?[7] After all, 80 percent of the citizens had voted for one of the three major parties of consensus in the 1988 parliamentary elections. There was, of course, the disquieting rise of the National Front, but this was attributed almost exclusively to anti-immigrant racism.[8] But how could the Socialists have betrayed the hopes they had fostered in the people of the Left without causing disenchantment?

Already the 1988 elections revealed the thin edge of a gap that was opening between the people and their representatives. This gap was not widely perceived because it was expressed by high rates of abstention and votes for marginal parties such as the ecologists and National Front. It took an anthropological historian to notice later that votes for the rogue businessman Bernard Tapie in the Midi were coterminous with those areas where the clergy had sworn allegiance to the Revolution in 1791—that they represented an egalitarian protest against the elites by those who were disappointed in Mitterrand.[9]

In 1988 Mitterrand was a candidate who portrayed himself as the embodiment of order and legitimacy; his main asset was his indifference to partisan politics. Concerned with unemployment, job training, and purchasing power, voters found the campaign lacking in real debate and substance. A record 34 percent abstained in protest at the narrow choice. Voters were not committed enough to give the Socialists an absolute majority in the legislative elections that followed; Socialists had to rely on ad hoc alliances with either Centrists or Communists to govern. The level of abstentions was high, and there was a loosening of support for all three major parties.[10]

Nonparticipation continued to be high for European and municipal elections in 1990, especially among working-class voters. In the regional elections of March 1992, the major parties received only 18 percent for the Socialists and 33 percent for the Right, with working-class votes scattered over the broad spectrum.[11] The consensus parties represented only one-third of registered voters compared with 63.6 percent in 1984. The legislative elections of 1993 confirmed the disenchantment; 31 percent of eligible voters abstained and there was a record 5 percent blank or spoiled ballots. With 3 percent less than they had received in 1986, the Right swept to the largest majority that any party had ever obtained under a French republic—some 84.7 percent of the seats, and that more out of voters' disgust with the Socialists than any enthusiasm for the Right.[12] The disillusionment underlying this vote was made obvious in the European elections of June 1994 when the government list obtained only 25.6 percent and the Socialist Rocard a dismal 14.5 percent of the vote.[13]

But the most pronounced manifestation of the social divide was the 1992 referendum on Maastricht. Mitterrand had expected easy approval for the treaty. Not only did the no vote nearly win, but it drew its largest percentages from the people of the Left who had elected Mitterrand in 1981— blue- and white-collar workers, and peasants from the traditional departments of the Left. They were not following the advice of the Communists, as unpopular as ever, nor that of Philippe Séguin, who objected to the growth of supranational power,[14] but rather their own instinct that the Europe of the open market created by technocratic elites was no friend to them. This was not a nationalist vote but a class protest by those who associated the single currency and monetarism with unemployment. Miners[15] and steel workers remembered that it was the Count Etienne Davignon who had programmed the shutdown of pits and steel mills; and farmers, the imposition of milk quotas and lower price supports. The European Community could not be blamed for the globalization of trade, which involved only 22.5 percent of national production, but it carried the message. Almost two-thirds of workers voted no. Only a third of voters queried thought that Maastricht would be helpful in combating unemployment.[16] Significantly, two-thirds of the managerial and professional class voted yes, signifying their acceptance of the wider European market.[17] In no other country was the disillusionment with Europe so great. The result, even though formally favorable to Maastricht, was a repudiation of the liberal Europe that Mitterrand and Jacques Delors had built.[18]

As electoral studies had shown, the working class had not disappeared but was merely poking up in odd places—in abstentions from voting and in no and National Front votes. The working class had been a rising class, peaking at 39 percent of the population in 1975. Since then, due to job losses and plant shutdowns, it had fallen to 27 percent, but almost all the losses came from the ranks of the unskilled. The number of skilled workers actually remained the same at 3.7 million, rising from 45 to 68 percent of the working class. Industrial production, of course, was rising constantly, and if there were fewer workers employed per unit of capital, these workers still had the capacity to arrest production or transport.[19] The professionalization of workers brought them closer in status, situation, and earnings to those of the so-called salariat—white-collar workers and technicians—who were growing in numbers. Treating lower-paid clerical staff as workers meant that over half of French families in 1990 were working class, representing by far the largest single bloc in the population.[20] These workers were subjected to the prospect of unemployment, which had risen from 6 percent in 1980 to 12 percent in 1995, with those on temporary contracts nearing 1.7 million.

The new element of the 1990s was the spread of the fear of unemployment to the middle class, including managerial personnel, whose jobs were no longer secure.[21] Over half of male voters feared job loss at the end of 1992.[22] Workers and white-collar workers had lost their natural representatives in the Communist and Socialist parties, but, while searching for a new identity and expression, they had not disappeared. A majority of workers, jobless, and those who considered themselves underprivileged (30 percent, 25 percent and 34 percent respectively), as well as those from previously left-wing areas from the north and Midi, voted for Jean-Marie Le Pen in the presidential election of 1995.[23] They displayed the same attitude toward state intervention and defense of wage earners as those of the Left. The National Front, not the Socialists or Communists, were the party of the disaffected working class.

Jacques Chirac knew that in order to win the presidency against Edouard Balladur, the comfortable bourgeois, he had to tap this working-class and popular discontent. A survey found that 74 percent of the middle class wanted the change from financial orthodoxy demanded by the Gaullist maverick Philippe Séguin. Chirac thus portrayed himself as the candidate of change focusing on wages, unemployment, and exclusion and what he called the "fracture sociale," or social divide, between the people and the elites. He promised to put finance at the service of employment and notably to protect social security from capping. Newcomers drawn from among the young, unemployed, and blue- and white-collar workers provided him the margin of victory over Balladur on the first round and over Lionel Jospin on the second. But these populist supporters, crucial for victory, were only 15 percent of his electorate on the second round, and he was blessed with one of the most conservative parliaments in French history.[24]

Little wonder that his new government, presented on May 15, 1995, reflected the broad spread of the parliamentary majority that was financially orthodox and pro-European in orientation—Gaullist Alain Juppé as prime minister, Centrists Jacques Barrot and François Bayrou at the Ministries of Transport and Education, the Giscardian Hervé de Charette as Foreign Minister, and Alain Madelin, free marketeer extraordinaire, at Finance.[25] Juppé, the consummate énarque—graduate of the school for high civil servants—started out without any clear direction, offering gifts to everyone in the budget, and worrying the financial markets and the Germans about his largesse. Commentators noted that he was trying to square the circle, aiming to satisfy the Maastricht convergence criteria for a budget deficit below 3 percent while tackling unemployment.[26] He raised the SMIC (the minimum wage) and introduced the *contrat initiative emploi,* a temporary job incentive contract, that not only exonerated employers from social charges but gave them a bonus of 2,000 francs for each job created. Madelin had to be dropped because of his remarks about the privileges of civil servants, but this did not prevent Juppé from declaring a freeze on their salaries. The latter prompted the first big quarrel with the unions, which carried out a highly successful and popular strike—55 percent strike rate—and demonstrations on October 10.[27]

Juppé's efforts had not won favor with either the Germans or financial markets. His standing at the polls hit record lows. Opinion was morose. A survey of young people in Germany and France showed that 54 percent of the French thought they would live more poorly than their parents, 80 percent felt that companies treated their employees unfairly, and 35 percent expressed a preference for work in the public sector.[28] Youngsters under 25 were condemned to precarious jobs, family handouts, and a tertiary education, which with the deterioration of the university faculties served merely to delay unemployment.[29] The distrust of the governing class was high. A survey found that 61 percent of the French thought the governing elite showed little concern for the public interest; 49 percent believed that the elite put European construction ahead of France.[30] The message from financial markets was equally bad. Like the financial markets, the Germans were looking for some sign of the government's determination to cut the budget deficit.[31]

On October 26, after conferring with Chancellor Helmut Kohl in Germany, Chirac announced that henceforth the government would give priority to budget cutting in conformity with its European commitment. The franc firmed immediately, the stock market rebounded, and conservatives rejoiced. To the public, however, the announcement was a betrayal of Chirac's pledges as a candidate to tackle unemployment and the social divide. The real consequences of the shift were not seen, however, until November 15, when Juppé suddenly announced a radical reform of the social security system.[32]

Social security was by far the largest-ticket item in the national budget. Since the sickness fund depended largely on payroll taxes, unemployment was the major cause of its large deficit. If the government was to reduce the national deficit below 3 percent to conform with Maastricht, something had to be done to balance contributions and benefits. Prepared in secret without consultation, the plan threatened many vested interests: union administrators, doctors and hospitals, and contributors and beneficiaries—nearly everyone.

Its main features were the transfer of the payroll tax on employers and employees to a proportional tax on all incomes—the *contribution sociale généralisée*—and the levy of a special tax—the *remboursement de la dette sociale*—to liquidate the existing debt, the imposition of parliamentary limits on spending—an increase of 2.1 percent for 1996—greater state control of the union-management boards that administer the funds, and last but not least the elimination of the special regimes for public-sector workers. Juppé's high-handed approach—he sought the reforms by way of the fast-track *ordonnance* (decree) procedure—which won the admiration of the parliamentary majority and many experts, was an audacious gamble that the resulting outcries would neutralize each other and that the rationality of the package would become visible to all; it surely was better than becoming bogged down in fruitless negotiations with the vested interests.[33]

The union movement, which was charged under the system with defending the interests of the public, was at a low ebb; less than 10 percent of salaried workers and less than 6 percent in the private sector were unionized, and strikes ran at a quarter of their rate in 1982. Except in the industrial public sector—rail, energy, mining—the CGT, which had lost two-thirds of its membership and most of its union outposts in the private sector since 1975, no longer dictated the rules.[34] The CFDT, which had suffered losses in the 1980s when it invested the Mauroy government, had rebounded somewhat in the 1990s, especially in the public service and service sectors.[35] Since the 1980s—really since its *recentrage* (move to the center) after the 1978 elections—the CFDT had switched position with the *Force ouvrière* (FO) to become the ratifier of accords and cooperative partner of government and business.[36] The FO, the anti-Communist product of the Cold War, had assumed a more oppositional stance especially since the election of the burly Marc Blondel, the Parisian son of a miner, with the help of the local Trotskyists. Chirac, it was said, had a particular desire to keep the FO, which welcomed Gaullists as members, on his side.[37]

The Juppé plan was a direct assault on the FO position, which benefited from controlling more than half of the local boards of the sickness fund. Having received assurances from Chirac and Barrot as late as November 11, Blondel called this betrayal "the biggest robbery in the history of the Republic, the end of Social Security."[38] With its patronage and reputation on the line, the FO went all out—all the way to calling an interprofessional general strike and to common action with its Cold War enemy, the CGT, to defeat the plan. As a result of its action, the FO was to become a new union of struggle.

The reaction of the CFDT was unexpected. Unlike the other two major confederations, which essentially defended the status quo, the CFDT had declared its interest in reform, mentioning the taxation of value added rather than wages and parliamentary control in particular, but it also had signed a common platform with the other confederations in defense of the existing system—against fiscalization and *étatisation* (putting it under government control). Yet the head of the CFDT, former school teacher Nicole Notat, found little fault, declaring that the Juppé plan "went in the right direction."[39] For breaking ranks Notat was hissed by members at a union meeting in Paris and railroaded out of the demonstration of November 24. Blondel said she was speaking "like a minister charged with managing the common interest."[40] The CFDT rail workers, who joined the other unions in the strike, called for an extraordinary congress to sanction the leadership; Notat responded by putting the Paris teachers' union under trusteeship and threatening to expel 13 members as leftist "agitators."[41] Many of these "leftists" ended up joining the breakaway union SUD (Solidaires, Unitaires et Démocratiques), which played a leading role in the strike.

The CGT, dominated by the Communists, played a subdued but directing role in the strike. The party had long abandoned socialism as its goal; for it, as for Edouard Bernstein, the movement was everything and the goal nothing.[42] Now that reformers predominated in the party, the CGT would no longer carry out political campaigns for the party; left to its own devices, it would be free to accompany the popular movement wherever it led. The congress of the CGT, held in the heat of battle, put its statutes in line with the party, abandoning its goal of socialization of the means of production. The CGT was still the majority union on the railroads, but it knew it had to cooperate with the other unions and conduct a democratic strike to win. While many members—Communist and non-Communist—chafed at the bit demanding a general strike,[43] the CGT had to avoid any hint of using the strike for political advantage. Thus it was that one of the most militant and politically orthodox CGT federations was able to lead a most democratic mass strike.

The strike began on the railroads on November 24, 1995, on the eve of the first big demonstration of public employees in defense of their special regimes. The rail workers were a proud corporation with a long tradition of militancy and solidarity, who were chafing under efficiency exercises, managerial rhetoric, and job losses—73,000 in the last ten years.[44] They were protesting not only the elimination of their special regime, with early retirement after 37.5 years of service, but also the five-year development plan that the government was preparing to sign with the railroad, allowing for continued job loss, the closure of lines, and the subcontracting of services. They were worried that privatization would occur as a result of the European directive 91/440 on competition in transportation.[45]

The CGT joined the FO for an interprofessional strike and demonstration on November 28. Trains and Parisian transport were totally paralyzed. Other public service workers, including postal and energy workers and teachers, joined the strike. The student strike against dilapidated faculty conditions, begun on October 8 at Rouen, spread to other universities. The demonstrations were particularly large, larger than in 1968, in the provinces, especially the west and the southwest, in Rouen with the students, in Toulouse where workers from Aérospatiale joined the public sector, and in Marseilles where the marchers were accompanied by contingents of the unemployed. The unprecedented strength of the movement in the provinces, especially the poorer south, was a token of the respect in which the public services, particularly as an avenue of social mobility and security, were held.

Juppé had said that he would resign when 2 million people hit the streets. On December 12 that figure was probably reached; 270 demonstrations took place, with over 200,000 persons in Paris, 130,000 in Toulouse, 100,000 in Marseilles, 70,000 in Grenoble, and demonstrations for the first time ever in some of the smallest provincial towns and backwaters. Unlike May-June 1968 when Danny the Red and the students took the lead of the march with "the Stalinist scum" in tow, rail workers led the marches in December as the heroes of the hour with students straggling in the rear. The crowds joined the CGT and the FO in demanding the complete withdrawal of the Juppé plan. "Ca ira, ira, ira," screamed the marchers, "les technocrates on les pendra." (So we'll go and hang the technocrats).[46]

Everywhere the strike met with the favor if not the solidarity of the public; it seemed as if the rail workers were proxies fighting the battle for jobs and public service for all. Parisians turned the inconvenience of the strike into a sociable and even festive occasion when they came out of their shells to help each other hitchhike, in-line skate, or bicycle to work. Even the police fraternized with the strikers, handing out handbills with their own demands rather than parking tickets in Paris. The strike was supported by a clear majority of the public, who spurned government attempts to turn them against the strikers. While the call of the CGT and the FO for the private sector to join the strike clearly failed, the government and the parliamentary majority could not but be impressed with the depth of the malaise and protest.[47]

The transport workers' daily general meetings were the strike's engine room. Strikers received food from local tradesmen, visits and financial contributions of solidarity. There was little sign that class resentment had disappeared. Workers were tired of being asked by successive Socialist and conservative governments to make sacrifices, to tighten their belts and work harder only to see employees on casual and low-paid contracts replace full-timers. The jobs crisis affected people at the two extremes of working life, from university students looking for their first job to workers who had contracted for an early retirement.[48] The fear of the future, of unemployment and social regression for the younger generation, was pervasive. People had lost confidence in the French economic machine to provide for them.

A Renault worker heard his son tell him, "Papa, it's no use working in school only to become unemployed."[49] A bus mechanic in Paris declared: "It's all a big joke. It only fills up the coffers of our bosses and deals us scraps to keep us quiet." A rail worker proud of his revolutionary heritage recalled the stories of 1936 and 1953 when police fired on strikers and hung up a sign saying "La Commune n'est pas morte [the Paris Commune is still alive]." Workers decried the liberal ideology that pervaded the public services with pressures for speedup and productivity. Pierre Bourdieu, the sociologist and author of *La Misère du monde*,[50] addressing railway workers denounced those official intellectuals who had decided what was best for the people, and urged support of the movement as the only alternative to liberalism or barbarism. It was clear from accounts of general meetings that French workers had not been normalized, that they still regarded the permanent employment contract and the nonprofit public service as a norm of civilization.

By December 12 it was obvious that the movement had reached its crest and could only subside for lack of a political alternative. The Mitterrand experience had left the parties of the Left incapable of picking up the gaunt-let. Unlike 1968, when everyone invoked his own personal utopia and called it socialism, socialism in 1995 was a hollow term that had been abandoned by Socialists and Communists alike. The abandonment of Marxism as a guide to practice did not mean that the Communists did not react to events with Marxist reflexes.[51] To the extent they influenced the strike through the CGT, they insisted this was not a political but only a social movement. What they meant was that they were too weak and the Socialists too unre-constructed to formulate a credible alternative. The Juppé plan was, after all, very similar to the Teullade project, which the Socialists had proposed, and reception to it was mixed; the Rocardian Claude Evin favored it, as did Nicole Notat and Lionel Jospin, and Jacques Delors castigated the govern-ment for lack of consultation. It was in response to Delors that the intellec-tuals of the Proudhonian "second left," such as Pierre Rosanvallon[52] and Jacques Julliard, circulated a petition hailing Notat for her courageous stand in defense of the Juppé plan.

As by-elections that occurred during the crisis had shown, a political cri-sis would mainly benefit a Socialist Party that had only just begun to con-sider alternatives—it was just beginning to question its support for the convergence criteria—after 13 years of collaboration with capitalism. PCF leaders debated holding talks with other left ginger groups—they received the Trotskyist *Ligue communiste* for the first time—or opening public fo-rums, but the best they could do was to cheer on the social movement.[53]

Even more confounded by the movement was the National Front, which suddenly disappeared from the scene. The best it could do was to damn both sides, the incompetent parties of government and the subversive agitators from the unions. The Front had nothing to say to the millions demonstrat-ing in the streets. The strike, it seemed, was the best antidote yet against the influence of the National Front,[54] which resumed its ascension after the strike ended.

The government, unable to sabotage the strike and unwilling to call new elections, had decided to compromise on the immediate issues facing the rail workers. Juppé called the unions on December 11 and told them that he was prepared to maintain the special regime, adjourn conclusion of the develop-ment plan, consult with unions on the decrees, and talk with the public sec-tor unions about jobs. That evening he told a television audience that he recognized the depth of public concern about his plans and vowed to defend the notion of public service in European negotiations and by amendment of the French Constitution. He reproached Brussels for its ideological ap-proach to public services and the head of the railways for failing to carry on the social dialogue. The main lines of his reform, however, remained.[55]

The FO and the CGT were not satisfied, but the moderate autonomous unions and the CFDT, which warned against politicization, called for a return to work. On December 13 the first assemblies of rail workers in the east voted to return. On December 14 the first metro made its run to La Défense in Paris. Workers regretted that their great movement had produced so little—that they had not carried the strike forward into the private sector—but Christmas was coming and there was no prospect of a change of government.[56] After one last *baroud d'honneur* (protest for honor's sake), a demonstration on December 16—a festive family affair—all transport workers went back with the CGT urging its members to continue the struggle by other means and the FO warning of the prospect of a new flare-up in the new year.[57]

Despite the Auroux labor reforms under Mitterrand and the multiplication of firm accords since 1982, real collective bargaining was a rarity in France.[58] The rail strike ended as French strikes normally do, without the give-and-take of negotiations but with unilateral and thus revocable concessions from government. A summit meeting was convened on December 21 on the broader issue of employment, but nothing came of these discussions, which were a display of goodwill by the government and a bit of face-saving for the CFDT. Chirac in his New Year's message told of his devotion to dialogue but indicated his intention to proceed with reform. Discontent was rife in the parliamentary majority, but no clear alternative to Chirac's plan emerged.[59] In January the government appeared to be listening to majority debate on parliamentary control of health expenses, the levy of the special deficit tax, and the tax on family benefit,[60] which was dropped due to Catholic pressure. But it soon became apparent that the government would introduce the decrees on social security with little alteration and without consulting the unions as promised. Nor was anything more heard about the promised constitutional and European amendment on public services. Public-sector wages were frozen, France-Telecom was semiprivatized, and EDF-GDF prepared for commercialization under an EU directive. The government's determination to reduce public expenditure and commercialize public services in conformity with EU directives and convergence criteria, the key to both its foreign and domestic policy, was unshakable.

Yet although the strike had achieved only limited goals, it had been an extraordinary affair for the French people. It was extraordinary as an expression of popular feelings—anguish and anger—that are normally repressed and ignored by political parties and media. With a Left and trade union movement at its nadir, it was extraordinary to see the spontaneous resurgence of anticapitalist sentiment—both relic of the past and harbinger of the future. The strike was extraordinary as a sectional conflict that had resonated favorably with an estimated 57 percent of the wider public, including 45 percent of the professional and administrative personnel.[61]

The French labor movement always has derived its dynamism from the linking of sectoral trade or corporate demands with larger class issues.[62] Some intellectuals had condemned demands for early retirement in December as "corporatist,"[63] but it was precisely their immediate and concrete nature, linked to more general concerns about employment, that attracted understanding and sympathy in contrast to the surrealist slogans—*l'imagination au pouvoir* (put imagination in power)—of May-June 1968, which alienated common people and drove them into the arms of the government.[64] Although the strikes of December 1995, limited to the public sector, were considerably smaller than those of 1968, the sympathy demonstrations, involving as many as 2 million at their height, were larger, especially in the provinces. Because it was based on concrete demands and a growing social divide, this movement was potentially more radical than the May-June 1968 one.

The strikes united the major unions—with the exception of the CFDT leadership—behind a social movement that ran ahead of the political parties, that raised questions about employment and the future to which they had no answer. If it did not produce any dramatic immediate effects, it did portend changes of policy toward Europe, and a rebirth and hardening of the Left—seen in recent union and by-elections and opinion surveys.[65] A survey in June 1996 found the Socialists with 30 percent and the Communists with 9 percent—a total of six points ahead of the majority. As in 1968, the greatest effect of the strike may have been on the nonparticipating Socialist Party, which since its effacement under Mitterrand is witnessing a revival of the Socialist Left. This current, which obtained 40 percent for an amendment to renegotiate Maastricht, succeeded in imposing the highly significant demand for the restoration of administrative control over collective dismissals.[66]

The movement thus challenged the liberal consensus of the *pensée unique* (one-track mind), which has paralyzed alternative thought over the past 13 years. Party reflection focused on the need to expand the convergence criteria that had caused the movement in the first place. The Socialists, including such moderates as Martine Aubry, daughter of Delors, and Laurent Fabius, conceded the failure of social policy in the European Union and conditioned their approval of European Monetary Union on inclusive membership, a competitive rate for the euro, and the creation of a truly European government that would control the independent bank and launch a Keynesian reflation to restore employment.[67] They proposed a series of radical reforms, including a youth employment pact and the 35-hour week without loss of pay, that were hardly compatible with the Maastricht criteria.

Conservatives too were talking about new functions for Europe. While admitting the impossibility of pulling out of Maastricht, Séguin urged a new Franco-German initiative that would provide a political basis for an interventionist "social" Europe.[68] Chirac, not to be outdone, defended the interventionist "third way" at a Group of Seven meeting on employment held in Lille.[69] Even Valéry Giscard d'Estaing called for a more flexible conjunctural evaluation of the deficit criterion.[70] None of these suggestions had the slightest chance of being adopted by Germany or the European Union,[71] but they showed that politicians at least were seeking a response to the movement—or were they merely fobbing their domestic failures off to Europe as Socialists have traditionally done?[72]

The reason the government was able to pursue its plans with impunity is that the circumstances that produced the explosion were not soon repeatable. The government would not repeat the mistake of seeking a comprehensive reform, while antagonizing the rail workers, the most militant and best organized in France. Even if the CGT were to renew its call to demonstrate, as it did with a response from about 55,000 in February 1996[73] and again without result during the truckers' strike of November of that year, it could attract few sympathizers. The millions who came out into the streets in December 1995 calling for a change of government if not of regime had been disabused by the absence of political alternatives. Despite the deterioration of economic conditions, public pessimism,[74] and the record unpopularity of the government, they were not likely to try again without a new program of the Left.

Much has been written about the crisis of trade unionism[75] and the CGT,[76] but precious little about the crisis of French society that Chirac identified and to which the crisis of trade unionism is linked. Has Chirac's diagnosis proved too radical for even the parties of the Left? The crisis of the CGT is largely a function of structural changes in the workforce and the debilitating effects of unemployment and labor flexibility on organization and action. Except during periods of mass mobilization like the Popular Front, working-class unionism has always been one of active minorities, of committed leaders rather than followers, in France.[77] What the CGT lacked as a trade union it usually has made up for as a class union. Criticism is often heard of excessive "politicization"[78] and of bureaucratic structures and practices.[79] The December strike in which a most orthodox CGT federation— rail—conducted a most democratic mass strike should lay much of this criticism to rest. Democracy cannot operate without leadership, especially in a period of economic and psychological depression. What was missing in December was not democracy but precisely "politicization"—the formulation of a sufficiently credible transformative program that could mobilize millions and offer the hope of an alternative regime.

It was ironic that in the midst of the greatest strike movement since 1968, the CGT abandoned the only transformative program—for the collectivization of the means of production—it has ever had. Given the CGT's historic leadership and ideological links with the PCF, the initiative for such a program must come from the party. But the PCF, which lost its moorings after the collapse of the Common Program in 1977,[80] is a "drunken boat," a party of reformers locked in battle with traditionalists, in which class reflexes hide revisionist perspectives. No less than the Socialists, the PCF must come to terms with its history, not just the Soviet Union, but the Common Program and the Mitterrand experience. Traumatized by the collapse of the Common Program, the PCF repudiated the notion not only of stages or transitional programs but even that of the great transformative project of socialism, which provided a framework and dynamic for reform. The current revisionist strategy—the movement is everything, the end nothing—leaves the movement open to the most opportunistic pragmatism (a repeat of the 1981 governing alliance with the Socialists)[81] as well as to the most marginalizing sectarianism (a "radical pole" with Ecologists, Trotskyists, and other *groupuscules*).

The consequence for the CGT of these choices is enormous. Disillusionment with the utopian project of the general strike in 1914 left the CGT open to collaboration with the state during and after World War I. As this experience demonstrated, the CGT cannot continue to practice a militant class struggle unionism that wins concessions while avoiding the traps of collaboration without a credible transformative strategy and purpose.

NOTES

The author would like to express his thanks to the trade unionists of the CGT, the CFDT, and the FO and to René Mouriaux of the Centre for the Study of French Political Institutions for their help.

1. Cf. David Hanley and A. P. Kerr, *May 68: Coming of Age* (Basingstoke: Macmillan, 1988), and Pierre Favre, *La Manifestation* (Paris: Presses de la FNSP, 1990).
2. The French movement was not without similarities to popular expressions of discontent in the United States that have appeared in opinion surveys, in the Pat Buchanan campaign for the Republican nomination, and in proposed legislation to impose standards of social responsibility upon major corporations. See Andrew Sullivan, *Sunday Times,* February 4, 1996, and the *International Herald Tribune,* March 6, 1996.
3. The best history is Thomas Christofferson, *The French Socialists in Power, 1981–1986: From Autogestion to Cohabitation* (Newark, Del.: University of Delaware Press, 1991). See also Julius Friend, *Seven Years in France: François Mitterrand and the Unintended Revolution* (Boulder, Colorado: Westview

Press, 1989), S. Halimi, J. Michie, and S. Milne, "The Mitterrand Experience," in Jonathan Michie and John Grieve Smith, eds., *Unemployment in Europe* (London: Academic Press, 1994), chap. 6; and Bernard H. Moss, "Labour under Mitterrand: The Failure of French Socialism," in Peter McPhee, ed., *Proceedings of the Fifth George Rudé Seminar in French History* (Victoria University of Wellington, N.Z., 1986), pp. 72–79.

On the battle for the mind of Mitterrand, see Jacques Attali, *Verbatim* (Paris: Fayard, 1993), vol. 1, 1981–1986; Philippe Bauchard, *La Guerre des deux roses: Du rêve à la réalité, 1981–85* (Paris: Bernard Grasset, 1986), and Franz-Olivier Giesbert, *Le Président* (Paris: Seuil, 1990).

On wages and profits see *Centre d'étude des revenus et des coûts,* nos. 100 and 107.

4. René Mouriaux and Guy Groux, *La C. G. T.: crises et alternatives* (Paris: Economica, 1992). *Analyses et Documents économiques,* no. 67 (December 1995): 20–21, 36, 43.

5. Cf. André Gorz, *Adieux au prolétariat* (Paris: Ed. Galilée, 1980); Alain Touraine, Michel Wieviorka, and François Dubet, *Le Mouvement ouvrier* (Paris: Fayard, 1984); and François Furet, Jacques Julliard, and Pierre Rosanvallon, *La République du centre* (Paris: Calmann-Lévy, 1988).

6. Cf. Henri Mendras and Alistair Cole, *Social Change in Modern France: Towards a Cultural Anthropology of the Fifth Republic* (Cambridge: Cambridge University Press, 1991), Valéry Giscard d'Estaing, *Deux Français sur trois,* 2nd ed. (Paris: Flammarion, 1984); Pierre Rosanvallon, Jacques Julliard, and François Furet, *La République du centre* (Paris: Calmann-Lévy, 1988). Jacques Delors estimates the middle class at 70 percent of the population, but admits its insecurity; *L'Unité d'un homme* (Paris: Odile Jacob, 1994), p. 74.

7. Cf. Francis Fukuyama, *The End of History and the Last Man* (New York: Free Press, 1992); and Steven Laurence Kaplan, *Farewell Revolution: The Historians' Feud, France, 1789/1989* (Ithaca: Cornell University Press, 1995).

8. Cf. Nonna Mayer and Pascal Perrineau, "Why do They Vote for Le Pen?" *European Journal of Political Research* 22 (1992): 123–141.

9. Emmanuel Todd, "Aux Origines du malaise politique français: les classes sociales et leur représentation," *Le Débat,* nos. 83–85 (1995): 106–109, and his original version in *Notes de la Fondation Saint-Simon* (November 1994), esp. pp. 29–31.

10. Gina Raymond, "The Decline of the Established Parties," in Gina Raymond, ed. *France during the Socialist Years* (Dartmouth, 1994), pp. 90–113.

11. Philippe Habert, Pascal Perrineau, and Colette Ysmal, *Le Vote éclaté: les élections régionales et cantonales des 22 et 29 mars 1992* (Paris: Presses de la FNSP, 1992).

12. Jérome Jaffré, "Les Grandes Vagues électorales sous la Cinquième République," in Habert, Perrineau, and Ysmal, *Le Vote sanction,* pp. 250–265.

13. Todd, "Aux Origines du Malaise," pp. 103–106.

14. *Le Figaro,* August 4, 1992.

15. *Le Monde,* October 6, 1992.
16. Bernard Denni, "Du référendum du 20 septembre 1992 aux élections législatives de mars 1993," in Habert, Perrineau, and Ysmal, *Le Vote sanction,* p. 95.
17. Cf. Annick Percheron, "Les Français et l'Europe: acquiescement de façade ou adhésion véritable," *Revue française de science politique* 41 (1991): 382–406.
18. Todd, "Aux Origines du Malaise," pp. 100–101, 106–109. *Politis,* October 1, 1992. Alain Prate, *La France en Europe* (Paris: Economica, 1995), pp. 80–87, 300–331.
19. Alex Callincos and Chris Harman, *The Changing Working Class: Essays in Class Structure Today* (London: Bookmarks, 1987), pp. 55–60.
20. Todd, "Aux Origines du Malaise," pp. 102–103.
21. *Le Monde,* June 11, 1996.
22. Todd, "Aux Origines du Malaise," pp. 113–116. Janine Mossuz-Lavau, *Les Français et la politique: enquête sur une crise* (Paris: Odile Jacob, 1994), pp. 349–351.
23. Pascal Perrineau, "Dynamique du vote Le Pen: le poids du 'gaucholepenisme,'" in Pascal Perrineau and Colette Ysmal, eds., *Le Vote de Crise: l'élection présidentielle de 1995* (Paris: Presses de la FNSP, 1995), pp.247–248.
24. J. Gerstlé, "La Dynamique sélective d'une campagne décisive," in Perrineau and Ysmal, *Le Vote de Crise,* pp. 21–45. See summary of programs in *Le Monde,* May 5, 1995.
25. *Le Monde,* May 20, 1995.
26. *International Herald Tribune,* September 15, 1995.
27. *Le Monde,* September 6, October 10, 1995; *Syndicalisme-hebdo,* October 19, 1995.
28. *Le Monde,* October 16, 1995.
29. *Le Monde,* October 25, 1995.
30. Erik Izraelewic, *Le Monde,* December 7, 1995.
31. *Le Monde,* October 7, 26, 1995. *International Herald Tribune,* October 27, 1995.
32. On social security, see J. Ambler, ed., *The French Welfare State* (New York: New York University Press, 1991).
33. *Le Monde,* October 26, November 17, 1995.
34. André Narritsens and Charles Demons, "Combien de syndiqués," *Analyse et Documents économiques,* no. 67 (December 1995): 28–36.
35. *Syndicalisme hebdo,* October 12, 1995.
36. Cf. Bernard H. Moss, "Ideology and Industrial Practice: Federations CGT, CFDT, and FO," in Mark Kesselman, ed. *The French Workers' Movement,1968–1982* (Boston: George Allen and Unwin, 1984), pp. 238–254.
37. *Le Monde,* November 23, December 9, 1995.
38. *Le Monde,* November 23, 1995.
39. *Le Monde,* November 17, 1995.
40. *Syndicalisme-hebdo,* November 23, 1995.
41. Interview with Federation of Transport, CFDT, January 6, 1996, and with Paris SGEN, January 7, 1996.

42. Robert Hue, *Communisme: la mutation* (Stock, 1995), pp. 309–342.

43. *Le Peuple,* December 5–7, 1995 (discussion at congress).

44. Jean-Pierre Le Goff and Alain Caillé, *Le Tournant de décembre* (Paris: La Découverte, 1996), pp. 43–48, 69–70.

45. Interviews with CGT and CFDT leaders, January 4, 6, 1996.

46. *Le Monde,* November 26, 30, December 6, 13, 1995. See table in Steve Jefferys, "France 1995: The Backward March of Labour Halted?" *Capital and Class,* no. 57 (Summer 1996): 15.

47. *Le Monde,* December 17, 1995 (statement of Pascale Robert-Diard).

48. Jean-Paul Fitoussi, *Le Monde,* December, 5, 1995.

49. The following quotations are taken from Dominique Le Guilledoux, "Les Paroles de grévistes," *Le Monde,* December 5, 1995, p. 14.

50. Pierre Bourdieu, *La Misère du Monde* (Paris: Seuil, 1993).

51. Cf. Peter Morris, "The French Communist Party and the End of Communism," in Martin Bull and Paul Heywood, eds., *West European Communist Parties after the Revolutions of 1989* (Basingstoke: Macmillan, 1994), pp. 31–55, fails to make the distinction.

52. See Pierre Rosanvallon, *La Nouvelle Question sociale: repenser l'Etat-Providence* (Paris: Seuil, 1995).

53. *Le Monde,* November 23, December 14, 1995.

54. Cf. Alain Bihr, *Pour en finir avec le Front national* (Paris: Syros, 1993); and David Martin-Castelnau, ed., *Combattre le Front national* (Paris: Vinci, 1995).

55. *Le Monde,* December 12, 1995.

56. *Libération,* December 14, 15, 1995.

57. *Le Monde,* December 16–19, 1995.

58. Steve Jefferys, "On the Road to 'Normalisation'? French Industrial Relations in the 1990s," *Work, Employment & Society* 10 (1996): 3–6; Bernard H. Moss, "Industrial Law Reform in an Era of Retreat: The Auroux Laws in France," *Work, Employment & Society* 2 (1988): 317–334; Janine Goetschy and Patrick Rozenblatt, "France: The Industrial Relations System at a Turning Point?" in Anthony Ferner and Richard Hyman, eds., *Industrial Relations in the New Europe* (Oxford: Blackwell, 1992), esp. p. 432.

59. *L'Express,* January 1, 1996.

60. *Le Monde,* January 24, 1996.

61. *Le Monde,* January 5, 1996.

62. See Bernard H. Moss, *The Origins of the French Labor Movement: The Socialism of Skilled Workers (1830–1914)* (Berkeley: University of California Press, 1976).

63. Pascal Perrineau and Michel Wieviorka, *Le Monde,* December 20, 1995. See reply of Christian Baudelot and Stéphane Israel, December 28, 1995. Also, A. Touraine, Michel Wieviorka et al., *Le Grand Refus* (Paris: Fayard, 1996). Touraine and Wieviorka in *Le Mouvement ouvrier* predicted that the decline of trade "corporatism" would spell the end of the labor movement.

64. I owe this point to Professor Sidney Tarrow of Cornell University.

65. *Le Monde,* March 1, 3–4, 19, May 9, June 11, 13, 21, 1996.

66. *A Gauche, l'hebdo de la Gauche Socialiste* (March-July 1996). *Le Monde,* July 2, 1996.

67. *Le Monde,* March 2, April 2, 1996. Convention nationale in *Vendredi, l'hebdomadaire des Socialistes,* April 5, 1996.

68. *Le Monde,* January 27, 1996.

69. *Le Monde,* April 3, 1996.

70. *Le Monde,* January 26, 1996.

71. Led by Germany, European leaders shelved a $1.5 billion public works proposal that was a miniedition of Delors' plan for a European transport network. *International Herald Tribune,* June 24, 1996.

72. "The myth of a supranational Europe was the way to flee unbearable reality by taking refuge in imaginary worlds." Maurice Duverger cited in Geneviève Lemaire-Prosche, *Le P.S. et l'Europe* (Paris: Editions universitaires, 1990), p. 34.

73. *Le Monde,* February 13, 1996.

74. *Le Monde,* October 11, 1996.

75. Pierre Rosanvallon, *La Question syndicale* (Paris: Hachette, 1988).

76. Groux and Mouriaux, *La CGT.*

77. See especially Michel Dreyfus, *Histoire de la C. G. T.* (Paris: Editions Complexes, 1995).

78. The classic statement is George Ross, *Workers and Communists in France: From Popular Front to Eurocommunism* (Berkeley: University of California Press, 1982).

79. Groux and Mouriaux, *La CGT,* pp. 222–230, 263–264.

80. Roger Martelli, *Le Rouge et le bleu: essai sur le Communisme dans l'histoire française* (Paris: Editions ouvrières, 1995), pp. 65–81. Bernard H. Moss, "Workers and the Common Program (1968–1978): The Failure of French Communism," *Science and Society* 54 (Spring 1990): 42–66.

81. *Le Monde,* June 23–24, 1966.

CHAPTER NINE

Women and French Unions: Historical Perspectives on the Current Crisis of Representation

Laura Levine Frader

s the CGT's one-hundredth year came to a close with an explosive and massive social mobilization in November-December 1995, French unions, like labor movements in many parts of the globe, were experiencing one of their worst crises ever. The conjunctural dimensions of this crisis have been evoked many times: recomposition of the labor force, the so-called diversification of the working class, the apparent triumph of neoliberalism, globalization, massive unemployment, and the increase in part-time, limited-term jobs that accentuate the increasing fragility and uncertainty of work in the post-Fordist, late-capitalist economy. All of these changes have had gender-specific dimensions with particular consequences for the French labor movement. The tendency for a large proportion of women to work in unstable or insecure jobs has posed major problems for the labor movement's capacity to mobilize women and has deprived the unions of new recruits.[1] Women now face a double crisis of representation in the French unions: They are severely underrepresented numerically in comparison with their presence in the labor force. At the same time, unions continue to experience difficulty in representing women's interests with respect to both employers and the state.

These problems are not new. Underlying the broad conjunctural dimensions of labor's current dilemma are the difficulties French unions have experienced for over a century in mobilizing large sectors of the working class that have included (and continue to include) some of the most disadvantaged and exploited workers, notably women. Historically, women's gender-specific demands have challenged supposedly gender-neutral labor discourses and practices, including the crucial notion of what constitutes legitimate demands and fields of action. In the past those challenges could be ignored, particularly when they came during periods of remobilization and growing union membership (as in the 1930s, for example). In the 1980s and 1990s, when union membership has fallen to an all-time low and basic labor and social *droits acquis* (entitlements) are being eroded by neoliberal state and employer politics of *rigeur* (austerity), the unions are no longer ignoring those challenges, but they have yet to respond fully to them in labor platforms and strategies. It is hardly news that the unions' difficulties are not only the result of the larger conjuncture, but have been, at least in part, specific to the politics of unions themselves. Despite hopeful signs of commitment to women's demands on the part of both the CGT and the CFDT in the 1970s, despite the emergence of new organizations, such as Force Ouvrière (FO), which have successfully organized women, and despite growth in the numbers of unionized women overall, women's integration into unions has remained problematic. Understanding the historical dimension of unions' difficulties in mobilizing women is important if unions are to move out of the doldrums.

Looking just at the period since the 1920s, three interrelated areas of organized labor's relationship to women and of women's relationship to unions have been particularly problematic: the integration of women into leadership positions in union organizations and structures; the extent to which women's specific demands could be incorporated into labor strategies; and the limited opportunities for women's autonomy as a specific constituency in negotiating the complex relations between unions and parties.[2] Apart from the fundamental problem of mobilizing women, the overarching dilemma of all three areas has been the basis on which they would be included. Would they be included under some universal model of the worker and under the assumption that all workers' interests were more or less identical, or would they be included on the basis of their specific status and specific interests as women? Would inclusion be gender-neutral or recognize the salience of gender difference? The persistence of beliefs in "the worker" as a universal category coded male and the failure to acknowledge gender difference as a key arena of social struggle and conflict has been costly for the French unions.[3]

ORGANIZATIONS AND STRUCTURES

Following World War I, both Communist and non-Communist unions made promising commitments to organizing women in the context of the failed strikes of 1919–1920 and the swift decline of union membership that followed upon the splitting of the Communist-affiliated Confédération Générale du Travail Unitaire (CGTU) from the Confédération Générale du Travail (CGT). Both *centrales* followed the strategy of establishing separate women's groups within each confederation. Following a directive of the Internationale Syndicale Rouge, the CGTU established the first Women's Commission in 1922. Designed primarily to bolster the membership of the new *centrale,* the Women's Commission coordinated the organization of working women, gave them a voice within the confederation, and represented women in national confederal congresses. The CGT, which at about the same time had appointed a women's organizer, followed suit and set up its own Women's Commission in 1927. The commissions of both confederations conducted organizing drives that, if not always successful, nonetheless permitted women's issues to reach the floor of confederation congresses with considerable regularity. Occasionally the commissions were replicated at the federal or local level in groups such as the Union des Syndicats de la Seine et la Seine-et-Oise (CGTU). Additionally, through a small body of female activists, the CGTU encouraged women's labor struggles, such as the strike of sardine packers in Douarnenez in 1925 and the massive textile workers' strikes of 1928–1929 in the Nord (the "strike of the ten sous") as targets of opportunity for the mobilization of female workers.[4]

The creation of the commissions marked a significant step forward for the potential inclusion of women in the labor movement and continued a trend already evident before World War I of acknowledging the legitimacy of women's presence in the labor market and the importance of organizing them. However, women's unionization failed to match the level of female employment, which stabilized between the wars at around 38 percent of the labor force. From an estimated 15 percent of the labor movement in 1920, women's declining unionization followed the general demobilization of organized labor in the wake of the 1919–1920 strikes. A 1925 estimate that women constituted 10 percent of CGTU members was probably overly optimistic.[5] Moreover, even in federations where women had a strong presence (as in primary school teaching, where they made up 33 percent of the members in the CGTU Fédération de l'Enseignement) or where they constituted a clear majority, as in the garment industry (between 60 percent and 70 percent of the membership of the Fédération de l'Habillement), women's presence in leadership posts (such as the administrative council or the federation council) was infinitesimal. Those who did hold positions in the confederations' administrative bodies held posts that had no real power: as treasurer, as *secrétaire de propagande* (propaganda secretary), or *secrétaire pédagogique* (education secretary).[6] Although women were in the majority on the provisional administrative commission of the Fédération de Textile et Habillement, which brought together the Textile Workers' Federation and the

Garment Workers' Federation in 1924, the debate on the nomination of a standing secretary for women at the fusion congress revealed men's ambivalence about accepting a female nominee. Although delegates accepted the principle of nominating a woman to the federal bureau *(bureau fédéral)*, the highest executive body of the new federation, action on the nomination was put off to a subsequent congress and no woman was ever nominated.[7]

Despite major political differences between the confederations and important corporative distinctions between federations, overall, between the two world wars, the women's commissions had mixed results for women. On the one hand, women used these bodies to articulate gender-based demands on a variety of issues that were particularly important to them. In the 1920s, in the context of national debates about pronatalism and as the government took the first steps to put in place a system of family allowances, women in the CGTU commissions debated the practices of employer-sponsored family wage bonuses to reward fertility and argued for state-managed social protections that would permit working women to combine motherhood and work. They demanded nursing rooms for mothers and canteens where women could take meals.[8] Within the CGT, women's organizer Jeanne Chevenard spoke out for the protection and organization of industrial homeworkers and against night work for women. She argued for family workshops that would allow women who could not afford to stop working while they were nursing to bring their children to a special nursery in the workshop. Women in both commissions protested wage inequalities and protested against unsafe conditions on the job. However, although the commissions permitted women's issues to reach the agendas of the confederation more easily, they also ghettoized women as a specific group or category of worker. Women's gender made their class status problematic for male workers. The gender specificity of women's demands challenged established labor practices that tended to treat the working class as homogeneous and male and failed to recognize the ways in which gender difference structured class interests. Moreover, although it was not always apparent from the beginning, tension between female activists in the commission and the Communist Party came into the open in the late 1920s and compromised the relative autonomy that CGTU women enjoyed in the Women's Commission.

A much more radical form of separatism was practiced by the Confédération Française des Travailleurs Chrétiens (CFTC), keen to use a labor organization to facilitate the rechristianization of the working class. From its origins in 1919 the CFTC actively organized women in entirely separate federations, following the practice of the earliest women's Christian unions dating from the end of the nineteenth century.[9] This level of separatism may have indeed facilitated women's organization: women counted for half of the members at the founding congress of the CFTC, and they were rapidly parachuted into the leadership of regional unions and trade federations. From 1920, two women sat on the confederal bureau, and a woman was vice-president of the confederation.[10] But between the wars the CFTC position with respect to women was thoroughly ambiguous. Although it defended the rights of female textile workers, employees, postal workers, and teachers in labor conflicts such as the postal workers' strike of 1925 and the textile workers strikes of 1927–1928, the CFTC treated women's work as an unfortunate accident. Proclaiming the family—not the individual—the fundamental unit of society, it made protection of the family one of its primary objectives. As often as possible the confederation condemned married women's presence in the labor force and supported the return of women to the home, a position that led it to support such measures as the unwaged mother's allowance in the 1930s. This, then, was the other face of women's surprisingly strong integration into the ranks of the Christian labor movement.[11] Hostility to the presence of married women in the labor force remained the official line of the CFTC until 1964, when the majority of the confederation abandoned its Christian identity and became the CFDT. From that point on, the CFDT position on women's rights, including all women's right to work, evolved rapidly.

Gender was not the only form of difference that challenged French labor activists' notions of a homogeneous working class marching forward to break the chains of exploitation. Although beyond the scope of this chapter, the ways in which labor organizations addressed immigrant workers provides a fascinating illustration of how gender shaped class and ethnicity with respect to the integration of immigrant workers into the French labor movement. Women's insertion into the unions differed from that of immigrant workers, and organizing strategies operated differently for the two groups. Whereas women were segregated in the women's commissions in the interwar period, immigrant male workers were not organized in separate organizations. Male immigrants were the subject of long debates in federation and confederation congresses; massive propaganda devoted to immigrant men— broadsides and appeals translated into multiple languages, meetings designed to address the "problem of the immigrant worker"—all spoke eloquently to the fact that French male workers, especially in trades such as building and metallurgy, were far more threatened by semiskilled and unskilled male immigrants than by women. Here was a good example of the relevance of gender difference in shaping organizing strategies. Male immigrant workers could not be dismissed within the framework of a "complementarist" discourse that relegated them to one sphere of the division of labor in the same way that women, in the rhetoric of some activists, were relegated to their complementary roles as wives and mothers. Immigrant men shared the same gender with French men even though their nationalities or ethnic identities were different. Gender did not render their class status problematic or questionable, nor did their class interests challenge accepted modes of labor struggle. The subtext in most discussions about immigrant labor was French male workers' concerns about how immigrant men (far more than women, given the gender division of labor) threatened to compete with them for jobs and undercut wages.

The strategy of providing separate organizations for women, therefore, was mixed. The CGT and CGTU Women's Commissions did permit women to be more easily included within the organizational frameworks of the *centrales* and provided them with a voice, but as separate and frankly peripheral structures within the larger confederations (or federations), whose position with respect to the *rapports de force* of these organizations was notoriously weak. They were not able to compel the confederations to change their analysis of women's place in the labor market or in the labor movement, union platforms, or agendas. Moreover, with the reunification of the labor movement in 1935–1936, the Women's Commissions disappeared.[12] The CFTC's radical separation of men and women may have facilitated women's integration into the Catholic labor movement, but only in the service of the larger christianizing objectives of the confederation and at the price of women's ideological autonomy.

PRACTICE

Three aspects of labor practice had important consequences for women: labor discourse that gave priority to masculine definitions of the worker and tended to emphasize maternity when speaking of women, men's attempts to protect male skill and maintain sexual divisions of labor, and unions' definitions of what was considered acceptable as a legitimate domain of action. Fundamental to the shaping of labor demands historically was the problem of labor discourses that defined labor action in masculine terms and attempted to delegitimize women's place in the labor market. The persistence of the notion that the right to work was fundamentally a male right, especially among those professional groups that wielded the most power within the labor movement—such as metalworkers, printers, and building workers—was one example of such discourses. Even though demands for a family wage had by and large disappeared from the agendas of most unions affiliated with the CGT and the CGTU, some male workers (for example, postal workers and electrical workers) still referred to the family wage as an ideal into the late 1920s.[13] Despite important differences between CGT and CGTU discourses on women—the CGT fell into step with the pronatalist stance of the government and social reformers in the interwar years, whereas the CGTU abstained from supporting pronatalism until 1935 and placed more stress on women's identity as workers—both confederations emphasized the links between maternity and work. Although after 1936 the reunified CGT resisted attempts on the part of Catholic women's organizations and other groups to return working women to the home, the emphasis on the ties between maternity and wage labor reappeared after World War II and persisted in the CGT into the 1970s with mixed consequences for women.[14] Because it was impossible for union activists to discuss women as workers without simultaneously invoking maternity, male activists could continue to question the legitimacy of women's status as workers. At the same time, the fact that women were primarily responsible for children and family meant that maternity, family, and the distribution of activity between work and family were fundamental issues of concern that differed from and disrupted unions' notions of the domain of labor practice. The tension evoked by women's dual status as both workers and mothers threw into relief the inadequacy of unitary or universalistic notions of the (male) worker and simultaneously made it difficult for women to make specific claims without being treated as unequal partners.

As we have already seen, such a tension was implicit in official CFTC discourse and labor practice with regard to women, although there was no ambiguity in its official position. The confederation continued to view women's work as deviant, and the return of working mothers to the home remained a priority. Thus the head of the CFTC Textile Workers' Federation, which had the largest number of female members of any CFTC federation in the 1930s, condemned modern industry for having torn women away from the family, and the local CFTC newspaper in the north, *Le Nord-Social,* regularly published statistics on the numbers of abortions and infant mortality in households where women worked in the textile industry to drive home the point about the nefarious consequences of married women's employment.[15] Of the illegitimacy of women's work there could be no question.

The post–World War II period also saw contradictory discourses on the part of parties and the state that undermined women's inclusion as equal partners. On one hand, the postwar agenda of rebuilding the French economy and reestablishing the republic on the ashes of *les années noires* was potentially advantageous to women. For the first time women enjoyed full citizenship rights, and, at the very least, their work was less of a public issue in the context of relatively high employment of the postwar period. Only the CFTC resisted the idea of a massive mobilization of women's labor after the war.[16] On the other hand, the postwar resurgence of pronatalism inherent in the family policies of the Fourth and Fifth republics assumed that women would bear the burden of reconstituting French families. The pronatalist, profamily agenda, largely defended by the CFTC, also received support from within the CGT. In 1935 the Communist Party had reversed its position of the 1920s and early 1930s by promoting the family and condemning contraception, following the more conservative shift in Soviet policy on the family and reproduction under Joseph Stalin.[17] In the 1950s and 1960s the same conservative position on reproductive rights powerfully influenced the labor movement's inability to dissociate women from motherhood but also enabled it to refuse to include the issue of reproductive rights as a claim that labor could support.[18]

An equally important problem concerned definitions of work and skill. In the 1920s and 1930s the unions tended to reinforce rather than challenge the gender dimension of the historical process of rationalization and degradation of work. Male activists persisted in defining skill in gendered terms and sought to maintain skill and wage differentiations on the basis of gender.[19] Even if men ceased to argue for the family wage and acknowledged women's right to work, they still could not acknowledge women's right to work on the same terms as men. In this respect it is questionable whether the reunification of the labor movement in 1936 constituted a step forward for women. Women's membership in the unions soared during the Popular Front period: Before June 1936, for example, the Textile and Garment Workers' Federation counted 741 women and over 5,096 men; by October 1936 it had grown to 83,187 women and 17,419 men, and more women were brought into the administrative structures of federations that had large numbers of women, although not at the highest levels.[20] On the other hand, not only did the reunified confederation fail to reinstitute a women's only (albeit imperfect) platform for challenging inequality, the Women's Commission, but male activists excluded women from mixed shops during sitdown strikes of 1936. As Jacques Kergoat has pointed out, in some cases women stayed at home to take care of children. But the main resistance to women's presence in mixed factory occupations came from considerations of morality. "Un femme visée à son tour dans une usine de travail, ça va. Mais une femme libre dans une usine occupée, cela vous a tout de suite un air subversif, alors qu'elles y passent la nuit. . . . La pudibonderie d'une partie du mouvement ouvrier se nourrit certes des descriptions des baccanales dont fourmille la presse bourgeoise." ("It was acceptable to see a woman working at her lathe in a factory, but a single woman in a sitdown strike immediately looked shady, and if she were to spend the night inside the occupied factory. . . . The prudishness of part of the labor movement fed on descriptions of the baccanalian orgies that the bourgeois press stirred up.")[21] Even if such a move were construed as strategically justifiable in the conduct of a strike, it rested on a sexualized representation of women that failed to construe them as serious labor activists. Rather than challenge this representation, male workers accepted and perpetuated it and demonstrated just how gender relations on the political left reproduced those in the larger culture. In the accords that eventually ended the strikes, even though wages increased overall, many unions negotiated different wages on the basis of gender. Thus *contrats collectifs* in textiles, electricity, aviation, and automobiles negotiated by the CGT and the CFTC reinforced women's secondary position in the wage structure.[22]

Finally, in the interwar years (although these practices were not new to the 1920s and 1930s), both the CGT and the CGTU often separated public-sphere issues or demands from private-sphere ones in their own analyses and thereby excluded issues of interest or importance to women. Thus unions' definition of what constituted a legitimate field of action was frequently at variance with what women considered to be important and/or legitimate issues.[23] Since many issues of importance to women in fact concerned the overlap between public and private spheres, although women could raise them in the Women's Commissions, they remained virtually absent from union action programs. One exception was seen when, in the context of both the Depression and the antifascist struggle in 1934, the CGTU launched an appeal to women, defending obligatory maternity leave at full pay for 16 weeks, increases in the nursing allowance, and obligatory creation of day care centers under the control of working women, alongside more classic wage demands. But this attempt to connect women's public and private interests within the framework of labor demands was relatively unusual.

The practice of the CFTC provides a contrast in the interwar period. The dual project of returning women to the home and rechristianizing the working class (complete with Christian references to women's "natural" function as mothers and wives) permitted the activities of CFTC activists to spill beyond the domain of traditional labor action. CFTC women organized consumer cooperation programs and women's restaurants, established libraries and study groups, and sponsored housekeeping courses, all designed to help women be better mothers. They maintained close ties with Catholic women's groups, such as the Union Féminine Civique et Sociale and the Jeunesse Ouvrière Catholique Féminine, that worked to raise the status of motherhood and supported an unwaged mother's allowance. However, bringing together public and private issues was not designed to advance women's position as workers as much as it was designed to valorize the private sphere. Thus, in the logic of the CFTC, the "femme au foyer" acquired the status of a right for all working women.[24]

After World War II, the notion that public and private were separate realms of unequal valence continued to mean that the willingness of non-Christian unions to integrate women's issues and demands depended on their definition of a legitimate field of action. In practical terms until recently this has meant the unions have been unable to stretch the domain of action beyond economistic workplace demands to include issues defined as "private" concerns, such as reproductive rights, sexual harassment, family allowances, or social security. Maintaining the fiction of a split between these two domains made it difficult for male activists to recognize that child care or reproductive rights were not private issues but were of fundamental importance for the workplace, as the 1974 unity-in-action accord between the CGT and the CFDT acknowledged.

The question of reproductive rights is a case in point. In its new identity as a progressive, non-Christian labor confederation, from about 1972, the CFDT was able to incorporate feminist concerns (including an analysis of the gender dimension of women's subordination) more successfully than the CGT. In fact, under the leadership of Jeannette Laot, national secretary of the CFDT from 1970 to 1981, the CFDT was the first labor organization to agitate for the abrogation of the 1920 law penalizing contraception and abortion.[25] Within the CGT, although abortion and contraception (as well as sexism, the domestic division of labor, and issues such as child rearing) were debated in the CGT women's magazine, *Antoinette,* and elsewhere (such as the *commissions sociales* in the workplace), these issues fell outside what the CGT had defined as the official domain of labor action. As one observer has pointed out, "Le champ de compétence reconnu repose sur le sort du travailleur dans l'entreprise, lieu d'exploitation . . ., et s'exprime en termes de 'rapports de classe.'" "L'extension (revendiquée par la CFDT à l'époque . . .) à des domaines considérés comme hors champ syndical était vu comme brisante l'identité de la CGT et donc dangereuse." ("[For the Confederation], what constitutes the recognized field of union competence revolves around workers' position in the workplace, the site of exploitation, and expresses itself in terms of 'class relations.'" "The CGT saw the expansion of labor action to domains outside of [what they believed was] the unions' legitimate sphere of interest (as the CFDT demanded at the time), as destructive of labor unity and therefore dangerous.")[26] Only when the CGT determined that it was electorally expedient to mobilize women's support in the context of the Common Program of the Left in the 1970s did it become more open to the inclusion of "private" domain issues on its agenda. Thus the 1974 unity-in-action agreement and the accord on wage-earning women between the CGT and the CFDT marked the CGT's willingness to address women's concerns more directly than it had done in the past. Even more important for the CGT was the 1977 conference on women wage earners, where CGT secretaries Christiane Gilles and Jean-Louis Moynot drew attention to men's role in the exploitation of women and called for the infrastructures necessary to establish gender equality. These interventions broke a long silence within the CGT on the subject of women's exploitation and opened a path to the inclusion of this general issue within the framework of union demands.[27] This commitment to address women's issues as a part of the Common Program, however, was closely tied to political and electoral objectives of the 1970s.

UNION-PARTY RELATIONS

The willingness of unions to place women's issues on their agendas also depended on political conjunctures and partisan strategies. Both historically and more recently, especially within the interwar CGTU and the postwar CGT, confederation attention to PCF strategy either opened or closed doors for women. Following World War I, in conjunction with attempts to rebuild the labor movement and build a mass-based, class-based political party, the Communist Party and the CGTU both had emphasized the recruitment of women and provided the organizational apparatus to facilitate recruitment into the unions. Yet women's independence within the framework of the *Commission féminine* was constrained by party strategies that demanded allegiance from labor women. Conflicts between female activists began at the very first national meeting of the CGTU Women's Commission in 1923 in debates over union autonomy and continued in bitter struggles through at least 1927. In 1925 and 1926 in the midst of the period of bolshevization—both in communications to the CGTU Women's Commission and in policy on the party's Women's Commission—male activists challenged women's autonomy and told women to work alongside men, whom they presumed would be better versed in organizing.[28]

One might also add that the party's strategy of organizing in factory cells, put in place in these years, may have operated differently for women than for men. Historical evidence suggests that whereas men found the workplace to be a favorable environment for organizing, labor mobilization of women in the workplace was more difficult. As M. J. Maynes has pointed out, women found the workplace "more problematic as a political space" than men.[29] The gender division of labor or women's exclusion from male shops made it harder to organize women at the point of production in mixed groups.

The late 1920s also marked the party's movement away from emphasizing gender equality and was followed by the party's attempt to contain women's activities in the unions as well as in other areas. In 1927, as the PCF entered its class-against-class strategy, its women's newspaper *L'Ouvrière*, originally designed to provide a forum for Communist working women, was closed down for being too much under the influence of "bourgeois" feminists.[30] When the paper was reopened a couple of years later, it was under a new editorial board more closely aligned with the party. The problem of women's autonomy did not disappear following World War II. Analysis of the relationship between labor women and the PCF in the 1960s and 1970s, for example, has suggested that the strategic responses of labor confederations to the electoral politics of the Left determined the confederations' positions on women. Thus it has been argued that the ability of the CGT and the CFDT to come together in promoting women's issues and the subsequent soft-pedaling of women's concerns by the CGT must be viewed in the context of PCF engagement in the Common Program of the Left and the failure of the Left to secure a victory in the 1978 elections.[31]

A NEW PATH FOR LABOR?

These three areas—organization, practice, and union-party relations—suggest that in both structural and cultural terms, gender tensions within the French unions have a long history. At the same time, over the past 20 years there have been important signs of change in all three areas. Unions finally have begun to abandon the notion of women as a special "category" and now address women as legitimate members of the working class. Second, since the 1970s, the unions have paid increasing attention to placing women in upper-level, leadership positions in the federations and in regional organizations, especially in sectors with large numbers of women, such as teaching, food industries, textile and garment industries, banking, and postal work.[32] In the CFDT, women make up 25 percent of the national executive committee and 31 percent of confederation officials; in the Force Ouvrière 8 percent of the national committee and 67 percent of the confederation officials are women.[33] Although activists complain that women do not have a strong presence in positions of importance outside of those areas in which they are in the majority, it is at the same time true that women are taking more responsibility for negotiations at both the federal and the confederal level and responsibility for issues such as employment.[34] Finally, the greater willingness of the political parties to address women's concerns and run women candidates (partly under the impulse of party-level decisions to run a quota of women candidates and more recently in response to the national movement for representational parity) has aroused the attention of the labor movement. Labor practices and discourses have been more inclusive of women not only as mothers but as workers. Thus the CGT, for example, recently has redoubled its efforts to mobilize women through workshops and discussions of women's issues in local organizations.

Despite this apparent progress, two recent labor mobilizations are suggestive (albeit in very different ways) of the difficulties unions continue to face in responding to women's interests. The historically unique *coordination* (collective organizing committee) in the nursing strike of 1989 was the first time women led a mass movement outside of formal union structures. (Women constituted 85 percent of the nursing profession; about 80 percent of the strikers were women.) The *coordination* attempted to include both unionized as well as non-unionized nurses and functioned as an autonomous organization on the basis of direct democracy. In general assemblies, striking nurses made decisions about the conduct of the strike, issued mandates to the coordinating committee, elected delegates, and controlled the work of the strike committee. Without expressing overt hostility to unions, the *coordination* spoke eloquently to the problems traditional labor unions have had in mobilizing women. Although it did not claim to pose a formal alternative to the unions or adopt an overtly antiunion stance, it refused to allow the unions to constitute the *only* representatives of the profession. Indeed in both real and symbolic terms, its very existence suggested that the unions did not represent the profession.[35] This was because women saw the unions as exclusionary, unfriendly, or unconcerned with their interests and demands.[36] Not only did the fiercely *autogestionnaire* character of the *coordination* respond to the historical dilemma of women's autonomy within union structures and organizations as well as within political parties, but the *coordination* also demonstrated how the discourses of struggle had changed. Nurses made demands for improving conditions at work not on the basis of their difference or specificity as women, despite the existence of a gender division of labor within the profession, but on the basis of their claims to exercise control over work and to defend professional identity and competence.[37]

A second case six years later shows how easy it has been to ignore women's interests in mixed movements where women are not in control. The massive strikes of December 1995 demonstrated how women's issues could be masked within the framework of a larger, mixed labor mobilization. This mobilization against Prime Minister Alain Juppé's proposed reduction of social security benefits for public-sector workers drew massive numbers of workers into the streets of Paris and most major French cities for almost a month, shutting down public transportation, post offices, schools, and hospital services. These broad-based strikes were preceded by a huge women's demonstration in Paris on November 25, where over 100 organizations, including numerous union federations and *collectivités* of the CGT, the CFDT, and the *Solidaires, Unitaires et Démocratiques* (SUD), mobilized for reproductive rights, the right to work, equality between men and women, and against the resurgence of "moral order." Yet in the strikes that followed in succeeding weeks, despite women's strong presence in the streets, the unions tended to treat all concerned as an undifferentiated mass and barely mentioned the specific issues of women in the government's attack on social security. These include issues such as the fact that women's discontinuous work patterns or their overwhelming presence in the ranks of part-time workers make it doubly hard to accumulate the *annuités* needed for full pensions or the fact that women, as the majority of single parents, have the most to lose by reductions in family allowances. The demonstrations illustrated how, within the framework of union structures and organizations, when gender shapes and defines workers' claims differently, women's specific interests still can be ignored.[38] The dilemma of specificity versus inclusion remains a problem for the gender politics of the unions.

Problems such as this will continue to shape the unions' capacity to respond to developments over the next decades. But beyond the internal problems of unions, 4 broad challenges have emerged for the French unions over the past 15 years, all of which have serious implications for the gender politics of unions and that likely will make the unions' ability to attract women difficult.

First, the evolution of the labor market and the gendered characteristics of certain forms of work will make it increasingly difficult to mobilize women. As the research of Danièle Kergoat, Margaret Maruani, Chantal Nicole, and Chantal Rogerat has shown, since the early 1970s increasing numbers of women are found among the lowest-paid and least secure workers as *ouvriers spécialisés* (semiskilled workers) and *employés* (white-collar workers). Still more consequential for the unions, more and more women are found in part-time work or on fixed or limited-term contracts, the results of neoliberal "flexible" solutions and the politics of "rigueur" since 1983.[39] The numbers in part-time work are particularly striking. In 1981, 15.5 percent of women in the labor force were employed at part-time jobs, by comparison with 1.9 percent of men; 13 years later, in 1994, 28 percent of women and 4.6 percent of men were employed in part-time work. Between 1982 and 1986 alone, 550,000 part-time jobs were created, of which 450,000 were occupied by women. It is probably no exaggeration to say that since 1982, women's labor force participation has grown because of the increase in part-time work.[40] Although the unions have uniformly rejected the creation of part-time jobs as a solution to unemployment, they have been powerless to reverse a trend that affects women so disproportionately.[41] Given that the difficulties unions have experienced in the past mobilizing part-time workers overall, it is to be expected that the gendered characteristics of part-time work will continue to pose obstacles to the unions' ability to mobilize women. The same is true of unemployment: Since the end of the 1960s, women's unemployment rates have been uniformly higher than men's, regardless of age, and have been increasing. In 1975, 5 percent of women in the labor force were listed as looking for work against 2.6 percent of men; in 1981 those figures had increased to 10 percent for women and 5 percent for men. In 1992, 13 percent of women were unemployed against 8 percent of men.[42] Again, to the extent that the French labor movement has been unable to mobilize the unemployed, unemployment, like part-time work, poses new challenges to labor's capacity to reach women. Unions thus will have to resist the neoliberal move toward flexible work that has affected women disproportionately, either by reducing them to part-time jobs or depriving them of work all together. But employment or unemployment can hardly be disassociated from state policies that have had important consequences for women in the labor market.

French unions face a second challenge with respect to their capacity to respond to state initiatives in the domain of employment that have particular consequences for women. During the Mitterrand years, a number of state employment policies—notably the Roudy law of 1984 on professional equality banning any form of sex discrimination in hiring or remuneration, the July 1989 law instructing the social partners to introduce the concept of "mixité" (gender inclusiveness) into labor contracts, and a policy of support for the creation of part-time jobs—directly addressed women in the labor market. However, most of these policies either have been ineffective at correcting inequalities or have promoted even greater inequalities (the support of part-time work).[43] The unions have an important role to play in forcing the application of these laws in ways that really do eliminate job discrimination and in resisting state policies that support the creation of part-time work whose gendered consequences are so clearly inegalitarian. But not all policies that affect the labor market do so under the label of "employment policy." The family policy elaborated under the Socialist government in 1984, the Allocation Parentale d'Education (APE), was designed to permit a parent to leave the labor force temporarily after the birth of a third child, and paid an allowance of about 2,900 francs. But the allowance was fixed at a level too low to allow fathers to benefit. Given women's lower wages, they, rather than men, dropped out of the labor force, making the APE more of a low-cost "mother's wage" than a real parental allowance.[44] Given attempts to reduce unemployment and the persistence of beliefs in the questionable status of women's work (beliefs that are reinforced by government support for part-time work, for example), the APE has become one way in which the state uses family policy to carry out employment objectives.[45] Although this policy elicited the staunch opposition of the major union confederations and Socialist deputies alike, in practical terms the weakness of the unions, among other factors, meant that the state has had free reign in this domain.[46]

Third, political party strategies will continue to challenge unions' capacities to address women's concerns. The experience of union-party relations in the 1970s suggests that labor unions' promotion of women's interests was strongly determined by their responses to the electoral politics of the Left under the Common Program. But after the dissolution of the Common Program, women faded from the agenda of the CGT in the late 1970s. It remains to be seen how the recent decline of the Left's electoral fortunes will influence confederation strategies and what the effects of those strategies on women will be. Here we can only gaze into our crystal ball. It is too soon to tell, for example, how the movement for representational parity will influence party strategies and the unions that are closely tied to them. It seems likely, however, that women's ability to prosper within the unions in the future will depend partly on their ability to liberate themselves from partisan struggles that historically have proved to be overtly constraining or have made addressing women's interests dependent on which way the winds of political fortune have been blowing.

Finally, unions face a continuing cultural challenge about which the history of labor in France has taught much: A revitalized labor movement will have to be one in which class interests and gender interests are no longer seen as oppositional or as contradictory but rather as overlapping and mutually constitutive. In this reconstituted labor movement, integration will not have to mean assimilation, and difference will not have to mean inequality.

NOTES

1. See "La Précarisation sociale. Précarités et Rapports Sociaux de Sexe, Rapport de l'Action scientifique fédérative IRESCO/INSERM 1995"; Laura L. Frader, "Précarité du travail et rapports sociaux de sexe: une perspective historique," forthcoming; Jean-Michel Bézat, "L'INSEE confirme que l'emploi progresse grâce au travail précaire," *Le Monde* (June 28, 1995), who cites the INSEE report: "L'écart entre les taux de chômage des hommes (9,8%) et des femmes (13,9%), 'se creuse à nouveau' et sa structure 's'est modifiée': il touche désormais plus les employés que les ouvriers." ("The gap between the unemployment rates for men [9.8 percent] and women [13.9 percent] is widening again and its structure is changed; it effects white-collar workers more than blue-collar workers.")

2. These problems of course predate the 1920s. For the period before 1914 they have been outlined by Marie-Hélène Zylberberg-Hocquard, *Féminisme et syndicalisme* (Paris: Anthropos, 1978); *Les Femmes et le féminisme dans le mouvement syndical français* (Paris: Les Editions ouvrières, 1981); and Madeleine Guilbert, *Les Femmes et l'Organisation syndicale avant 1914* (Paris: CNRS, 1966).

3. Clearly, other forms of difference—race and ethnicity, to name just two— have been important. This chapter focuses on the problem of gender blindness as one problem.

4. On the Commissions Féminines and the early attempts to bring women into the CGTU, see "La Conférence sur l'Organisation des femmes," *L'Humanité,*

December 27, 1921, p. 2; CGTU, *Congrès national extraordinaire, 2ième congrès de la CGTU tenu à Bourges du 12 au 17 novembre 1923 et Conférence féminine du 11 novembre 1923* (Paris: Maison des Syndicats, 1924). The first mention of a "Commission d'Etudes féminines" in the CGT was in the Congrès confédéral of 1927. CGT, *Congrès confédéral de Paris, 1927. Compterendu des Débats du XXV Congrès national corporatif XIX de la CGT, les 26–29 juillet 1927* (Paris: CGT, 1927); prior to the formation of a CGT Commission Jeanne Chevenard was the *rapporteur* for women's issues. Union des Syndicats de la Région parisienne, *Vième Congrès de l'Union des Syndicats de la Seine et Ier congrès des Unions des Syndicats de la Seine et Seine-et-Oise, tenus les 25 janvier, 1–22 février 1925* (Paris: Maison des Syndicats, Service de l'Imprimerie, 1925), pp. 243–264, 358–360; Lucie Colliard, *Une Belle Grève de Femmes: Douarnenez* (Paris: Librairie de l'Humanitié, 1925). On the "strike of the ten sous" in the Nord, see press coverage in *L'Humanité* (July 1929-April 1929); Archives départementales du Nord (ADN) M 617/ 30–31, M 619/ 78–79; M 595 /47, 60–61; and Philippe Manie, "Recit de Vie. Martha Desrumeaux. Femme, ouvrière, syndicaliste, communiste du Nord," Maîtrise d'Histoire contemporaine. University of Lille, III (1978–1979).

5. This estimate was made by Alice Brisset at the 1925 Congress of the CGTU. CGTU, *Congrès national ordinaire. 3ième de la CGTU, Paris, 26 au 31 août 1925 et Conférence féminine du 25 août 1925* (Paris: Maison des Syndicats, Service de l'Imprimerie, 1926), p. 439. For labor force participation rates see T. Deldyke, H. Gelders and J-M. Limbor, *La Population active et sa Structure* (Brussels: Institut de Sociologie de l'Université libre de Bruxelles, 1968), and Jean Daric, *L'Activité professionnelle des femmes en France* (Paris: Presses universitaires de France, 1947).

6. Françoise Blum, "Les Femmes de la Fédération de l'Habillement 1919–1935," Mémoire de Maîtrise, Université de Paris I, 1977; Anne-Marie Sohn, "Exemplarité et Limites de la Participation féminine à la vie syndicale: les institutrices de la CGTU," *Revue d'Histoire moderne et Contemporaine* (Julu-September, 1977): 392–394.

7. Blum, "Les Femmes," pp.73–76; Fédération unitaire du Textile-Vêtement de France . . . Congrès de Fusion . . . Compte-Rendu sténographique des séances (Courbevoie: La Cootypographie [1924]), pp. 215–216.

8. On working women's demands for expanded, paid maternity leaves, child care, and family allowances, see Laura L. Frader, "Gender and Social Policy in France Between the Two World Wars," *Social Politics* 3 (Summer/Fall, 1996): 111–135.

9. See, for example, Henry Boisgontier, *Les syndicats professionnels de l'Abbaye* (Paris: Jouve, 1927); Emile Guerry, *Les syndicats libres féminins de l'Isère* (Grenoble: Fédération des syndicats libres féminins de l'Isère, 1921); Michel Launay, *La CFTC, origines et développement, 1919–1940* (Paris: Publications de la Sorbonne, 1987); Christine Bard, "La non-mixité dans le mouvement syndical chrétien en France de 1900 à 1939," in Claudine Baudoux and Claude Zaidman, eds., *L'égalité entre les sexes. Mixité et démocratie* (Paris:

l'Harmattan, 1992), and Bard, "L'Apôtre sociale et l'ange du foyer: les femmes et la CFTC à travers le *Le Nord-Social* (1920–1936)," *Le Mouvement social,* no. 165 (October-December 1993): 23–41; Joceline Chabot, "Les syndicats féminins chrétiens et la formation militante de 1913 à 1936: 'proagandistes idéales' et 'héroïnes identitielle,'" *Le Mouvement social* no.165 (October-December 1993): 7–21.

10. Bard, "La non-mixité," p. 218 and Guy Groux and René Mouriaux, *La CFDT* (Paris: Economica, 1989), p. 21. Bard argues that the relative success of the CFTC in recruiting women had much to do with its political stance (the confederation rejected the notion of class struggle and favored cooperation with employers; strikes were seen as a last resort when all other options for conciliation had been exhausted), the congeniality of all-woman's organizations, and the fact that recruitment occurred "between Catholics." Bard, "L'apôtre sociale," p. 29.

11. See Groux and Mouriaux, *La CEDT,* p. 14.

12. Although it is not entirely clear why the commissions were not carried over to the newly united CGT, the CGT may have been even more reluctant to give a place to women as a separate constituency in the context of large-scale male unemployment during the Depression, when many rank-and-file members questioned anew women's right to work. It is also possible that as membership in the confederation grew during the Popular Front in 1936, the CGT felt less compelled to address or organize women as a separate or specific constituency. In federations with large numbers of women, reunification in 1935–1936 did not mark a major step forward for women with respect to their position within the organizations' structures of power. In the Fédération du Textile-Habillement, for example, although the administrative commission, a study and oversight body ("chargée d'étudier et d'expédier les affaires courantes et de veiller à l'application des décisions du congrès") included four women, the more powerful federal bureau remained entirely male. Blum, "Les Femmes," p. 76.

13. On the family wage ideal in France, see Laura Levine Frader, "Engendering Work and Wages: the French Labor Movement and the Family Wage," in Frader and Sonya O. Rose, eds., *Gender and Class in Modern Europe* (Ithaca, NY: Cornell University Press, 1996), pp. 142–164.

14. The Catholic *Union féminine civique et sociale* supported women's return to home and family from about 1930 on. See Susan Pedersen, *Family, Dependence, and the Origins of the Welfare State in Britain and France, 1919–1945* (Cambridge: Cambridge University Press, 1993). See also Laura Levine Frader, "Gender, Class, and Social Policy in Interwar France," *Social Politics* (Fall 1996): 111–135, on the labor movement's reaction to these proposals; *La Question féminine dans les Congrès confédéraux et les Conférences nationales de la CGT (1948–1982)* (Institut C.G.T. d'Histoire sociale, 1983); Jenson, "The 'Problem' of Women," in Mark Kesselman, ed., *The French Workers' Movement. Economic Crisis and Political Change* (London: George Allen and Unwin, 1984), p. 162.

15. Bard, "L'apôtre sociale," p. 30.

16. In response to the Monnet plan, CFTC activists denounced the "menace grave que représent pour la femme, la famille, et pour le pays la mise à l'ordre du jour . . . de la question de l'emploi massif de la main d'oeuvre féminin en vue de la reconstruction." ("serious threat that the massive use of female labor for reconstruction poses for women, the family, and the country.") Marie-Noëlle Thibault, "Politiques familiales, politiques d'emploi," *Nouvelles Questions féministes* 14–15 (Winter 1986): 156.

17. On the shifts in Soviet family policy in the 1930s, see Richard Stites, "Women and the Revolutionary Process in Russia," in Renate Bridenthal, Claudia Koonz, and Susan Stuard, eds., *Becoming Visible. Women in European History* (Boston: Houghton Mifflin, 1987), pp. 464–465.

18. See Jane Jenson, "One Robin Doesn't Make Spring: French Communist Alliance Strategies and the Women's Movement," *Radical History Review* 23 (Spring 1980):74, n. 5; Claire Duchen, *Women's Rights and Women's Lives in France, 1945–1968* (London: Routledge, 1993).

19. See, for example, Laura Downs, *Manufacturing Inequality: Gender Division in the French and British Metalworking Industries, 1914–1939* (Ithaca, NY: Cornell University Press, 1995); Annie Fourcaut, *Femmes à l'Usine en France dans l'Entre-Deux-Guerres* (Paris: Maspero, 1982); Mathilde Dubesset and Michelle Zancarini-Fournel, *Parcours de femmes. Réalités et représentations, Saint Etienne 1880–1950* (Lyon: Presses Universitaires de Lyon, 1993), Helen Harden Chenut, "The Gendering of Skill as Historical Process: The Case of French Knitters in Industrial Troyes, 1880–1930," in Laura L. Frader and Sonya O. Rose, eds., *Gender and Class in Modern Europe* (Ithaca, NY: Cornell University Press, 1996), pp. 77–107.

20. See Jacques Kergoat, *La France du Front populaire* (Paris: Editions de la Découverte, 1986), p. 130.

21. Ibid., p. 141.

22. Michel Dreyfus shows how the CGT defended gender-based wage differences in the wage scales established for electrical workers in the 1920s and 1930s in "Les femmes dans les luttes et les activités sociales des électriciens-gaziers," *Bulletin d'histoire de l'électricité*, nos. 19–20 (June-December, 1992): 113–114. See also Chenu, "The Gendering of Skill"; Herrick Chapman, *State Capitalism and Working-Class Radicalism in the French Aircraft Industry* (Berkeley: University of California Press, 1991), p. 88. It is worth noting that the state played an important role in setting wage parity for teachers before World War I and eventually for postal workers after the war. Judith Wishnia, *The Proletarianization of the Functionnaires. Civil Service Workers and the Labor Movement Under the Third Republic* (Baton Rouge: Louisiana State University Press, 1990); Georges Frischmann, *Histoire de la Fédération CGT des PTT* (Paris: Editions Sociales, 1967). Although the CFTC women's unions supported the principle of equal wages for equal work, this position was undermined by the CFTC's gender-based distinction between different forms of the wage: the "salaire vital," a full-fledged wage,

designed to support single women; and the "salaire d'apoint," acceptable for certain married women, for young girls living with their families, and for privileged women who worked "without real economic need." Bard, "L'apôtre sociale," p. 33.

23. An excellent statement of this dilemma for the 1970s is found in Margaret Maruani, *Les Syndicats à l'Epreuve du féminisme* (Paris: Syros, 1979).

24. Bard, "L'apôtre sociale," pp. 28, 34.

25. On the CFDT's position, see Jeannette Laot, *Stratégie Pour les Femmes* (Paris: Stock, 1981), pp. 86–92 and 219–221; Margaret Maruani and Marie-Noëlle Thibault, "Féminisme et syndicalisme de la Libération aux années soixante-dix," in FEN, *Le Féminisme et ses enjeux* (Paris: FEN-Edilig, 1988), pp. 103–106. For discussion of the ways in which women were incorporated in the agendas of both the CGT and the CFDT in the 1970s, see Maruani, *Les Syndicats*. See also Jane Jenson, "The 'Problem' of Women." Again Danièle Kergoat's more recent critique of the unity-in-action accords of 1974 raises questions about the consequences of these initiatives.

26. Chantal Rogerat, "Femmes et syndicalistes: Assimilation ou intégration? La dynamique du compromis," in Pierre Cours-Salies, ed., *La Liberté du Travail* (Paris: Editions Syllepse, 1995), p. 176.

27. See Danièle Kergoat's analysis of the consequences of the unity-in-action accords for women in "Les Femmes dans l'organisation syndicale: entre le «générale» et le «spécifique,»" *Cahiers du GEDISST*, no. 15 (1996): 109–126. Kergoat criticizes the CGT, for example, for failing to challenge the principle of the "double day" for women: "Parler de la double journée, en fait avait pour conséquence de ne pas combattre pour qu'il n'ait pas une double journée, mais pour qu'on compense. La division sexuelle du travail n'était pas mise en cause (121)." ("Discussion of the double day in fact, resulted not in fighting for the elimination of the double day but in fighting for its remuneration. The sexual division of labor was not called into question.") On the unity-in-action accords, see also Maruani, *Les Syndicats*, chap. 2. For a view of the theoretical foundations of the new CGT position, see Jean-Louis Moynot, "La Force du Travail féminine dans la production et la société," in *La Condition féminine* (Paris: Editions sociales, 1978), pp. 131–184.

28. CGTU, *Congrès national extraordinaire... tenu à Bourges du 12 au 17 novembre 1923 et Conférence féminine du 11 novembre* (Paris: Maison des Syndicats, Service de l'Imprimerie, 1923), pp. 156–161, 621–639; "Le Travail Parmi les Femmes," *L'Humanité*, January 21, 1925, p. 2; CGTU, *Congrès national ordinaire, 3ième Congrès de laa CGTU, Paris, 26 au 31 août, 1925* (Paris: Maison des Syndicats, Service de l'Imprimerie, 1925), p. 540; CGTU, Congrès national ordinaire, Bordeaux, 19 au 24 septembre 1927. Conférence nationale féminine. *Conférence des Jeunes travailleurs* (Paris: Maison des Syndicats. Service de l'Imprimerie, 1927), pp. 134–144, 162–165; Danielle Tartakowsky, "Le PCF et les Femmes (1926)," *Cahiers d'Histoire de l'Institut Maurice Thorez*, no. 14 (1975): 194–225; PCF, *Ve Congrès national*

du Parti communist français tenu à Lille du 20 au 26 juin 1926 (Paris: Bureau des Editions, 1927), p. 693.

29. M. J. Maynes, *Taking the Hard Road. Life Course in French and German Workers' Autobiographies in the Era of Industrialization* (Chapel Hill: University of North Carolina Press, 1995), p. 159.

30. Jacqueline Tardivel, "Des Pacifistes aux Résistantes: les Militantes communistes en France dans l'Entre-Deux-Guerres," Doctoral thesis, University of Paris VII, 1994.

31. Jenson, "The 'Problem' of Women," tells the complex story of why this happened. She argues that CGT retreated from openness to women's issues in the process of beating a retreat from the Union de la Gauche. This retreat was accompanied by an internal battle within the CGT between the advocates of decentralization of decision making and more independence from the PCF (which could give more power to the rank-and-file, and potentially to women, to define issues and labor practice) on the one hand and advocates of continuity of a strong relationship with the party on the other. See especially pp. 168–174.

32. Rogerat, "Femmes et syndicalistes," p. 177.

33. Mary Braithwaite and Catherine Byrne, *Women in Decision-Making in Trade Unions* (Brussels: European Trade Union Confederation, n.d. [1994]), pp. 26–27. Apparently the CGT did not respond to Braithwaite's and Byrne's survey.

34. Rogerat, "Femmes et syndicalistes," p.178. As Rogerat is quick to point out, if women's presence in these positions has begun to change the power relations within the unions, there are still debates over the conditions of women's representation (do they represent all workers or only women?) and over the desirability of retaining specific women's organizations.

35. This is the analysis of Danièle Kergoat, Françoise Imbert, Hélène Le Doare, and Danièle Senotier, *Les Infirmières et leur Coordination* (Paris: CNRS-PIRTTEM, 1990), p. 208.

36. Danièle Kergoat, "La Gestion de la Mixité dans un Mouvement social: le cas de la coordination infirmière," in Claudine Baudoux and Claude Zaidman, eds., *Egalité Entre les Sexes. Mixité et Démocratie* (Paris: L'Harmattan, 1992), pp. 268–269. See also Danièle Kergoat, "Réflexion sur les Conditions de l'Exercise du Pouvoir par des Femmes dans la Conduite des Luttes. Le Cas de la Coordination infirmière," in Michelle Riot-Sarcey, ed., *Femmes, Pouvoirs* (Paris: Kimé, 1993), pp. 124–139.

37. See D. Kergoat, "Réflexion," p. 129.

38. See also Josette Trat, "Autumn 1995: a Social Storm Blows Over France," *Social Politics* 3 (Summer/Fall, 1996): 223–236. She stresses the solidarity between men and women in the demonstrations.

39. Danièle Kergoat, *Les Ouvrières* (Paris: Sycamore, 1982); Margaret Maruani, *Les Syndicats à l'Epreuve du Féminisme* (Paris: Syros, 1979); Chantal Rogerat and Danièle Senotier, *Le Chômage de longue durée: le cas des femmes* 1993; see also INSEE, *Les Femmes. Portrait Social* (Paris: INSEE, 1995), pp. 132–133;

Patricia Bouillaguet-Bernard and Annie Gauvin, "Les Effets de la Restructuration de l'Appareil de Production sur le Travail féminin et les perspectives de l'activité féminine," *Problèmes économiques*, no. 1669, April 16, 1980, pp. 18–26; Michèle Aulagnon, "La Place des femmes sur le marché du travail ravive le clivage droite-gauche," *Le Monde*, March 8, 1995, p. 10; Margaret Maruani and Chantal Rogerat, "Introduction. La Recompositions du Marché du Travail: Problèmes sociaux et questions de recherches," Marianne Berthod-Wurmser, Michel Bozon, Jacques Commaille, and Monique Dental, et al., eds. ("EPHESIA"), *La Place des Femmes. Les Enjeux de l'identité et de l'égalité au regard des sciences sociales* (Paris: Editions de la Découverte, 1995), pp. 524–528; Danièle Meulders, "Flexibilités," EPHESIA, pp. 534–538; Jane Jenson, "Le Travail à Temps partiel pour les femmes: choix de qui, solution à quoi?" EPHESIA, pp. 539–545; Rachel Silvera, "Les Inégalités de salaires entre hommes et femmes, ou comment expliquer ce qui reste «inexplicable»?" EPHESIA, pp. 546–551; Nicole Gadrey, "Formation, Qualification et Mixité," EPHESIA, pp. 552–556; Annie Gauvin, "Emploi des Femmes, Tertiarisation de l'Emploi et de la Société," EPHESIA, pp. 562–568; and Marie-Hélène Zylberberg-Hocquard, "Métiers ouvriers: approches historiques," EPHESIA, pp. 569–573.

40. *Les Femmes en France dans une société des inégalités* (Paris: La Documentation française, 1982), p. 47; INSEE, *Les Femmes. Contours et Caractères* (Paris: INSEE. Service des Droits des Femmes, 1995), pp. 132–133; Margaret Maruani and Chantal Nicole, *Au Labeur des dames. Métiers masculins, emplois féminins* (Paris: Syros/Alternatives, 1989), p. 93.

41. On the unions' position, see Maruani and Nicole, *Au Labeur des dames,* p. 85.

42. *Les Femmes en France dans une société des inégalités,* p. 45. and INSEE, *Les Femmes. Contours et Caractères,* pp. 136–137.

43. See the analysis of Jane Jenson and Mariette Sineau, *Mitterrand et les Françaises: un Rendez-Vous Manqué* (Paris: Presses de la Fondation nationale des Sciences politiques, 1995), pp. 209–238. As Jenson and Sineau point out, Mitterrand, shifting his position since the presidential campaign of 1981, supported part-time work from 1984 with women specifically in mind: "Ce mode du travail répond à la fois à une attente des femmes et à une amélioration du marché du travail." ("This mode of work was a response both to the expectations of women and to an improvement in the labor market.") (p. 231).

44. Ibid., pp. 261–265.

45. See Marie-Noëlle Thibault, "Politiques familiales, politiques d'emploi," *Nouvelles Questions féministes*, no. 14/15 (Winter 1986): 147, 158.

46. Jenson and Sineau, *Mitterand et les Françaises,* p. 266.

Part IV

Unions, Public Opinion, and the State

CHAPTER TEN

One Century Later: Unions in French Public Opinion— Representations, Images, and Expectations

Roland Cayrol

This chapter summarizes the results of qualitative surveys conducted by the CSA Institute about the image and role of French unions. These studies were conducted between 1991 and 1994 using in-depth personal interviews and mostly projective group meetings. The tables of quantitative materials are drawn from national representative surveys conducted by CSA between 1990 and 1995, commissioned either by the CFDT or the CGT.[1]

UNIONISM: A COMMON RESPECT FOR A RICH AND USEFUL HISTORY

In our qualitative materials, no one expresses any doubt about the important and decisively useful role of the unions in certain areas, including:

• The creation of social justice at the beginning and during the industrial era as a counterpower to the owners, in fighting against child labor, for weekly leave, and the like. Frequently invoked mental associations include Zola's *Germinal,* class struggle, oppression, and abuses.

The unions were born of mass industry—that must not be forgotten—and, in order to confront the strength of the employers, at that time powerful unions were necessary, unions that could respond in a similar fashion. There-

fore, when you see metalworkers, for example, in confronting the mine owners, they had . . . then, they had to have a force in order to be able to negotiate, to discuss, to have something.

—Male, 57 years old, retired cadre, Nancy

In the beginning the unions had an enormous task: social protection, child
labor, all of that was indispensable. Those were laudable goals.

—Female, 34 years old, teacher, Nancy

• A positive role in the amelioration of social conditions and working
conditions such as social security, paid holidays, reduction of working time,
and the like, mainly in the periods of 1936 and 1945.

They [the unions] had an image that they had earned with all the social gains
they achieved and this image wasn't tarnished.

—Female, 29 years old, technician, Paris

The unions that had labored so much before the war for paid vacation just
after the war labored a lot for the defense of the workers and for social
protection.

—Male, 57 years old, retired cadre, Paris

We would not deny that—absolutely not—but we deplore what they have
now become.

—Female, 48 years old, executive secretary, Paris

These references to the glory of unionism constitute a strong and very
vivid reference point. They provide respectful roots to French unionism and
furnish a "golden age" point of reference that contrasts with the present situation. Respondents perceived that in earlier times unions clearly identified
the problems of the people, were strong, representative, and united. They
were fighting for an ideal.

It was a mass phenomenon, there were major things to change. It was heading toward an ideal, it was large demonstrations, it was beautiful even. In '36
that's how it was.

—Male, 26 years old, independent professional, Nancy

These historic references are consistently present in the in-depth interviews and group discussions. They are shared by all classes of society, among
those who approve of the present state of unionist action as well as among
those who criticize this action. A recent poll, conducted on the occasion of
the centennial of French unionism, confirms this retrospective approval (see
table 10.1).

Table 10.1   Achievements of the Trade Union Movement

This year, the national trade union movement celebrates its centennial. What are, in your opinion, the three most important achievements to which it has contributed in the past century?

	All French (%)	Salaried Workers (%)
Improvement of working conditions	61	64
Defense of rights and liberties of salaried workers	51	53
Development of social protections	34	34
Increasing buying power	22	24
Better inclusion of social rights in the democracy	11	12
Better training for salaried workers	9	9
Higher solidarity among salaried workers	9	9
Promotion of peace/solidarity among people	6	6
No response	9	8

One can see that a strong majority of the French population in general and salaried workers in particular cite the improvement of working conditions and the defense of salaried worker's rights as the main achievements of the union movement during the century. The improvement of working conditions is cited by 56 percent of the blue-collar workers and 61 percent of salaried workers, but also by 65 percent of executives and 60 percent of the self-employed.

TODAY: UNIONS SEEM RIGID, WITHOUT SUFFICIENT ABILITY TO ADAPT

When questioned now, public opinion judges the unions with reference to this "golden age" and to current social and economic concerns: unemployment, fears about the future and the future of today's children, social exclusion, and the inability to envision a better world in the coming years.

According to these criteria, the unions are often seen as having been able to play their appropriate role (defense of workers' rights, social welfare, redistribution of the benefits of growth) in the period of economic growth. At that time, unions had rights to defend, claims and demands to support, an ideal to promote.

> There was some hope that there no longer is at all.
> —Female, 48 years old, executive secretary

There was a force.

>—Female, 31 years old, receptionist

The crisis also didn't exist then. There was much less unemployment, so people were much less distressed.

>—Female, 29 years old, bank technician, Paris

Before, they were useful—they had more faith then, they were defending an ideal.

>—White-collar workers, Paris

At that time, it was valid, a union was necessary in all societies, still that brought many things.

>—White-collar workers, Nantes

Within the "crisis," unions seem to have kept the same approach, the same strategy, the same discourse. Respondents sense the existence of a crisis, characterized mainly by increasing unemployment, and they view the classic strategy of the unions as ineffective.

The big difference between 15 years ago and now is primarily on the level of hope. The union said, "If we do this, that will happen," we tried to do "this" and nothing happened. Now they are confronted with the fact that they have nothing left to propose, in the sense that what they proposed did not bring the results they hoped for. Thus the problem is posed differently. They have certainly started to reformulate the question. I don't know if they have completely done that.

>—Male, 60 years old, middle manager, social service agency

I think that they have rested a bit on the idea of 1936 with all the social gains, so they had that image thinking that inevitably it was that image that was the best and now it is clear that that is no longer the case. Now I think that people have no more illusions. People have the social benefits, but now we are in an inverse period where they are being suppressed.

>—Female, 29, bank technician, Paris

There is a lack of conviction brought about by lack of projects.

>—Female, 29, bank technician, Paris

There were five weeks of vacation, after the 39-hour work week. We have all of that now. It was attempted to reduce the work week to 32 hours, but there is point at which it is going to have to stop. Therefore, they must find other solutions. There they are cornered. Now working conditions, I would say, are good. The problem is that there is not work for everyone. There they don't have a solution.

—Female, 29, bank technician, Paris

The unions are not accused of being responsible for this situation, but they are mainly seen as no longer able to sustain hope among the workers. The present reality is not seen as a period for new demands for those who work but rather as a period to ensure jobs for the unemployed, to promote adequate education and professional training for youth, and to work on ways to find an exit from the economic crisis. On these issues the unions are mainly perceived as "stuck," "without a solution."

They are perplexed because they don't quite know what to do.
—Male, 60, manager of social service agency, Paris

They are worn out.
—Male, 57, sales representative

They lost their illusions.
—Female, 28, business assistant

Completely worn out.
—Female, 48, executive secretary

They are stymied. They have no more solutions.
—Male, 57, sales representative

In fact, people often perceive the unions in ways that they feel about themselves: without solutions, without perspective, without ability to transmit hope. But they tend to transfer the accusation to the unions and to charge them of remaining distant from the problems of people's daily lives.

In most of the interviews with salaried people, respondents do not say that the situation is hopeless; on the contrary, they think that the unions are aware of their failures and that they are preoccupied with trying to find a new role. The unions are perceived as conscious of their errors and delays, and are in a process of desirable change (but without many visible results to date).

Disappointed hope leads to [unions] not being credible. Now the people [in the unions] reflect, are perplexed because they are looking for a new hope that is inevitably completely different from the old one, because the old one . . . doesn't hold together. Therefore, we must find something else.
—Male, 60, middle manager, social service agency, Paris

THE MAIN COMPONENTS OF THE
CURRENT IMAGES OF THE UNIONS

The first common image, linked with the preceding comments, is, of course, an image of the lack of adaptation to the present state of society. According to white-collar workers in Paris, unions are: "out of date," "has-beens," "old-fashioned," "obsolete," "bored," "not with it," "an image of the nineteenth century," "anachronistic," "poorly adapted," "they have lost control of the situation."

The unions seem to lack new solutions and projects: "overtaken by events"; "It's a rear-guard fight rather than a search [for new solutions]"; "one no longer senses that they are 'on top of things'"; "They don't have solutions for the future"; "lack of leaders, lack of projects, lack of convictions"; "They no longer have anything to propose. Other things must be found. They are perplexed because they no longer know quite what to do"; "loss of ideal, loss of ideology"; "They must find some ideas because with that they are going to continue to run out of steam."

They give the impression of a decline: "less impact," "loss of strength," "loss of power," "not involved," "minority," "slowed down," "10 percent of salaried workers," "out of stream," "timid."

Finally, there is an image of an inability to move, an inability to understand the new environment: "They are stuck"; "They're worn out"; "They're trapped"; "The unions don't move much"; "There is boredom, gloominess, inaction compared to 12 years ago, there is a big difference in any case!" "It's the weight of unemployment that anesthetizes everything"; "The unions have not evolved. On the contrary, one has the impression that they block, that there is a barrier"; "They fight for things that in the end . . ." "It is not very understandable"; "They fight primarily for social gains that were considered normal 30 years ago . . . now we need national solidarity, multisolidarity between the multisyndicates"; "We need to reconsider several positions"; "to make some concessions."

This image structures the vision of the majority of every professional category.

The unions are seen as bodies defending their own "boutique" more than the salaried people as a whole. Everyone is aware that there has been a decline in union membership. Therefore, the unions are increasingly seen as unrepresentative of "the base."

> The union leaders are no longer with it, since at given moments the base is in need of coordination that is different than the unions, that is to say there is . . . a dichotomy between the base and union leadership in general.
>
> —Managers, Paris

Unionism is a minority, there are few union members. It's becoming a minority of the salaried class.

—Managers, Paris

I am sad, however, that in our time there aren't any unions that are somewhat representative of what people think.

—Female, 29, bank technician, Paris

The commonly reported representation of a union member is someone belonging to the public sector, either the administration or large publicly owned companies—that is, relatively privileged salaried persons, protected by a "statute."

The union member comes from an old establishment, former public service enterprises.

I also see him often in public service, that is to say, with no threat of dismissal.

At Renault, at Citroën, there are mostly robots.

He is at SNCF [nationalized railways], at Air France.

—Middle managers, Paris

Therefore, salaried workers in the private sector are not likely to feel they are "represented" by these militants. The more informed respondents advance the idea that the union fulfill a function of "legal representation" within the bipartite bodies or vis-à-vis the state, the government, or business organizations.

Currently at the union level, It is all legal representation. This role is well-known but the defense of rights, on the contrary, is slipping. Most working people are organized differently. At the level of bi-partite representation they may appeal to traditional union representation, while at the level of the defense of rights of the rank and file they are wary of the union.

—Female, 44, social worker, Nancy

In any case, the unions make propositions to the government in the context of [negotiations about] bills; the unions make the first move, contact the deputies in order to say, "Hey, Here's our position."

Let's say they have a very political function.

Politics with a big P.

It's a link of democracy, there it is, indispensable.

—Managers, Paris

The lack of unity, the fighting among unions, is another important common theme. Unions are even less accepted in a period of great difficulties, when problems obviously demand a strong united front to defend salaried workers:

> [The union] defends the union interests rather than those of its members.
> —White-collar workers, Paris

> I have the feeling that the unions intrinsically try to keep their gains for themselves.
> —Salaried workers, Paris

> Today and for some time, I think that all the bosses (because there are union bosses: Blondel [for example])—all of those people want to hold their troops together because it's human even though, in fact, I think we need to break the system apart, otherwise that will not be able to function.
> —Male, 34, manager, Nancy

> They are searching for a good power niche, unfortunately.
> —Middle manager, Paris

> Arguments, they argue all the time.
> —Middle manager, Paris

> There is no unity. They argue amongst themselves over minor points and don't lead any common action.
> —White-collar worker, Paris

> They're all the same, in fact, they defend their own union instead of calling for unification.
> —White-collar worker, Nantes

Another idea is also very widespread and common to every category: that the gap is growing wider between the "base" and the "summit" and that the unions act only as actors of "recuperation" of spontaneous conflicts. These two criticisms could seem contradictory, but they usually converge as a proof of a growing distance of the unions from the general population—being distant from their natural base, the unions have to "recuperate" actions of the base which they were not able to carry out themselves.

> At the present time, the problem of the unions is the head who decides that it is necessary to strike and not the rank and file. That is perhaps the problem of unionism. I would say that the roles have been reversed.
> In general, it is the delegates, the officials that make the decision and then more or less impose them on the others: we must strike on such and such a subject. Therefore, it is "I think for you."
> —Middle- and high-level managers, Nancy

There were a certain number of [strike] movements these last years where the unions were overwhelmed, where the people organized independently, outside of the unions since the unions were no longer adequate for their demands. That damaged and hurt the unions.

—White-collar workers, Paris

Now there are also the acts where it was recognized that the unions had been overtaken and that they no longer controlled the base—"the coordination."

—Managers, Nancy

In other places, "the base" was not spoken of, the famous base, they always say that they were outflanked by the base and, in the end, this base appears more active, more combative, more effective than the traditional unions.

—Worker, Nantes

The lack of adaptation or the obsolescence of the unions' means of action is also stressed very frequently. This does not mean that the interviewees object in principle to strikes or mass demonstrations. But the impression is that the unions use them systematically—as was normal in previous historical periods—without trying to invent more appropriate forms of action. This "systematic" use reinforces the perception of "archaic" structures and, even more, of unions' difficulty to develop new and more efficient methods of social dialogue.

I think the union should be a partner—in fact, one has the impression that the bosses and the union delegates are "enemy/brothers" in an enterprise.
They are condemned to work together. They can't always be in opposition. It's like in a family, the children of 14 or 15 are always contrary.
It is the crisis of adolescence that is now found in enterprises.

—Managers, Paris

We want something, we strike! That becomes systematic, there's no longer direct negotiation. It's: We strike; we'll see afterwards. That becomes a method of blackmail.

—Male, 28, foreman

That's one way, but that would show, if [action] is launched by the unions, that they have not found the system that permits dialogue. That means that they are not very open to dialogue. That means that they are a generation or a generation and a half behind.
What's needed are less explosive and more effective actions, some basis work.
The big demonstrations mobilize people but it stops there. When it's over, the problem remains until the next demonstration—it's demagoguery.

—White-collar workers, Paris

If they could discuss real problems there wouldn't be all these strikes. What's bothersome is that contrary to [other] European unions, . . . every time there's a discussion, there's a strike. . . . Therefore, there's an enormous difference. The German unions, for example, there are no strikes . . . at the level of the national economy; it's enormous what a strike can do.

—White-collar worker, Paris

If you look at English unions, they're rather brutal as they were immediately after the war in France. They engaged in demonstrations of force while the German unions, on the contrary, veered the other way and avoided conflicts and defended their members in a more effective manner than the French and British unions.

—Male, 57, high-level manager, retired

The German unions, they manage.

—Male, 55, manager SNCF (nationalized railways), Nancy

Last but not least, unions are widely depicted—even, very often, by their own supporters—as too politicized. This opinion is expressed in regards to all the unions as a general statement, although it is more frequently attached to the CGT. But since the image of the CGT is seen as structuring the whole landscape of the union world (the CGT is, in terms of image, the union par excellence), the description of the "transmission belt" about the CGT has immediate repercussions on the image of unions in general.

I am sad that during our time there are no unions that are representative of what people think because I feel that [unions] are a force that should exist in a country; it's for that reason that for me the ideal union is "non-politicized."

—Female, 29, bank technician

Apolitical—absolutely.

—Male, 60, middle manager

I would emphasize politicized because for me a union is inevitably political, but it would not be associated with a political party . . .

—Female, 31, receptionist, Paris

[Nicole Notat, television excerpt, 1986] You see her, you say to yourself: She has concerns that I also have. [Television excerpt 1992] There is already the union leader, no longer really concerned . . . and still! She is almost already *the politician*. You sense well-formed ideas . . . well-reflected, but something tricky. Phrases that we have already heard hundreds of times—pretty unoriginal!

—White-collar workers, Paris

CONFIDENCE IN THE UNIONS AND
THE IMAGES OF DIFFERENT UNIONS

In France today a majority of workers are not prepared to join a union, which is understandable if we take into account our preceding observations.

As we can see in table 10.2, only a third of the French population—but six out of ten salaried people—could envisage joining a union in order to defend their personal interests. There is a significant difference between the public sector, in which the union environment is stronger (48 percent), and the private sector (only 34 percent). Salaried workers appear to be slightly more ready to join (43 percent) than blue-collar workers (38 percent).

The proportion of people having confidence in the unions to defend their interests is a little higher: 41 percent of the population, 44 percent of salaried workers.

One can see in table 10.3 that the unions are given a confidence score equal to that given the hierarchy within companies, in both the public and the private sectors, and that there was an increase of confidence toward unions in 1993 to 1995, during the cohabitation period, and after the election of Jacques Chirac. This tends to confirm what appears to be a rule: Confidence in the unions tends to be reinforced when the Right is in power, and to decline when the Left governs. It seems that a number of workers fear the attacks, or at least the threats of, the parties of the Right against the social conquests. In these periods, these workers understand the unions as more useful.

As mentioned in our discussion of workers' readiness to join unions, there is a significant difference in the level of confidence in unions between the public and the private sectors. An absolute majority of the salaried people in the public sector (53 percent) confirm their confidence in the unions (whereas 41 percent say they are not confident); it is the reverse in the private sector (56 percent not confident, 38 percent confident).

Table 10.2   Readiness to Join a Union

In order to defend your interests, would you currently be ready to join a union?

	All French (%)	Salaried Workers (%)	Salaried (Public Sector) (%)	Salaried (Private Sector) (%)
Ready	35	40	48	34
Not ready	56	55	47	60
No response	9	5	5	6

Table 10.3 Confidence in Unions

To defend your interests, how confident are you in . . .

	the unions?			the hierarchy within companies?		
	1995 (%)	1994 (%)	1993 (%)	1995 (%)	1994 (%)	1993 (%)
Very confident	8	6	7	8	5	8
Somewhat confident	36	37	29	39	35	29
A little confident	26	31	33	28	34	34
Not at all confident	24	22	27	21	20	22
Don't know	6	4	4	4	6	7

To defend your interests, how confident are you in . . .

	the unions?				the hierarchy within companies?			
	All French (%)	Salaried Workers (%)	Public Sector (%)	Private Sector (%)	All French (%)	Salaried Workers (%)	Public Sector (%)	Private Sector (%)
Very confident	8	8	11	6	6	8	6	9
Somewhat confident	33	36	42	32	35	39	38	39
A little confident	24	26	24	27	25	28	31	26
Not at all confident	25	24	17	29	20	21	22	21
Don't know	10	6	6	6	14	4	3	5

*These responses are for salaried workers.

It should be noted that there are some expected differences in the level of confidence according to social categories:

Salaried workers:	50 percent
Blue collar:	46 percent
Intermediate professions:	46 percent
Executives:	37 percent
Self-employed:	27 percent

These differences are less pronounced than the important discrepancies of the answers along the Left/Right scale:

Extreme Left:	74 percent
Left:	55 percent
Center Left:	43 percent
Center Right:	29 percent
Right:	15 percent
Extreme Right:	35 percent

or according to party preferences:

Communist Party:	72 percent
Socialist Party:	52 percent
Ecologists:	52 percent
UDF (Centrists):	30 percent
RPR (Gaullists):	25 percent
National Front (extreme Right):	36 percent

In France today, confidence in unions is much more linked with political attitudes than with social stratification (not an intuitive result): The more people lean toward or vote to the left of the spectrum, the more they support the unions.

One can assume that this was also the case at the beginning of the century. But at that time, there was a much stronger linkage between class structure and political preferences. Today the class/politics link is much weaker. One may have thought the preferential linkage for unions—which are social organizations—would have been the class linkage. This is not the case. Politics constitute a better explanation of union proximity than social class.

Finally, there is a relative exception to the Left/Right rule: Compared to the moderate Right families, a higher proportion of self-defined "extreme Right" individuals and of the National Front supporters state their confidence in the unions. This is probably due to the new ex-Leftist part of the FN electorate and to the fact that a number of the FN sympathizers see themselves more as "antisystem" than as belonging to the Right.

If we go from the general judgments about unions and their role to their actual place at the company, factory, or workshop level, and the concerns of the workplace, we see a new increase in the positive statements. Even people who say they would never join a union, who profess they do not have any confidence in the unions, not only accept the existence of unions but wish the unions could exert more influence at the workplace level. This explains the results of table 10.4.

At this level—where the daily life of the people is concerned—it is important to note that union action is not only accepted but also that more union influence is desired by, for instance, 74 percent of blue-collar workers,

Table 10.4 Should Unions Exert More Influence?

Would you wish that the unions exert more or less influence on your workplace?

	All French (%)	Salaried Workers (%)	Salaried (Public Sector) (%)	Salaried (Private Sector) (%)
More influence	44	52	59	48
Less influence	19	18	15	19
Neither (same amount)	21	23	21	24
Undecided	16	7	5	9

62 percent of salaried workers, 68 percent of the intermediate professions, and 67 percent of executives. There is, therefore, a real and in some dimensions consensual legitimacy of the unions in France. Even if they are seen as "too politicized," "archaic," "bureaucratized," they are also legitimate. They play a role that is part of French democracy; it is their function to help and defend people. Their main place of action is the workplace: "I could need them some day"—we find such phrases in the qualitative surveys. At this level the difficulties of the current period even reinforce the legitimacy of the unions.

> Don't exaggerate! Fortunately the unions are there for certain actions. They are indispensable to protect the rights of the wage earners.
> —White-collar worker, Paris

> We should hope that there will always be these [union] functions because otherwise that would mean that it was a dictatorship and that the unions would no longer have the right to do all that.
> —Manager, Paris

> The associations that are stronger than a single man, in the end if there are problems it's better to call upon a union than to be alone with one's problems.
> —Male, 22, white-collar worker, Paris

One wonders if for us, unemployment, all of that, concerns the unions. I think that countries where there are no unions are countries where the vise is tightening on inhabitants of these countries. It seems to me that the possibility of having several patterns of expression and the possibility of being able to defend workers is also the guarantee of a certain democracy. There are no unions in totalitarian countries; thus, in my opinion, everything that concerns

salaried and nonsalaried workers concerns the unions. To whom would one go
if one had problems with employers.

—Male, 26, professional

There are countries where it doesn't exist.

—Male, 43, manager, Nancy

I think that the expectations of people at the present time is to think of them
[unions] because there are words, unemployment, etc., that are frightening. I
am not a union member, but if one day . . . I want to think of myself!

—Male, 29, salaried worker, Paris

As in many other aspects of social life, a "consumer" view of the role of
unions is at work: It is not useful that I join a union; I think they are not
adapted to the situation, but their existence could (who knows?) be helpful
to me tomorrow, in case of difficulties.

LEVEL OF CONFIDENCE IN EACH UNION

The "fight" for the best grade in the union classroom is not of interest here.
Let us just remind the reader that, in the contemporary period, a trio of large
confederations lead the race: the CFDT, the CGT, and the CGT-FO.

In terms of image, the CFDT gets approval ratings above its mean with
executives, intermediate professions, salaried workers, socialist (and since the
December conflict, UDF and RPR) supporters, ages 35 to 55. The CGT has
greater support from blue-collar workers, Communist and Socialist supporters, ages 35 to 55. The Force Ouvrière receives support from those in
the public sector, Socialist and Rightist supporters, and retired salaried
workers, ages 35 to 55.

OBJECTIVES ASSIGNED TO THE UNIONS

During the present period, the priorities assigned to the unions by the
French reflect citizens' major preoccupations, mainly based on the growing
unemployment crisis.

Defending employment and protecting the unemployed now appear
much more important than the traditional objectives of the unions in
French culture: The improvement of working conditions is only in third position (19 points behind the defense of employment); the fight for buying
power comes only in fourth position (fifth among salaried people), about at
the same level as a better management of social protection. The guarantee of
buying power comes 24 points behind the defense of employment.

Table 10.5 Confidence in Specific Unions

How confident are you that each of the following unions is able to defend your interests?

	FO (%)	CFTC (%)	CFDT (%)	Autonomous (%)	CGT (%)	CGC (%)
Very confident	5	2	5	3	7	1
Somewhat confident	27	19	28	18	24	17
A little confident	24	22	21	21	23	23
Not at all confident	31	37	31	33	33	39
Don't know	13	20	15	27	27	20

Note: These responses are for salaried workers.

Table 10.6 Priorities for Unions

Which objectives should take priority today for the unions?

Defend employment	58 (%)
Protect the unemployed	42
Improve working conditions	39
Better management of social protections	34
Maintain buying power	34
Reincorporation of marginalized groups	30
Retraining of skilled workers	26
Solidarity between French and immigrants	22
Reform of professional qualifications	20
Intervention in company management	20
Don't know	7

Note: These responses are for the entire population.

A growing theme, the "reinsertion" of the "excluded," is now close to the issue of buying power in the hierarchy of French preoccupations. This obviously means a new challenge for the unions, their role, and their perceived image.

It might be useful to note some more precise demands from specific categories: Among young people (ages 18 to 24), the gap between the protection of the unemployed (quoted as a priority by 50 percent) and the guarantee of buying power (31 percent) reaches 19 points (as opposed to 8 in the general population). The improvement of working conditions ranks significantly stronger among the salaried and also among the intermediate white-collar professions, where it surpasses the need to protect the unemployed. The improvement of the management of social protection is particularly important among executives, where it appears as the second priority for unions (quoted by 42 percent) after the defense of employment. Of course, among the unemployed, the defense of employment (65 percent) and the protection of the unemployed (50 percent) are very high priorities.

PRIORITIES OF THE PERIOD AND THE IMAGES OF THE VARIOUS UNIONS

Table 10.7 has been calculated using only the people who say that a particular issue in question should constitute a priority for the unions. For instance, 25 percent of the people who think that buying power should be a priority believe that the CGT is the most efficient union to reach that objective.

This table shows, among other things, that the CGT has a strong image of efficiency. While on many topics the CGT is challenged by its partners/opponents in the unionist universe, it remains the "powerful," "strong," union par excellence even if, in many data, the CFDT appears

Table 10.7   Effectiveness of Unions

Which union do you believe to be the most effective in reaching each of the following objectives?

	CGT (%)	CFDT (%)	FO (%)	Don't Know (%)
Maintain buying power	25	19	11	45
Defend employment	23	20	9	48
Reincorporation of marginalized workers	23	16	13	48
Improvement of working conditions	22	20	14	44
Solidarity between French and immigrants	22	15	12	51
Protection of the unemployed	21	20	10	49
Better management of social protections	19	17	15	49
Retraining of skilled workers	16	17	15	52
Participation or intervention in company management	17	22	15	46
Profound internal restructuring	13	15	14	58

Note: These responses are for the entire population.

more "modern," more the "union of the future," more "open to the transformations in society," and the FO more "open to compromise," more "dialogue oriented," more "reasonable."

THE FUTURE OF THE CONFEDERATIONS

Within the last five years, French public opinion about unions has evolved. I will use here only one example, comparing the words that, for salaried people, correspond with "what union action should be today."

It is clear from table 10.8 that the words "negotiation" and "solidarity" increasingly characterize the expectations, that "defense" is still very strong (but comes now behind "negotiation"), and that "revindication" and "contestation" are declining. This is, of course, very important as a new challenge to the various confederations. Under these circumstances, the CFDT often is regarded as the confederation the most capable of representing this "new unionism." If we compare the words describing the expectations regarding union action today (table 10.8) and those that characterize CFDT action among the same salaried people (table 10.9), we can see the correspondence is very high.

Even if many respondents are unable to answer, it is clear that the CFDT appears to be a union acting in favor of "negotiation," "solidarity,"

Table 10.8   The Role of Unions

Which of the following words do you feel best describes the role that unions should play today?

	1990 (%)	1995 (%)
Defense	47	52
Making proposals	23	25
Innovation	8	Not asked
Change	18	Not asked
Solidarity	35	56
Emancipation	3	Not asked
Contestation	29	6
Management	9	Not asked
Making demands	47	22
Negotiation	43	60
Don't know	5	2

Note: These responses are for salaried workers.
Source: CSA polls for CFDT, June 1990 and April 1995.

Table 10.9   Characterizing the Action of the CFDT

Which of the following words would you say best defines the action of the CFDT?

Negotiation	37 (%)
Defense	28
Solidarity	24
Making demands	21
Making proposals	16
Contestation	12
Don't know	31

Note: These responses are for salaried workers.
Source: CSA Poll for CFDT, April 1995.

and "defense." But, of course, the story has not ended. The FO also has its zones of strength in public opinion.

This volume marks a century of confederated trade unionism, and, thus, tends to emphasize the CGT's role. It must be added, as a provisional conclusion to this ongoing history, that, seen from the viewpoint of public opinion, the CGT has a real ability to adapt but still needs to meet a few decisive expectations. In an October 1995 CSA poll for the CGT, 52 percent of French people (and the same proportion of salaried people) said "the CGT can still adapt," as opposed to 32 percent saying "the CGT is incapable of adapting" (28 percent among salaried workers). As for the CGT, should this confederation want to increase its influence, the data shown in table 10.10 seem clear enough:

The union must begin a process of breaking ties with political influence, be more realistic in negotiation processes, be nearer to workers' preoccupations,

Table 10.10   Priorities for the CGT

In your opinion, what should the CGT do as a priority in order to gain influence?

Cut every political influence	43 (%)
Be more realistic in negotiations	43
Listen more to workers' concerns	38
Find innovative solutions	27
Democratize	21
Be more aggressive	18
Cooperate more with other unions	14
Don't know	11

and find new solutions to problems. These are the challenges of the future for both the CGT and the entire French unionist movement.

NOTES

1. I would like to thank both of these organizations for permission to use the results of these surveys for this chapter. Unless otherwise indicated, all tables are from the CSA poll for CGT, October 1995.

CHAPTER ELEVEN

Labor, Power, and the State in France: Lessons of Industrial Restructuring

W. Rand Smith

The massive strikes of late 1995 raised again the enduring question of French labor's problematic relationship with the state. Since 1945, that relationship usually has been portrayed as one of extreme disproportion: on the one hand, a strong, centralized state, commanded by a cohesive elite and able to conceive and carry out such long-term aims as indicative planning and strategic high-technology projects; on the other hand, a weak, divided labor movement, unable to recruit members and to control strike action decisively and thus largely excluded from the corridors and negotiating tables of power.

Yet the events of 1995, like the events of May-June 1968, revealed something wrong with this picture. The Chirac government, shaken and paralyzed by masses of protesting citizens in the streets, appeared ineffectual and intimidated, while the labor movement, quickly claiming credit for the unforeseen uprisings, suddenly seemed to have the whip hand. Weak state? Strong labor (or at least strong working class)? These strikes suggest that the classic portraits of state dominance and labor impotence need to be retouched, if not completely redrawn.

The relationship between the state and organized labor has at least two dimensions. The first has to do with the union movement's participation in governmental decision making. What patterns of interaction and integration mark labor's role in various decision-making venues? The second dimension is that of organized labor's effective *power* as a political actor—that is, labor's ability to affect the actions of political leaders and therefore policy outcomes.

Historical experience suggests that these two dimensions are distinct. Patterns of "routine" decision making from which labor is largely excluded have alternated with sudden, unpredictable upheavals in which unions typically seek, often effectively, to channel mass mobilization into concrete gains. Moreover, even during routine periods, the *threat* of uncontrolled mobilization has deterred political leaders from treating unions with complete disdain, since the latter may be needed in crisis situations precisely because they can contain and channel mass protests. Political exclusion, therefore, does not necessarily spell powerlessness.

What, then, is the nature of organized labor's political role and influence? I address this question through the prism of a key political-economic process of recent years: industrial restructuring. During the 14 years of the Mitterrand presidency (1981 to 1995), restructuring encompassed several measures designed to help the French economy adjust to basic transformations in the global and regional (European) economy. These measures included extensive nationalizations, modernization plans for specific sectors such as textiles and electronics, reconversion programs for state-owned firms dominant in such sectors as steel and shipbuilding, and, finally, after 1984, a shift toward public-enterprise autonomy and even privatization. Industrial restructuring during this period provides a useful venue for assessing state-labor relations because it constituted an arena in which fundamental interests were at stake: the state's interest in enhancing the efficiency and competitiveness of industrial firms versus labor's interest in protecting the jobs and livelihoods of workers in those firms. How, if at all, was labor able to influence this process?

This analysis proceeds in three steps. The next section examines the nature of the Mitterrand government's industrial restructuring strategy, an approach I call Market-Adapting. The following section identifies the policy logic of this approach, particularly its implications for labor's role in the restructuring process. Finally, I assess state-labor relations in two important industries undergoing restructuring: steel and automobiles.

THE MITTERRAND GOVERNMENT AND INDUSTRIAL RESTRUCTURING: A MARKET-ADAPTING APPROACH

One of the central aims of François Mitterrand's presidency was to improve the eroding performance of the nation's principal industries. Thanks in part to imbalances inherent in Charles de Gaulle's "national champion" strategy of the 1960s, French industry had responded poorly to global conditions in the 1970s, especially in foreign trade. While some industries were conquering foreign markets, whole sectors were succumbing to manufactured imports at home. Moreover, the policy responses of the Giscard government

(1974 to 1981) tended to worsen these problems, with the result that key industries developed persistent trade deficits with those of chief competitors such as the United States, Japan, and West Germany, while industry as a whole suffered drops in profit margins and investment.[1]

While part of the Mitterrand government's industrial policy entailed the promotion of emerging, technology-intensive industries such as electronics and telecommunications, an equally important focus was the restructuring of older industries experiencing long-term market decline. In such industries as coal, steel, shipbuilding, automobiles, and textiles, the government sought to boost productivity and restore profitability, goals that often entailed significant and rapid reductions in the labor force.

How did the Mitterrand government approach this task? To address this question, we must first ask: What choices did it have? Generally speaking, any restructuring strategy consists of two interrelated tasks: *capital* adjustment and *labor* adjustment. The former refers to firms' efforts to restructure their capital stock or supply—including such aspects as technology, product lines, productive capacity, and relations with suppliers—to respond to changes in market demand. Labor adjustment encompasses the (usually simultaneous) adjustment of labor supply, including such aspects as total manning levels, workforce composition and qualification, pay levels, and work organization.

Given this basic distinction, table 11.1 presents four ideal types of adjustment approaches potentially available to any government, distinguished by the degree and nature of government intervention and proceeding roughly from lesser to greater market regulation by public authorities.[2] For each of these, I note the core goal along with the main capital and labor adjustment measures.

The first approach, Type A (Market-Embracing), stresses rapid market-driven adjustment that, far from avoiding or delaying adjustment, welcomes it. Inspired by a neoliberal belief in the market as an efficient allocation mechanism, this approach eschews government intervention that would mitigate or cushion labor displacement and thus countenances no government subsidies to maintain production or postpone labor adjustment. This approach does, however, permit government intervention in order to create more flexible labor markets that would enable employers to respond more quickly and fully to market shifts. Given its stress on market exposure, this approach encourages privatization of public-sector firms and economic deregulation in general.

The Type B (Market-Adapting) approach, like Type A, accepts the market as the final arbiter of restructuring strategy but, unlike Type A, permits government intervention to effect an "orderly exit" of workers whose jobs must be eliminated. Thus this approach sets a longer time

Table 11.1 Government Approaches to Industrial Restructuring: Four Ideal Types

A. Market-Embracing

Core Goal: Promote rapid market-driven adjustment in response to international and domestic market forces with minimal government intervention.

Capital Adjustment Measures: Attempt to deregulate "inefficient" capital markets while adjusting supply (especially productive capacity) in line with prevailing market trends.

Labor Adjustment Measures: Attempt, through deregulation, to create more flexible and "efficient" labor markets. No special measures for dislocated workers—labor market clears through market processes.

B. Market-Adapting

Core Goal: Bring about gradual adjustment of capital and labor to market forces using government measures to cushion shocks.

Capital Adjustment Measures: Policies to expose firms to market competition gradually in order to avoid sudden crisis or collapse.

Labor Adjustment Measures: Measures to achieve "orderly exit" of labor. *Active* measures include job retraining, incentives to establish own businesses, systems for better matching labor supply and demand, and relocation incentives. *Passive* measures emphasize income support such as severance payments and pre-retirement regimes.

C. Market-Modifying

Core Goal: Same as Type B.

Capital Adjustment Measures: Same as Type B.

Labor Adjustment Measures: Same as Type B (to achieve "orderly" labor exit), but on the basis of explicit exchange with organized labor designed to reinforce latter's institutional power. In exchange for labor's compliance with adjustment measures, government seeks to strengthen labor representation in economic decision making at micro- (firm) and macro- (national) levels.

D. Market-Resisting

Core Goal: Avoid and/or delay adjustment of productive capacity and labor.

Capital Adjustment Measures: Subsidies to cover firms' operating losses, discriminatory trade policies to protect domestic market, use of public contracts and projects to favor domestic firms and sectors, price controls.

Labor Adjustment Measures: Subsidies to preserve jobs.

frame for adjustment than Type A, since the goal is to restructure without causing widespread economic distress and/or community upheaval. The Market-Adapting strategy is also clearly more labor-friendly than a Market-Embracing one in that it seeks to absorb (but not eliminate) the shocks of labor displacement. It is therefore willing to employ temporary and even long-term subsidies to labor. Labor measures can be of two types, active and passive, with the former encouraging redeployment (through retraining, relocation incentives, etc.) and the latter providing income maintenance through such means as severance and early-retirement benefits.

The Type C (Market-Modifying) approach is a qualitative variant of Type B. While Type C, like B, accepts the need for labor adjustment—and thus accepts market-equilibrium outcomes in the long term—it offers a different kind of quid pro quo to labor than Type B. Whereas the latter approach provides mainly quantitative trade-offs to labor—for example, income support and job retraining—a Market-Modifying one extends to labor the prospect of enhanced institutional power. Thus in exchange for labor's compliance with restructuring measures, this approach also seeks to "restructure" institutions for governing capital and labor markets. Labor representation thus would be extended to new sites—at the firm level (for example, codetermination) as well as within policy-determining bodies at the national level (as in wage-earner funds).

Finally, a Type D (Market-Resisting) approach privileges labor and social stability over other goals and thus seeks to protect threatened industries. Adjustment would be delayed for as long as possible or avoided altogether. In the process, governments would employ such protectionist measures as operating subsidies and discriminatory trade practices to favor domestic firms. Given its emphasis on maintaining labor stability, a Market-Resisting approach would tend to favor nationalizations of "lame ducks" as an alternative to outright collapse.

Given these four general possibilities, how can the Mitterrand government's adjustment strategy be characterized? After flirting with a Type D (Market-Resisting) approach during its first two years, the government opted, from 1983 on, for a version of a Type B, or Market-Adapting, strategy. Faced with market failures in older industries such as steel and automobiles, the government took measures that, directly or indirectly, eliminated the jobs of thousands of workers who constituted an important base of Socialist support. At the same time, the government accompanied its drive to facilitate labor reductions with generous programs to soften unemployment shocks for affected workers. Most notably, it relied heavily on passive measures that would maintain the purchasing power of laid-off workers. By contrast, active labor policies such as worker retraining, while present, were of only secondary importance and effect.

It is worth underlining what this adjustment strategy was *not*. As mentioned, the government ultimately rejected a Market-Resisting strategy that would seek to avoid or delay adjustment; market discipline was accepted as the guiding logic of adjustment. Moreover, the government rejected a neoliberal or Market-Embracing (Type A) approach. While the Mitterrand government has been accused of betraying its own workers, evidence does not support the claim that affected workers were abandoned to the vicissitudes of unregulated labor markets. Finally, the government showed no interest in a Market-Modifying (Type C) approach to empower organized labor in exchange for the latter's support for adjustment.

In comparative perspective, the Mitterrand-Socialist approach was both unprecedented and unexceptional. On one hand, whereas the Giscard government largely failed in its adjustment efforts, the Mitterrand government took sustained, effective measures to strengthen industrial capacity by seeking to channel financial resources to private firms while stimulating investment and profits—whatever the employment consequences. On the other hand, this strategy was unexceptional in that it differed little from practices of other European governments. Most Western European governments used a comparable mix of labor adjustment cum compensation that sought to restore market performance while maintaining workers' living standards, if not their jobs.[3] Thus Mitterrand and his Socialists joined the mainstream European approach to adjustment, which was neither liberal nor socialist but rather sought to strike a balance between social solidarity and economic efficiency.

Why did the Mitterrand government adopt a Market-Adapting approach to restructuring? There are several reasons, including the French economy's relatively weak industrial capacity coupled with the state's relatively strong capacity to influence the actions of industrial firms, mainly through direct financial and ownership control in key sectors. But a critically important factor was the nature of Mitterrand's governing coalition, especially during the periods of 1981 to 1986 and 1988 to 1993 when Socialists also controlled parliament. At various points that coalition included not only the Socialist Party (PS) but the Communists and the two largest labor confederations, the CGT and the CFDT.

Put simply, this coalition was unwilling or unable to counteract the constraints imposed by limited industrial capacity by mobilizing decisively in favor of an alternative to a Market-Adapting approach. The PS itself was unwilling to challenge prevailing orthodoxy. Not only was its leader, Mitterrand, not committed to contesting capitalist power, but the party's elitist membership and leadership structures largely excluded from representation some of the very groups most directly affected by restructuring. Thus the PS had little inclination to press for adjustment measures that would depart radically from those adopted elsewhere. At the same time, other elements of the governing coalition, including the CGT and the CFDT, were unable to mobilize in favor of an alternative to a Market-Adapting strategy, in large part because of their own weakness, division, and exclusion from policy making.[4]

THE POLICY LOGIC OF
MARKET-ADAPTING RESTRUCTURING:
IMPLICATIONS FOR STATE-LABOR RELATIONS

Any restructuring strategy carries with it a particular policy logic in the sense of privileging certain types of state-group interactions over others. Just as any particular strategy creates specific groups of winners and losers, so does that strategy define which groups (or sectors or interests) will have effective policy access and influence and which groups will not. What kind of policy access and influence did organized labor have in the restructuring process during the Mitterrand years?

Given the earlier distinction between capital and labor adjustment, a Market-Adapting approach carries a "dualistic" policy logic. In the domain of capital adjustment, this approach privileges the interests of capital and thus gives primacy of access and influence to agents of financial and industrial enterprises. Put simply, since the goal is to maximize market competitiveness, organized labor is given little or no opportunity to hinder or otherwise influence market adjustment.

In the domain of labor adjustment, a Market-Adapting (and therefore relatively labor-friendly) approach is more solicitous of organized labor. In effect, the state seeks to make an implicit exchange with labor:

> We (the state) will encourage firms to carry out capital adjustment in line with market constraints, and you (labor) will neither influence the process nor protest too much. In return, we will take care of workers whose jobs must disappear. We will largely maintain their income at present levels, and we will undertake some retraining and other measures to ensure orderly exits and adaptations. Moreover, we will consult you on these issues and even give you some administrative authority over retraining and redevelopment programs.

Given this division of labor, a Market-Adapting strategy will tend to manifest a dualistic pattern of state-labor relations. Within the domain of capital adjustment, state officials and corporate managers collude to set goals and measures, while labor is largely excluded. Unions thus have no guaranteed or recognized voice and must contend, often vociferously, for influence. In regard to labor adjustment, the state seeks to enlist unions to help restructure the labor force. For state officials, union support plays a useful, and even essential, legitimation function. In acquiescing in, and even giving explicit approval to, measures that produce massive layoffs, unions help convince workers that today's "dirty job" is tomorrow's healthy industry.[5] In many cases, unions are even brought in to assume some of the administrative tasks of retraining, reclassifying, and relocating displaced workers. Thus labor adjustment under a Market-Adapting approach encourages a limited version of neocorporatism whereby the state recognizes unions, along with employers, as de facto partners.

These hypothesized differences in capital versus labor adjustment are, of course, tendencies that in practice will be affected by such factors as the relative power resources and strategic interests of various actors. For example, in the "pluralist" realm of capital adjustment, union influence will likely vary according to labor's organizational and mobilizational capacity. Stated simply, all else being equal, the more vigorously labor can press its demands through collective action (or the threat thereof), the more likely that state officials will pursue strategies to co-opt unions through consultations and the like.

The domain of labor adjustment is especially subject to the influence of specific factors, notably the types of incentives underlying the political exchange just outlined. Incentives to corporatize relations with labor may diminish for state officials to the degree that they perceive such corporatization as unnecessary to the successful implementation of labor adjustment. As we shall see, this applied in the case of restructuring at Renault after 1984. For unions as well, incentives to cooperate in labor adjustment also are subject to change. While cooperation may bring clout, it may bring organizational risk as well. This is especially true in France's competitive "plural-union" environment where the well-known dynamic of "higher bidding" *(surenchère)* renders cooperative behavior hazardous. Specifically, any union assenting to such an exchange invites attacks by unions on its left for betraying workers' interests. Thus unions may well reject the neocorporatist trend, finding it dangerous to their organizational health.

TWO CASES: AUTOMOBILES AND STEEL

How well does this dualistic policy logic apply in specific cases? The following examines two industries that were at the heart of the Mitterrand government's restructuring strategy: automobiles and steel. As "mature" industries facing slowly expanding (or even declining) markets, rapidly changing technologies, and new sources of supply from newly industrializing countries, both autos and steel also developed problems of excess labor and productive capacity. Given these industries' importance as exporters and employers, government officials pursued restructuring measures aimed at restoring market performance.

What influence did labor exert in the process? In both industries, capital adjustment decisions, especially after the economic policy U-turn of 1983, were formulated largely between government and business leaders, with unions being "consulted" only after the fact. Unions thus were largely ineffectual in influencing capital adjustment decisions and their implementation. By contrast, unions were more influential vis-à-vis labor adjustment, notably in helping define and implement such measures as income support and retraining for displaced workers.[6] Thus these cases reflect the basic policy logic identified earlier. Yet the reflection is far from perfect, with the cases diverging considerably, especially regarding labor adjustment. As we shall see, government officials and employers used different strategies to manage relations with organized labor, and thus the latter's role and influence varied across our cases.

AUTOMOBILES

Restructuring in this industry centered on the two major producers, privately held Peugeot Société Anonyme (PSA) and nationalized Renault. Both firms, following the second oil shock in 1979, had lost market share to their main European competitors (Volkswagen, Fiat, General Motors, and Ford), and their decline drew the government increasingly into managing adjustment. The cases were far from identical, however. PSA's restructuring preceded that of Renault and came at the firm's initiative rather than the government's. Moreover, PSA's adjustment was more protracted and contested than Renault's, for not only did the government have to negotiate with a private firm, it also had to confront a more highly mobilized workforce. Because of these differences in timing and dynamics, we shall consider the two firms separately, beginning with PSA.

The context for PSA restructuring was one of deteriorating finances and growing worker mobilization. Owing to strategic errors during the 1970s (notably acquisitions of Citroën and Chrysler's European operations, renamed Talbot) and declining markets (notably the 1979 oil shock), the firm was forced to eliminate about 24,000 jobs during 1980, mainly through preretirement and buyout payments to immigrant workers, especially North Africans. (By contrast, Renault, of comparable size, cut only 4,000 jobs during that year.)[7] Moreover, after the Left's election in 1981, with workers' worries over job security rising, a newly militant CGT sought to increase its own influence by mobilizing work stoppages, especially at two plants in the Paris region: a Citroën facility of 6,500 workers in Aulnay-sous-Bois and a Talbot plant of 17,000 in Poissy. Although both conflicts were resolved through a government-appointed mediator, these settlements brought only a temporary truce and did little to restore calm in the plants.

By mid-1983 the combination of work disruptions and declining performance had produced massive operating losses and debt that required drastic adjustment measures. Thus beginning in July, management initiated a restructuring program, centered first on Talbot and then on Citroën, to cut 12,500 jobs. The Talbot plan proved to be explosive, ultimately requiring government intervention at the highest levels and souring relations between the government and both of the major unions, the CGT and the CFDT.

This plan called for dismissal of nearly 3,000 workers, mainly production workers at the Poissy plant. Because labor law required government approval for all collective layoffs, the plan became politicized, as government officials negotiated with management and top union officials while local unions sought to mobilize workers against the job cuts. To understand the government's response, one must recall the context of that period: Although the Mitterrand government already had made its famous U-turn, the Communist Party (PCF) still remained in the government. Thus policy-makers sought to satisfy PSA's capital-adjustment needs while not alienating the Communists and CGT as well as other unions, such as the CFDT. The result was an attempt by Communist Employment minister Jack Ralite to negotiate the dismissals and accompanying "exit conditions" with the CGT metalworkers federation led by André Sainjon. Largely excluded from this limited neocorporatist effort were the CFDT metalworkers federation as well as the two confederations' local sections at Poissy.[8]

By late 1983 Ralite, Sainjon, and the PSA had reached agreement on the layoffs (which were reduced to 1,900); however, the agreement fell apart when it was rejected by the Poissy rank-and-file led by the local CFDT section. Amid fights among striking and nonstriking workers, CGT-CFDT splits, and even sharp differences between local and federation leaders within these two confederations, the government eventually was able to restore order in the plant and establish the precedent of unconditional mass layoffs.

The "lessons of Talbot," which became an unofficial template for restructuring in other sectors, were threefold. First, after Talbot, government officials sought to engage unions in wider consultations concerning labor adjustment. There were no further attempts to employ peak-level concertation between the PCF and the CGT while excluding the CGT's local units or other unions, such as the CFDT. Rather, ad hoc and unofficial but widespread consultation became the pattern. Second, the Talbot conflict initiated an eventual divorce between the government and both major unions. Despite subsequent efforts to involve unions in labor-adjustment questions, the government was never able to repair the rupture, especially with the CGT. Within six months, the PCF had left the government, and the CGT had become a constant critic of government restructuring measures. Finally, Talbot set a precedent for future adjustment, namely that large-scale layoffs would be tolerated. Thus within months the government approved, either directly or indirectly, restructuring plans for Citroën as well as for the steel, coal, and shipbuilding industries that entailed drastic labor reductions. In virtually all future cases, managements were given carte blanche on the number of labor reductions, while the government sought to bring in unions to negotiate such issues as worker reclassification, retraining, and income support.

In the case of Renault, although restructuring began in 1985, two years later than PSA's, the firm's problems were no less severe, including a failure to control production costs, pricing structures that provided inadequate margins, and an illusory sense of market dominance. The firm was especially slow to adjust, however, in large part because of its relation to the Mitterrand government. As a publicly owned corporation, Renault has received periodic state subsidies, and its head is named by the government; nevertheless, the firm traditionally has enjoyed wide operational autonomy. Some observers claim, however, that its chief executive officer, Bernard Hanon, was under pressure from the early Mitterrand government to help fight unemployment and thus to avoid massive layoffs. According to a top Renault executive:

> Hanon wasn't free to do as he wished. For political reasons, since he was CEO during the first years of the Left in power, Hanon wasn't allowed to lay off workers in response to the market. Thus to claim that Hanon let Renault lose millions isn't accurate, because the government was preventing him from making the necessary adjustments.[9]

By 1984, however, restructuring had become imperative, as Renault faced the scissors of escalating investment costs and shrinking markets. Thus in the spring Hanon, in the wake of the Talbot fiasco and at the urging of Prime Minister Mauroy, began consulting with the unions over personnel cuts.[10] At the same time, the firm hired a new director of planning, a man who had crafted Fiat's 1980 restructuring plan involving 20,000 layoffs, and charged him with devising a restructuring plan. During the summer he drew up a strategy, which was then approved by Hanon and presented to the unions for negotiation. Unlike PSA's approach, which included mass layoffs, Hanon's plan sought to cut up to 10,000 jobs without layoffs, mainly through pre-retirements and departure incentives (for example, for immigrants to return home).[11]

Hanon apparently believed that his good relations with the CGT would enable him to gain union backing for his "soft" approach to labor adjustment; however, by late 1984, with the Communist Party now out of the government and staunchly opposing its economic policies, the CGT refused any agreement, as did the much smaller CFDT. According to the planning director, Hanon also met opposition from many of Renault's managers and executives. Thus the "Hanon plan" remained stillborn throughout 1984.

Hanon's failure to reverse Renault's slide led directly to his dismissal early the following year, for by 1985 the government was firmly committed to reducing subsidies to public firms, whatever the political cost. Thus in January Prime Minister Laurent Fabius replaced Hanon with Georges Besse, an engineer who had guided restructuring at newly nationalized Péchiney. According to the director of planning, Besse took a hard-line approach to restructuring: "Besse . . . didn't see any particular role for the unions. For him it was his plan or nothing."[12] Largely ignoring or bypassing the unions and making decisions unilaterally, Besse did not unveil a "grand plan" but rather carried out restructuring in incremental, unannounced steps.[13]

The CGT, by then completely hostile to the government, sought to mobilize opposition to Besse's plan in an October 1985 strike wave but failed to garner significant support. By late 1985, then, Renault's basic trajectory was set: The government expected management to make profits, regardless of the impact on the workforce. Unlike Hanon, Besse himself exercised virtually full independence from government pressure. By the time of Besse's assassination by *Action Directe* terrorists in November 1986, Renault had reduced its workforce by nearly 20,000 in less than two years.[14]

The Renault case, in an intriguing contrast with that of PSA, reveals a stiffening government attitude toward the unions. Recall that Hanon, during 1984, had sought to apply the "lessons of Talbot" by seeking to enlist unions as de facto partners regarding labor adjustment. By 1985, however, two things had changed: First, the government, now firmly committed to restoring financial viability in public firms, ordered these firms, including Renault, to break even within two years; second, the CGT, along with the Communists, had left the governing coalition. As a result, the government's tolerance for Hanon's neocorporatist approach ended, and Hanon's successor, Besse, had a free hand to impose labor-adjustment conditions on the unions. The Renault case thus reveals the fragility of neocorporatist attempts to enlist unions in labor adjustment. By definition, such attempts require that both government and unions have an incentive to cooperate. By the mid-1980s, that incentive had vanished on both sides.

STEEL

Steel adjustment followed yet a third trajectory, one strongly influenced by the industry's structure. After three major government restructuring plans during the preceding 15 years, the Mitterrand government finally nationalized the two main steel producers, Usinor and Sacilor, in 1981. As a result, the government could exercise direct and virtually uncontested control over the industry; however, given the firms' dire competitive and financial condition, the government had limited restructuring options.

After an initial adjustment plan in 1982 failed to reverse the firms' performance, in March 1984 the government announced more rigorous measures to eliminate up to 40,000 of the industry's 100,000 jobs within four years. It is important to note this plan's timing, for it came on the heels of the Talbot debacle. As in the Talbot case, although the government feared social explosions in the plants and regions affected—and thus sought to co-opt unions as cosponsors of generous layoff benefits—union mobilization was incomplete and uneven due to both interunion and intraunion divisions. Not only did CGT and CFDT leadership differ fundamentally over whether restructuring was even necessary,[15] but each confederation was riven by region-based splits between local unions of Usinor (based in the Nord) and Sacilor (based in Lorraine).

For all its stress on market efficiency, the Mitterrand government's steel policy after 1984 also devoted close attention to the labor-market consequences of adjustment, since the government wanted to avoid a repeat of the bitter strikes and mass demonstrations that had occurred in Lorraine over the Giscard-Barre government's 1979 restructuring plan. Thus officials consulted and negotiated extensively with unions (including the CGT) over early retirement and other income-support programs. The government also sought to attract new investment into distressed regions and to help retrain and find new jobs for laid-off workers.

A key element of government strategy for Lorraine was to enlist union support in this "reconversion." Heading this effort was a top CFDT official (and former Lorraine steelworker), Jacques Chérèque, whom the government appointed as its steel "czar" in the region. Chérèque focused on two tasks: (1) redevelopment of abandoned industrial sites (including that of his own previous firm in Pompey) into industrial parks containing light manufacturing plants and office buildings; and (2) creation of the European Development Pole (EDP), a 1,200-acre industrial park on the French-Belgian-Luxembourg border that planned to create 8,000 jobs. Vilified at first by most of his union colleagues for selling out, Chérèque eventually gained grudging respect for his role in stimulating new investment and jobs.

Restructuring in the steel industry thus generally followed the dual logic of Market-Adapting adjustment. On one hand, organized labor played little effective role in determining *capital* adjustment at either the "macro" level of investment, technological change, and overall manpower reductions or at the "micro" level of work reorganization. Such decisions remained in the hands of either government officials (from 1981 to 1984) or firm executives (from 1985 to 1995). As in the past, labor's relative lack of power derived largely from its own organizational weakness and division. On the other hand, unions played a significant role in *labor* adjustment regarding the fate of displaced workers. State officials were sufficiently concerned with the explosive potential of worker discontent that they sought to corporatize, at least partially, the administration of labor-adjustment programs. Both state and firm officials sought to co-opt unions into helping manage industrial contraction. This effort was only partially successful, however, as the CGT largely refused to cooperate, while the CFDT's own participation provoked controversy within the confederation itself.

CONCLUSION

The central argument can be summarized as follows: After its 1983 U-turn, the Mitterrand government generally followed a Market-Adapting restructuring approach that gave primacy to market competitiveness but also sought to mitigate social and political disruption by providing generous programs of income support, early retirement, retraining, and other measures. State-labor relations thereby followed a broadly dualistic logic. The state largely excluded unions from decisions regarding capital adjustment, with such strategy being decided largely by the state (mainly before 1984) or firm management (after 1984). However, the state did seek to include or associate unions in decisions concerning labor adjustment. Specifically, unions participated with the state and management in negotiating and administering relatively generous systems of income support and retraining for affected workers; thus a limited version of neocorporatism emerged in this domain.

To return to our original query concerning organized labor's political role and influence, this analysis underlines the difficulty, if not impossibility, of describing state-labor relations in singular, static terms, for these relations are both variable and unstable. First, state-labor relations are variable in that both dimensions of these relations—labor's participation in government decision making as well as its ability to influence government actions—differ from one policy domain to another. As we have seen, both of these dimensions contrasted in the cases of capital versus labor adjustment. Excluded and ineffectual vis-à-vis capital adjustment, labor was both more incorporated into decision making and efficacious concerning labor adjustment. Thus this analysis cautions against using such terms as "pluralism" and "neocorporatism" as blanket characterizations of state-labor relations. Rather, we need to take account of variations in these relations, not only across time and economic sectors but also across phases of the policy process.[16]

Second, state-labor relations are also unstable because of constant shifts in a key determinant: incentives to engage in entangling alliances. As these cases of labor adjustment revealed, the willingness of government and labor officials to enter into neocorporatist arrangements changed over time as their perceptions of the costs and benefits of such arrangements altered. Especially striking is the Talbot case, in which the CGT's collaboration with Employment Minister Jack Ralite backfired when the local CFDT section sparked a grass-roots rejection of the adjustment plan. Thereafter the CGT refused to enter into peak-level agreements. The Renault case also demonstrates changing incentives on the part of the state, as Hanon's replacement by Besse signaled a stiffening of the state's resolve to push through restructuring, regardless of union support or opposition. The ultimate lesson of industrial restructuring is that state-labor relations are forever in flux, driven in large measure by leaders' continual strategic reassessments of the risks and rewards of conflict and cooperation.

NOTES

1. I discuss this decline in detail in "'We Can Make the Ariane, But We Can't Make Washing Machines': The State and Industrial Performance in Postwar France," in George Ross and Jolyon Howarth, eds., *Contemporary France* (London: Frances Pinter, 1989), pp. 175–202.
2. As with any ideal type, the ones proposed here are not meant to be fully descriptive of any particular government. In practice, governments can be expected to combine elements of these four approaches and vary over time in the relative weight given to one or more of these elements.
3. See Susan N. Houseman, *Industrial Restructuring with Job Security: The Case of European Steel* (Cambridge, MA: Harvard University Press, 1991); Bo Strath, *The Politics of De-Industrialization: The Contraction of the West European Shipbuilding Industry* (London: Croom Helm, 1987).
4. I expand this argument in a forthcoming book, *Dirty Job: Dilemmas of Industrial Restructuring in France and Spain.*
5. Laurent Fabius, industry minister (1983 to 1984) and prime minister (1984 to 1986), confided in an interview: "When a Left government makes an industrial decision that has human costs, it does so because if it does not make that decision the costs will be even greater. This is what I once called the Left's 'dirty job.'" Interview with the author, Paris, December 9, 1987.
6. I analyze restructuring in these industries at greater length in the following: "Industrial Crisis and the Left: Adjustment Strategies in Socialist France and Spain," *Comparative Politics* 28, no. 1 (October 1995): 1–24; and "The Left's Response to Industrial Crisis: Restructuring in the Steel and Automobiles Industries," in Anthony Daley, ed., *The Mitterrand Era: Policy Alternatives and Political Mobilization in France* (New York: New York University Press, 1996), pp. 97–113.
7. *Le Monde,* December 21–22, 1980.
8. The third largest confederation, Force Ouvrière, was a negligible presence in both the automobile and steel industries. Hence its role and influence will not be discussed.
9. Interview with author, Paris, December 13, 1990.

10. It will be recalled that following the Talbot conflict in early January 1984, the government became much more "consultative" in order to avoid a repeat of the Talbot explosion.

11. *Le Monde,* September 25, 1984, October 17, 1984; *Financial Times,* October 3, 1984.

12. Interview with author, Paris, December 17, 1990.

13. *Le Matin,* May 10, 1985.

14. Le Monde, November 9, 1990.

15. Throughout the crises of the 1980s, CGT leadership, especially in the metalworkers' federation, generally argued that France's industrial malaise stemmed from *insufficient* capacity, production, and consumption rather than an excess thereof. The CFDT supported restructuring but pressured, in vain, for a Market-Modifying approach. Its critique of government adjustment policy centered on the decision-making process, especially on the lack of union input, rather than on the measures themselves.

16. One promising path is the concept of the "statist" model of policy making, as developed by Vivien Schmidt, that posits different state-group patterns and dynamics at the policy formulation and policy implementation stages. See Vivien A. Schmidt, *From State to Market? The Transformation of French Business and Government* (Cambridge: Cambridge University Press, 1996), esp. chap. 2.

CHAPTER TWELVE

Virtual Trade Unionism in France: A Commentary on the Question of Unions, Public Opinion, and the State

Chris Howell

How are we to characterize the French labor movement? How we do so has important consequences for understanding the dynamics and the practice of trade unions and for state-society relations. The orthodox, and long-standing, characterization of French trade unionism is one in which there are two mutually reinforcing sources of weakness. First, politicization, in the form of close ties to political parties, ideological radicalism, and an undue focus on the political sphere, to the detriment of industrial activity, have combined to produce a divided and ultimately weak labor movement. Second, employer and state hostility combine to make union recruitment and organizational implantation in the workplace extremely difficult.

One can quibble with elements of this account. Certainly employer hostility has deeply marked the development of French unions, but the politicization charge is more dubious. The highly successful Swedish Landsorganisation (LO) has been much more closely tied to a political party and has consistently subordinated industrial to political action. The real sin of French trade unionism, in the eyes of most commentators, has been communism, rather than politicization or a preference for political action. But in any case, however accurate this historical portrait, it does not get us very far in understanding the nature of French trade unionism in the 1990s. The characterization is too static, resting on an unchanging essence that pervades all discussion of the labor movement, and tends to extrapolate from the past into the present.

Most important, it does not help explain the paradox of the French labor movement, which is its material weakness and simultaneous broad societal influence. French unions are, on one hand, weak along almost any conventional measure of labor strength. They organize less than one in ten workers, and those are concentrated in the public sector. Thus, to all intents and purposes, trade unionism has disappeared from the private sector in France. And the small unionized portion of the labor force is shared among several bitterly divided trade union confederations. Even more so than in the past, France anchors the other end of the spectrum of labor strength, familiar to comparative political economists, from the centralized, high-trade-union density countries of northern and Central Europe.

On the other hand, the labor movement remains extremely influential within France's political economy. Why, if unions are so weak along every conventional measure, are more than 90 percent of French wage earners covered by collective bargaining? Why do employers and the state bother to negotiate restructuring plans with trade unions, and why, if French unions speak for so few, are they the state's privileged interlocutors during periodic strike waves? The paradox is that trade unions remain as influential as they do, despite their obvious weakness. Certainly, from a comparative perspective, it is hard to imagine right-wing governments in Britain or the United States privileging collective bargaining or negotiating with trade unions were they to represent less than one in ten of the workforce. Indeed, unions are more important social and political actors in France than in the United States, a nation with double the union density, and in Britain, with four times the union density.

The answer to this paradox is that France has evolved a distinctive type of trade unionism, one that is not easily amenable to being arrayed along the familiar spectrum of organizational concentration and centralization. This we might call "virtual unionism." Virtual unionism has a very different set of dynamics and potentialities in which trade unions serve two related functions: first, as a vehicle representing labor *as an interest* to the state, and second, allowing the state to manage conflicts that originate in the industrial sphere. Chapters 10 and 11 in this volume provide clues that help to flesh out this argument.

Chapter 11, by Rand Smith, poses the central question of how to characterize state-labor relations in France. He rejects the stock "there is no corporatism in France" argument, providing a much more nuanced argument about the role of labor. Smith demonstrates the particular nature of union influence through a study of restructuring in the steel and automobile industries under post-1981 Socialist governments. Smith's conclusion is that labor was consulted, and was able to influence restructuring plans, but only on issues of labor adjustment—jobs, benefit packages, retraining—and not wider issues of capital adjustment and the direction of industrial restructuring. Particularly after widespread industrial disruption at Talbot-Poissy, the French state sought to consult and include trade unions in the restructuring plans. Smith's chapter illustrates one of the two functions of virtual unionism: the use of trade unions by the state to manage conflicts which result from economic change.

Chapter 10, by Roland Cayrol, is based on fascinating interview data concerning French attitudes toward trade unionism. The data are in the form of surveys and in-depth interviews, and together they provide an unparalleled picture of the position of unions in French society. To a certain extent the data tell us what we might expect, that unions are considered old-fashioned, divided, too political, and poorly adapted to modern conditions. But what is startling about the chapter is the evidence it provides of the extent of public acceptance and support for trade unions. About two-thirds of all social groups wish that unions were more influential than they are, close to half of all social categories have confidence in unions, and more than a third of the French population could envisage joining a union.

The conclusion that Cayrol draws is that there is "a real, and in some dimensions, *consensual* legitimacy of unions in France" (my emphasis). Two further points are important about the evidence provided here: First, social class is a not a good predictor of attitudes toward unions, and their legitimacy appears to be an expression of genuine broad public support rather than sharply differentiated class views; second, there is a huge gap between trade union membership and trade union support. It would be nice to have comparative data here, but even in its absence it is clear that orthodox notions of representation have limited purchase under these conditions.

What these two chapters suggest is, first and foremost, that trade unions are much more influential than their membership figures would lead one to expect. Under these circumstances it makes little sense to decry their weakness. A much more interesting and important question is why French trade unions remain as influential as they do. Influence is not the same thing as power.

Power, for my purposes, implies that unions possess autonomous resources derived from their strategic location within the economy and the capacity to disrupt production and therefore accumulation. This is power because it provides the potential for occasions on which unions can pursue their own interests, against those of employers and/or the state, backed up with the threat of sanctions. French trade unions do not have power in this sense. The term "virtual trade unionism" is designed to capture a labor movement that lacks real membership and a clear material base. To paraphrase Mark Kesselman, this is trade unionism without the workers. But virtual unionism is not the same thing as no unionism. Unions do have influence because they retain two important, even crucial, functions.

The first function is to act as virtual representatives of the state in the world of work. In France trade unions, *as institutions,* are sustained in very concrete terms, and through a range of resources and mechanisms, by the state. Why is there such a high degree of institutional support for unions at a time when so few workers choose to belong to them? Trade unions serve, in the classic sense used by C. Wright Mills, as "managers of discontent." They act to give legitimacy to the economic policies of governments that involve significant dislocation for workers. This was clear in the case of Talbot-Poissy, when bargaining between the state and the unions served to manage economic crisis. The illusion of bargaining and the symbolism of negotiations—even in the absence of significant content—is tremendously powerful. Indeed, it is a public ritual. In the second half of the 1970s Jacques Delors characterized collective bargaining as "all that is left of a mass celebrated at the eleventh hour without faith: a liturgy empty of sense."[1] But this missed the point of the grand social meetings between union leaders and government ministers. It was the fact rather than the content of bargaining that was important. Ritual mattered more than faith. After the events of May-June 1968 a weakened state itself bestowed a legitimate social role on trade unions in order to channel social protest away from posing a threat to the regime.

This situation has been repeated in the various strike waves since 1968. Rarely have unions initiated these strikes, but once begun, the state needs someone to negotiate with and someone to reach a settlement with. So a solemn ritual is duly played out: A strike begins, various agencies of the state (depending on the seriousness of the strike) hold talks with the trade unions, and a settlement is announced. The settlement may be repudiated by the strikers, in which case more talks follow. The irony is that it is precisely the weakness of the trade unions—their lack of meaningful control over the strike and the consequent threat of industrial chaos—that gives them leverage over the state in negotiations. It is precisely the fact that French unions cannot—in good corporatist fashion—deliver their members, still less other protesters, that allows them to negotiate from strength because the state knows that any concessions it offers must satisfy the workers themselves, not the union.

The point is that even late capitalism needs mechanisms for channeling the inevitable discontent that results from economic change into orderly industrial relations, and France is no exception. That nine out of ten French workers are covered by collective bargaining mechanisms is a direct result of state action: first to make bargaining obligatory in certain workplaces and then to extend collective agreements across entire industries and regions.

The Socialist industrial relations reforms embodied in the Auroux laws had the effect of permitting flexibility in the workplace that could not have been achieved in any other way. The rapid increase in firm-level bargaining in the 1980s, despite being deeply one-sided, often signed by minority unions and containing little by the way of quid pro quo in return for flexibility, legitimized the state's withdrawal from active regulation of the labor market. Thus the high level of collective bargaining coverage in France is an indication of the need of employers and the state for cover for deregulation rather than of strong, well-implanted trade unionism.

The second function of trade unions in France is to act as virtual representatives for the workforce *as a whole* to the state. By this I mean that trade unions represent labor as a quasi-abstract societal interest rather than clearly identifiable sectional groups of workers. French unions are only tangentially craft unions, occupational unions, or industrial unions. Instead, they engage in virtual representation in the same sense that the British government argued that the American colonies were virtually represented in the British Parliament; they were not directly represented through election but rather were represented *as an interest* by British parliamentarians.

In France, it is the weakness of viable alternative institutions for representing civil society to the state that provides a role for unions. Trade unions are, by and large, ignored by working people in ordinary times. But they retain a residual historical legitimacy. What unions do have is not members, or even much loyalty, but a historical tradition of opposition to capitalist restructuring and defense of workers' interests. Trade unions have access to a vivid and highly symbolic narrative of oppositionalism that makes it possible for them to emerge as the representatives of a labor interest in moments of great social unrest.

Regarding chapter 10, I am normally skeptical of the value of polling data concerning opinions about trade unions because they miss the point that people act and even think very differently in different spheres of their lives and that, for example, a generalized public mistrust of unions is perfectly compatible with strong union membership and high levels of labor militancy. But in the French case polling data are exactly where one should look to understand the role of trade unions in the political economy, because unions perform a public representational function and because public confidence is a crucial resource for unions.

As a result, trade unions in France can be seen, in almost a feudal sense, as an estate in which the unions represent an interest—that of labor—by virtue of state sponsorship and public confidence rather than deep roots within the working class. French trade unions are *interest* organizations rather than *class* organizations. Representation here means something fundamentally different from that associated with most other labor movements. And it follows that understanding labor strength is bound to be different. Trade union strength in France does not derive from union membership, and only partly does it derive from elections to the *comités d'entreprise* and other industrial institutions. Instead it is conjunctural, a function of the need that wage earners and the state have of organizations capable of speaking, bargaining, and saber-rattling on their behalf.

Virtual unionism is not an entirely new phenomenon in France, nor are elements of it unknown elsewhere in the advanced capitalist world, but it has reached a particularly high state of development in post-Fordist France. It has long been the case, as Charles Tilly and Edward Shorter famously argued, that French trade unions have aimed industrial action at the state, using strikes as political weapons.[2] The very weakness of the Left in France, and the absence of a class compromise along postwar British or 1930s Swedish lines, has meant that unions have, to some degree, substituted for political parties as agents representing the concerns of working people to the state.

It is the collapse of the postwar political-economic model in France that has encouraged the transition of trade unionism from this familiar state to what I am calling virtual unionism. Since the second half of the 1970s a market model has come, little by little, to dominate political discourse, and the state has been less and less willing to take responsibility for managing economic restructuring and dislocation. (Whether it was able to do so is a different matter.)

This has made the state ever more anxious to search out societal interlocutors who are willing to share the responsibility and *legitimize* change. Closely related has been the decline in the legitimacy and cohesion of the French state's planning mission, so well elaborated by Peter Hall.[3] The *capacity* of the state to manage change and to claim to speak for French society as a whole—however ludicrous the claim was even in the 1950s and 1960s—has weakened. The year 1968 is a crucial date because it marks the point at which both the contradictions of the postwar model of economic growth became clear and the French state began to use the labor movement to help it *manage* the working class. After 1968 the state came increasingly to underpin the industrial relations system, encouraging collective bargaining, providing concrete organizational resources for unions, and creating a quasi-corportatist system of consultation on every issue of industrial significance.

The 1980s took this process to a new level by virtue of two factors. First, the virulence with which economic restructuring has hit France, and the extent of the sacrifices that the working class has been expected to make—in job loss and insecurity, in pay restraint, and in changes in working practices and *droits aquis* (entitlements) inside the workplace—has made a mediating role between the state and wage earners absolutely central to political management. The state needs some agency to perform this function all the more. Second, the "normalization" of the French Left with the ideological reversal and reconfiguration of French Socialism, combined with the marginalization of the French Communist Party, has meant that there is now no political force advocating radical change. (On the Left, the Front National is another matter.) Protest against economic change now can come only from outside the main political parties. Thus in moments of crisis, society, or at least wage earners, use unions to represent the world of work to the state.

It is this particular set of state-society relations that gives French trade unionism its comparative specificity. Virtual unionism is not an appropriate description for the labor movements of any other advanced capitalist societies. However, I do think that there is something of a common trajectory to labor movements. The two factors encouraging virtual unionism in 1980s France—rapid economic restructuring with adverse implication for jobs, wages, and conditions, and the eclipse of the Socialist, social democratic, and Communist left—are common, and highly advanced, across the advanced capitalist world. As trade unions lose members and weaken everywhere, albeit at different speeds, the questions for other countries are: (1) Will mass, extra-parliamentary protest against economic change develop? (2) Which societal actors will channel it? and (3) How will states choose to respond to it? The answers to these questions will determine whether virtual unionism escapes the national boundaries of France.

It follows from the argument made here that trade unions are primarily *political* actors, even quasi-state actors, in that their main function is to act in the political sphere. This is not the same oft-repeated argument about the politicization of French unions. The issue is not the ideological maps of French unions but the *function* played by unions in the political economy. Trade unions have not so much politicized the sphere of industrial relations as been politicized by the state.

We should not look to French trade unions to be oppositional, still less revolutionary, actors. French unions lack resources independent of the state. They survive by virtue of the function they play, not their own autonomous resources. The two sources of weakness outlined earlier are, paradoxically, the same sources of current influence. The political role of mediator between economy and the state and the need of employers and the state to legitimize massive industrial dislocation and its consequences are the basis of virtual unionism in France.

Part V

The International Challenge:
Globalization and the European Union

CHAPTER THIRTEEN

The CGT's Internationalism: What Europe, What World?

George Ross

Most, if not all, union movements, as they grew, recognized the need for internationalism. Labor had little difficulty understanding intellectually that capital had much greater mobility, including transnational mobility. Labor needed to construct international ties for this reason alone, but its internationalist concerns often were broader than this. Marx's notions that the logic of capital over time would rapidly destroy national identity among workers and lead to internationalism were widely shared.

Labor's early internationalism was paradoxical. It saw itself embracing workers wherever they were, yet at the same time, the materials out of which labor built its strength over time were local. Originally, local meant parochial, but as the twentieth century came it was redefined to become ever more primarily national. The central fact about modern unions, working-class social movements, and, indeed, socialism itself is thus their nationalization.[1] Over the twentieth century the logics of capitalist development have ever more profoundly enracinated laborers in national contexts, in direct contrast to Marx's projections. Ultimately it has been capital, much more than labor, that has thrown off its chains of patriotism.

Despite internationalist claims, unions needed national identities as one source of solidarity. Political development, perhaps most important the halting development of national democratic systems, reinforced these needs. The national state came to be seen as an important source of resources. The contradiction between claimed internationalism and de facto nationalization became clear in the early twentieth century, most notably through the events surrounding the outbreak of World War I, the assassination of Jean Jaurès, and the alacrity with which workers slaughtered one another in hellish trenches to gain a few yards of polluted mud. However desirable—indeed needed—effective internationalism might have been, the underlying social, economic, and political logics that shaped labor movements worked against it.

Union movements responded to pressures toward nationalization in different ways. Most social democratic and "bread-and-butter" union movements gave in to them and henceforth did little but give lip service to internationalism.[2] The Confédération Générale du Travail (CGT) had its own particular strategies in this general context. It already had a long history by the time of the great union divisions that occurred after World War I. The modern CGT, however, was created out of the organizational core of the CGTU, which in the aftermath of the Popular Front and World War II subordinated the post-1920 CGT. The CGTU was acutely aware that the creeping nationalization of union movements would, other things being equal, lead to a point where internationalism would be an insignificant part of union identity and action. It thus made extraordinary efforts to tie its national actions to a coherent vision of internationalism.

The vision, officially, was "proletarian internationalism." In fact, it very quickly turned out to be Leninist. Leninism, as it came to be defined in the 1920s, sought to counteract reformism by subordinating unionism to vanguard national political parties while simultaneously subordinating these parties and these union movements to Communist international organizations. All of this was meant initially to coordinate and focus available resources on strategies to pursue the kinds of policies that the international movement deemed appropriate to advance the cause of transcending capitalism.

The new CGTU quickly joined the new international Communist-sponsored union movement. Historically this meant that the CGTU, prior to the (first) reunification of the CGT in the 1930s, was officially affiliated to the Profintern. After World War II the CGT, now controlled by the descendants of the CGTU, then joined, and became a mainstay of, the World Federation of Trade Unions (FSM).[3] There is no point in mincing words about the politics of such affiliations. They both reproduced the "double subordination" just defined. The CGTU and the post-1945 CGT both had a relationship of particular importance with the Parti Communiste Français (PCF). The biased nature of much scholarship about these relationships rarely admits that they have varied considerably over time, but almost all of the variants involved strategic subordination of union actions to the PCF.[4] Moreover, the PCF itself very quickly became strategically subordinate to the Comintern until its dissolution in World War II and to the Kominform after 1947. Beyond this both the

Profintern and the World Federation of Trade Unions (WFTU) themselves had relationships of particular importance with the Soviet-dominated international organizations of Communist parties in general.

This chapter focuses on the changing meanings and logics of these "doubly subordinate" relationships in two parts. The first reviews the complex period through the high Cold War (roughly until the Khruschchev era), where the CGT's particular definition of internationalism seemed to serve it reasonably well. The second part considers the period between 1962 or so and 1989, a moment that ends in precipitous CGT decline. By the end of this period the CGT's particular form of internationalism had become extremely costly, both in terms of what the CGT did do, often ineffectively, in siding with a more and more decadent bloc of "existing socialist" countries and what it did not do to confront the important changes going on in the political economies of advanced capitalist societies.

THE LEGACIES OF A LENINIST PAST

The long period from the 1920s to the 1960s is neatly divided by World War II and, in terms of the CGT's internationalism, by the shift between the Profintern and the WFTU that occurred during the war. The Profintern/Popular Front moment was extraordinary to the degree to which CGTU/CGT internationalism, despite its ups and downs and the eager pursuit of very dangerous strategies, met general good fortune. Militant, internationalist, and pro-Soviet trade unionism survived and, on occasion, actually thrived.

This form of unionism had its chronic costs, to be sure. French unionism has almost always been divided organizationally among rival groups rather than unified. This situation has created a chronic competitive pluralism. Simply put, from the tactical vantage point of any specific French union organization, it often has made sense to seek advantage over rival union organizations more than to benefit the labor movement as a whole. In the game that came to exist each union organization has sought to capitalize on any and all vulnerabilities in others' positions. The CGTU's and the CGT's internationalism added yet another dimension to these usually destructive games of French union "pluralism" and constituted yet another reason for divisions among organizations to be more important than the unity without which union movements quite simply do not succeed.

INTERNATIONALISM AND GREAT-POWER POLITICS

The creation of the CGTU and its affiliation to the Profintern occurred after the Soviet Revolution, the Great War, and the division of the French Left in

1920–1921. The split of the existing CGT at Lille in 1921 followed the Tours congress, which divided France's political Left between Socialists and Communists and occurred for similar reasons. The moderate French Left had compromised itself in participating in a government during a war whose long, murderous trajectory became ever more unpopular among French workers. Moreover, the course of the war stretched to a breaking point a Left that always had had deep schismatic tendencies. The Russian Revolution, greeted enthusiastically by many who could not be aware of what would ensue, divided the Left even more. The failure of strikes in the immediate aftermath of the war and the role of "moderates" in this failure ultimately precipitated the party and union splits that followed. In these splits the new PCF and the CGTU gathered in a wide range of different activists and members, far beyond the circles who were more intimately acquainted with the logics at work in the new Soviet Union.[5]

The Profintern, along with the broader Leninist package that contained it, very quickly proved to be more than many had originally bargained for. Lenin's own 21 conditions and the ways in which they were imposed in the years following the PCF's and the CGTU's founding were troublesome. The strict discipline and subordination of both to strategies centralized in the new Soviet Union were too much for anarcho-syndicalists and others who initially had signed on with the CGTU because of their opposition to compromised reformism and their enthusiasm about making the revolution in France, not because they had any desire to participate in a rigid army whose commanders spoke another language. Thus in the 1920s, as a result of the Profintern's iron direction of the CGTU on international matters, the new union was involved in a wide range of highly politicized actions that were often sectarian and isolated, whatever one thinks of their political values. There were hard-line actions against the occupation of the Ruhr and against the Rif war, among others.

In the abstract, the problems that became evident stemmed first from specific lines chosen more than from the larger fact of subordinating CGTU unionism to strident political concerns, and second, from the extra-heavy dose of international political concerns in the general mix of CGTU activities. Unionism prospers when unions are in touch with and able to respond to needs of workers for defense in the workplace and in their material existence. Unions generate solidarity and accumulate resources of support and mobilization by helping workers to expand workplace and economic citizenship in tangible ways. Strident politicization on top of such matters sometimes can be made congruent with these needs, provided the needs remain a primary concern. But politicization for overtly international purposes with little evident connection to matters of wages, hours, and job security can tend to seem particularly removed. This has always been the characteristic danger of CGTU/CGT internationalism. Beyond this, the heavy dose of international policy concerns in CGTU activities added another dimension of potential conflict into the already volatile equations of competitive pluralist conflict among French unions.

The sectarianism of the 1920s degenerated with the class-against-class period as Joseph Stalin consolidated power in the Soviet Union. In this instance the hyperpoliticization of CGTU action, including politicization on international matters, was a function of positions that Stalin assumed in internal Soviet struggles to marginalize rivals, Leon Trotsky in particular, in the succession to Lenin and had little to do with the concerns of French workers. The results for the CGTU were contradictory, however. The rule that overpoliticization for remote causes is risky for union support held true. The CGTU, which had begun quite strong in terms of membership and mobilizing capacity, shrank to near extinction, partly as a consequence of its internationalist sectarianism. But there was a hidden positive dimension. Those who stuck it out in the CGTU (like those who stuck it out in the PCF) became solid, hardened, and skilled organizers. This was important, because these cadre were particularly well placed in the mass production, Fordist areas of the economy where the reformist CGT was unable or unwilling to organize. When mass production workers unionized in the 1930s and 1940s, these CGTU cadre were there to do work while others tended to be absent.

Comintern internationalism played the central role in making this, the PCF's most important labor organizing success, possible.[6] The Comintern's line shift away from class-against-class sectarianism toward Popular Front coalition politics, dutifully followed by Profintern, was the key. The French situation, the PCF, and the CGTU probably played an important role in prodding the belated Soviet recognition that fascism and Nazism were something more ominous than the last authoritarian gasps of capitalism before European revolution. Popular Frontism in general shifted international Communist energies toward mobilization to promote national antifascist social and political coalitions that might forestall and/or mobilize to protect the Soviet Union's interests, which were clearly threatened by German expansionism. As such it was clearly a Soviet—and Stalinist—great-power strategy. But the strategic change paid off handsomely for the PCF and the CGTU because it dismantled the high walls between what had been their declining little world and the broader world of French republican politics. In particular, the Popular Front "renationalized" the CGTU, gave it access to national legitimacy through antifascism. It also lowered boundaries between the CGTU's strong core of cadre and France's theretofore largely ununionized Fordist semiskilled workers, particularly as they became caught up in Popular Front mobilizations and strikes.[7] It led to the reunification of the

CGT at Toulouse in 1936 with the ex-CGTU faction in a much more powerful position.[8]

The contradictions and good luck persisted over the next decade or so. The reunified CGT did not stay unified for very long—a mere three years—and an issue of union internationalism—what position to take about the coming of World War II—was what tore it apart again. After a brief period of urging French mobilization on the side of the Spanish Republicans and rearmament, the ex-CGTU fraction in the CGT followed the PCF in supporting the Nazi-Soviet agreement. It could have destroyed itself in this process, and not only because the shift involved an almost overnight 180 degree change of direction. The shift exposed a rather abject political dependence on the PCF and the Soviet Union and left France diplomatically and strategically to shift for itself in the face of imminent Nazi aggression. The national legitimacy won so quickly in the Popular Front was lost again quite as quickly. The ex-CGTU fraction was expelled from the CGT, while the line in question was highly unpopular even among Communist unionists.[9]

Developments in the war itself, in particular the changed position of the Soviet Union after 1941 when the Germans invaded, opened space to repair the damage. Once more, Stalin's redefinition of "proletarian internationalism" saved the ex-CGTU and the PCF, yet not before the same Stalin had brought both unionists and party to the brink of complete catastrophe. The dissolution of the Profintern and the parallel dissolution of the Comintern were important in this regard. The Soviet Union was willing to do virtually everything to secure westward alliances against the Germans. In France this meant the rapid commitment of the CGTU and the PCF to the Resistance and the pursuit of coalitions with others in their Resistance efforts. From this point (although the roots had grown earlier, thanks to Benoît Frachon) the ex-CGTU fraction compiled an extraordinarily brave resistance record. Because of this the CGT eventually reunified in 1943 in the Perreux accords. By the Liberation in 1944, with the CGTU fraction poised to take over leadership of a majority of key CGT locals and federations, things looked better than ever.

CONSOLIDATION DESPITE COLD WAR—TO THE 1960S

The period from 1944 to the early 1960s—the "high Cold War-WFTU" period—posed the same general questions about the CGT's internationalism. How could the CGT succeed in imposing its own particular notions of union internationalism—tied to the promotion of the Soviet Union's diplomatic interests—onto the important day-to-day tasks of trade unionism? A priori, the context—that of insuperable Cold War divisions which crossed French union and political life—seemed unpromising. Yet the CGT succeeded remarkably well in the short term. Alas, these successes were to reinforce the ultimately tragic organizational patterns and habits that have led the CGT to its desperate situation.

The very brief period after the Liberation was critical for setting the general lines of the next decades. Until 1947 the CGT's international line coincided very well with its domestic goals, much as it had in the Popular Front period, and for similar reasons. At this point the Soviet Union was trying to maintain the wartime alliance pattern of the last months of the war and immediately thereafter, at least long enough to consolidate its security position and its predominance in the areas that the Red Army had liberated from the Nazis. This meant that both the PCF and the CGT were enjoined to pursue a patriotic, cooperative line in domestic French matters. Given their Resistance records and the resources that these granted, both organizations could do so with some energy, contributing significantly to the building of postwar France. The PCF thus became the most electorally successful single party in the immediate postwar period. The ex-CGTU fraction came to dominate the CGT during the same short period.

For both party and union, the opening to united front coalition action was brief, from 1942 to 1947, but both made the most of it. The CGT was reunified in 1943 and its internal unity was undisturbed for a critical few years, granting enough time for the ex-CGTU fraction to consolidate its control over the bulk of the confederation. In effect, the return of the kind of political conditions that had prevailed briefly in the Popular Front period allowed the ex-CGTUers to pursue their organizational efforts among Fordist factory operatives and to use their capital of organizing talent, which had been considerably enhanced in the Resistance experience. They did similar work in the new public-sector areas created by nationalizations. The renewed Republican legitimacy acquired in the Resistance, quickly spun into grandiose mythology by the ex-CGTU fraction along with everyone else who had played roles in the fight against Nazis, was reinforced in the immediate postwar months as the CGT moved to play a key role in very important, and much maligned, efforts to put postwar reconstruction in France on a firm footing.[10] In consequence, the ex-CGTU fraction was able to maintain and expand strong control over the bulk of the CGT. Thus, when the inevitable splits tied to the Cold War gestated in 1946–1947, that faction was in a position to continue leading the CGT, controlling all of its symbolic and organizational assets and obliging its new Cold War opponents to leave. Thus, with American aid, the CGT-Force Ouvrière was formed on the principles of anticommunism and bread-and-butter unionism while the very important teachers' federation (the Fédération de l'Education Nationale, or FEN), unable to resolve its internal Cold War disputes one way or the other, became autonomous.[11]

The period also saw the foundation of an international trade union organization, the WFTU (FSM), which eventually replaced the Profintern. The process, which began in early 1945, has been reviewed so well by René Mouriaux elsewhere that we can here overlook the details and go to the punch lines.[12] There was unquestionably widespread desire emerging from the war and the alliance to form a worldwide union organization that would unite pro-Soviet and non-Soviet organizations. Initially there was some hope that this might work, because the American CIO was interested, as was the British Trade Union Congress (TUC)—even if the American Federation of Labor (AFL) was not. At the founding congress Louis Saillant of the CGT became secretary general. But very quickly, with the coming of Cold War tensions, reservations, arguments, then departures, began. In consequence, the WFTU split on Cold War lines. A pro-Soviet WFTU thereafter confronted a new pro-American International Confederation of Free Trade Unions (ICFTU) in whose consolidation the politics and funding of the U.S. government were nearly as important as Soviet support was for WFTU. The stakes on both sides were huge, and little expense, espionage, and muscle were spared. The result was a reformulated Manichean internationalism that no one could avoid. The CGT, because it existed in a nation that was central to the divide between East and West, inevitably became a key player. Its inordinately devoted attachment to WFTU was conceived in this period.

The high Cold War period, which lasted roughly to the end of the Fourth Republic, was an extraordinary moment. The PCF faithfully reproduced the worst of the Soviet commitments during the capricious last period of Stalin's life and the confusion after his death in 1953.[13] Despite the very large problems that this posed for CGT unionism, the CGT often was very good at combining strong, no-holds-barred, pro-Soviet internationalism and its domestic duties. That the massive strikes of autumn 1947 and 1948 were based on serious grievances held by large numbers of French workers is undeniable. The immediate postwar period was one of shortages and penury, which hit workers particularly hard.[14] That the CGT skillfully used these grievance to inject an internationalist content is equally clear, however. These strikes occurred at the precise moment when the Cold War was actually "declared," and strikes in France were meant as an important factor in their declaration from the anti-American side. The CGT, in other words, was trying its best to use industrial discontent to make it difficult for French governments to commit to American plans and to "socialize" its base to anti-American positions, in particular using the French nationalist credibility that it had gained in the Resistance.

The actions were quite successful—even though their political objectives were not fully attained—because they were based on deep domestic grievances rather than being artificially contrived for WFTU purposes. At the same time they were clearly connected to the establishment of the Kominform in 1947. Indeed, the French were roundly denounced by the Soviets at the Kominform's founding sessions for having behaved much too moderately right after the war. However unjust these accusations were, for the PCF had been as dutiful in following Soviet injunctions prior to 1947 as it would prove to be afterward, the PCF took them to heart, and the 1947 worker unrest provided an ideal opportunity to demonstrate loyalty to the new hard line. Subsequent mobilizations against the French war in Indochina, which were designed to communicate an anti-American, anti-NATO message, had considerable effect. The CGT also devoted its energies to post-1949 "peace" campaigns such as the Stockholm petition (for which the CGT helped gather an enormous number of signatures in France).

Over time, however, these highly "internationalized" movements, which brought fewer and fewer material returns to workers (partly because governments and employers could disqualify and ignore CGT actions as the work of outside agitators) tended to become ever more cadre-shaped and their mass base declined. By the early 1950s much done in the name of the CGT had become de facto the work of tightly organized PCF militants. The low-point mobilizations of winter and spring 1952, culminating in support of a PCF demonstration against NATO ("Ridgeway la Peste"), were a disaster. The PCF leadership itself was in chaos, wracked by factional infighting that burgeoned into unrealistic sectarianism and spread rapidly to the CGT. The 1952 movements were unpopular cadre actions by apparatchiks prepared to engage in street battles with the police. Unsurprisingly, they were successfully outmaneuvered by the government and police. The isolation that resulted for the CGT was so evident that in the autumn the government felt emboldened enough to indict Frachon, the CGT secretary-general, plus a number of others, for "undermining the morale of the armed forces," obliging Frachon to go underground until the indictment was quashed months later.[15] Despite official PCF rhetoric about "victory," this was the low point of deep CGT Cold War politicization. Frachon, aware of the danger at hand, was reported to have said "victory . . . one or two more victories like this and there won't be any more CGT."[16]

Very quickly there was some rectification. By later 1953 the PCF's internal mess had been sorted out with the return of Secretary-General Maurice Thorez from sick leave in Moscow and with the death of Stalin. Frachon's relative independence from the party and his awareness of the CGT's problems helped the confederation to pull back from its exposed position. Finally, the beginnings of postwar economic change and expansion contributed to a resurgence of industrial conflict that allowed the CGT to "recenter" itself on industrial issues. There was a significant public-sector strike wave in the summer of 1953, for example, which the CGT leadership handled shrewdly. Politicization around international matters did not go away, to be sure, and overpoliticization on domestic issues remained a problem, particularly in the heated months around the Mendès-France government (since the PCF regarded Mendès's progressivism as a serious turf threat). Throughout the mid-1950s the CGT participated in many campaigns against German rearmament (anti-European Defense Community, or EDC, then against the integration of German forces into NATO). But the campaigns were more discreet and took place in a context where real trade unionism was much more evident. Moreover, opposing German rearmament was a matter where CGT politics played into a broad current of French opinion, for obvious reasons. The confederation even managed to avoid following the PCF into support for the Soviet crushing of the Hungarian rebellion in 1956. But by this point the decline of the Fourth Republic and the coming of the Algerian war were beginning to change the playing field altogether. The crisis of 1958 and the coming of the Fifth Republic dramatically altered French politics in ways that eventually prompted major changes in PCF and CGT strategy.

Balance Sheet for Two Epochs

The underlying narrative about CGT internationalism in the interwar and Cold War periods carries two somewhat contradictory messages. The first, which everyone can recite from memory, is about the Stalinization of CGT international outlooks in both periods. At times, indeed most of the time, the international Communist movement, including the Profintern and the WFTU and especially including the PCF and the CGTU fraction of the French labor movement, were prone to schematic strategic reflection, illiberal extremism, and intolerance. Blindness at best, approval at worst, of the mass liquidation of kulaks, the development of a police state dictatorship in the Soviet Union, and events such as the Moscow trials, along with grotesque characterizations of Social Democrats as "social fascists" and the cynicism of the Nazi-Soviet pact only begin to illustrate the perversities of the rote reaction. Concerning the second, closer to our time, it is sufficient to recall the attacks on Titoist Trotskyists and alleged Western spies that the French Communist world supported, its approval of things such as proletarian science, adulation of Stalin, the official version of the Doctors' Plot, and other such monstrous practices. The evidence is clear.

It is not an excuse, but rather an empirically verifiable proposition, however, to acknowledge that the CGTU fraction that evolved in the second period into the CGT leadership usually was able to attenuate the political effects of high Stalinism. Most of the time, Benoît Frachon and others

around him were able to insist on the specificity of trade unionism and resist the worst of the pressures coming from the PCF to turn the CGT into
a political claque. When they were unable to do so, trade union membership
declined and the viability of the PCF's labor base was threatened. This in itself was a sufficiently dangerous indicator to constrain Communist union
leaders against jumping over the cliff. The real core of this first message is,
therefore, that the CGTU-CGT was able to maintain its base and credibility as a union despite the political cocoon within which it had to operate.
Here many factors would need to be explored before any final explanation
could be proposed, including the needs and desires of important parts of the
French working class itself. But one cannot overlook Frachon's tough and
smart leadership.

The second message is about legacies, however, and it is less positive.
Four decades of practice within this political cocoon consolidated a number
of outlooks and practices that marked the CGT indelibly and that have
turned out to be hugely costly. First, and most important, there was a much
too uncritical understanding of the Soviet Union and "existing socialism."
While the CGT may have sheltered itself from some of the more patent and
horrifying crimes and absurdities of the Stalin period, it was not sufficiently
free of these things to realize the need for deep rethinking after the mid-
1950s. Here, it must be said, the Italians in the CGIL (the Italian equivalent
of the CGT) did much better.[17] Second, there was an absolute unwillingness
to confront the fact that the policy orientations that the Soviets imposed on
the international Communist movement and, to a lesser extent, on Profintern and WFTU were manifestations less of revolutionary internationalism
than of great-power politics. Both in form and in content the Soviet approach to balances of power was not that different from what the British and
French did in the interwar period or than what the hegemonic Americans
did after 1945, claims to universal progressivism notwithstanding. The third
legacy was an almost blind faith in the WFTU as an organization. Past a certain point it ought to have been evident that the union movements of the
Socialist bloc that were central in the WFTU were not trade unions in the
same sense that the CGT was, and, if one had even a mildly critical eye, perhaps not real trade unions at all (but transmission belts for politics from
above for Communist elites).

Connected with these matters, and perhaps even more important, the
CGT displayed a genuine inability to understand how rapidly and profoundly Western societies were changing in the postwar boom and what this
meant for trade unionism. The CGT managed for quite a while to run a
rather conventional "Fordist" union operation fitted to French circumstances—this was Frachon's triumph. France was a slow modernizer, with
the full triumph of mass-production capitalism, Fordist style, not occurring

until the 1950s. But even this change was accompanied by persistent public and internal denial that anything was changing.

Capitalism was changing rapidly, however. The boom of the 30 years of economic growth from 1946 to 1975—the *trente glorieuses*—was a serious business, bringing huge social shifts with which the CGT's traditional *ouvriérisme* was ill-equipped to cope. Consumerism, changes in social geography that broke down traditional working-class communities, the coming of mass secondary and higher education, television, increased leisure, the slow "white collarization" and feminization of important parts of the labor force, the rise of technobureaucratic new middle strata, and a host of other things created a new world. Insecurity, frustration, and even considerable misery were built into this new world, albeit usually in different ways than they had been in the old. The CGT, however, approached this new world through a haze of nineteenth-century notions about dichotomous class conflict to the finish between capitalists and industrial workers. These notions were, in turn, glued onto French antiauthoritarian passions derived from popular experiences with French statism and authoritarian hierarchies. Finally, both were "refined" by the simplifications of twentieth-century Soviet ideology. While some parts of this ideological mélange may have been alluring and others quite congruent with success, the evolution of advancing capitalism in France made the package more and more antiquated.

One particular dimension to this general problem merits further reflection because it is connected to an important flaw in the CGT's international outlook, the CGT's "It's all a capitalist plot" attitude toward European integration. The irony here is that the CGT's general perception of the logic behind European integration was quite to the point. It is not difficult to see the "Common Market" created after the Rome Treaty precisely as a capitalist plot—an effort more often than not carried out by political stealth (that is, out of sight of democratic scrutiny) to use European integration to create a broader market for European capital that felt constrained by national boundaries. One part of this feeling of constraint also was nourished by growing capitalist impatience with the costs tied to the success of reforms from the postwar period.

The CGT understood all this and might have made something quite constructive out of it had its understanding not been filtered through a Cold War political line. European integration was always seen as a threat by the Soviets, since it was likely to consolidate the position of the Americans in Western Europe, making Soviet positions more difficult in Eastern Europe. Thus, rather than adapting its approaches to allow some kind of workable confrontation within the European Community, the CGT instead used its resources to denounce Europe. The position that there could be no compromise with European integration, that it had to be rejected absolutely, was a dangerous one from the outset. If, indeed, capital would increasingly use Europe as a new space to transcend national economic problems and, even more to the point, the obstacles that national organizations such as unions presented within national arenas, then the CGT was likely eventually to find itself disarmed in a new arena where creative trade union energy was indispensable.

PAST LEGACIES AND PRESENT CRISIS

The Fifth Republic period, up to the end of existing socialism in 1989, was another story where the legacies we have just reviewed became an important part of the CGT's inability to adapt to rapidly changing circumstances. Here again there are two moments. The first, one of missed opportunities, went from the early 1960s to 1978–1979 and the aftermath of the confederation's fortieth congress. The second, the decade to 1989, involved the combination of legacies and significant strategic mistakes and led to near disaster.

MODERNIZE OR DECLINE? FROM DE GAULLE TO MITTERRAND

The years between the end of the Algerian war and the electoral defeat of the Union de la Gauche in 1978 were open-ended for the CGT and for French unionism more generally. To begin with, there was significant decline in the salience of traditional international issues. French colonial warfare came to an end in 1962, removing the obstacle that domestic political divisions over decolonization had posed since 1946. More important, détente between the United States and the Soviet Union moved most Cold War issues away from Europe and somewhat into the background. American-Soviet great-power tensions shifted to what was then called the Third World of the decolonizing and modernizing nations. Here, to be sure, there was a chess game of blood and bribery between two superpowers, but the game was much more removed from the European arena than the high Cold War confrontation about Europe had been.

The imprimatur of General de Gaulle's international "third forcism" on French foreign policy underlined the changed international setting. De Gaulle sought to use the European Economic Community (EEC) and French nuclear autonomy to diminish the American hold over European diplomatic allegiances; while by and large he was unsuccessful, the CGT (and the PCF) could hardly risk discrediting the effort by trying to be more anti-American than the president. This meant that the international matters that the CGT did attempt to mobilize around could not isolate it any more. It was stridently against the American war in Indochina, for example. But so too were General de Gaulle and, to varying degrees, the French public.

Quite as important, the evolution of French domestic politics and economic life pushed the CGT away from strongly distinctive mobilizing efforts that might isolate it, including those involving international political themes, toward efforts to reduce conflict and multiply common action with other trade union organizations. The primary impetus behind this was the PCF's changed strategy. The party saw clearly that the political and electoral logics of the Gaullist Fifth Republic implied new Left coalitions, provided that it itself was willing to take steps to make such coalitions happen. In addition, the PCF began to understand that it needed to modernize its own image, even if it involved changing important things, to make this new united front line work.

Most important among the political steps in the new strategy were those that minimized Cold War differences and stressed new Communist moderation to facilitate a new Union de la Gauche with the Socialists and others. The story, too familiar to need retelling in any detail, began in the early 1960s, made great strides forward in the 1965 presidential elections, and ultimately reached initial success in the signature in 1972 of the Common Program for Left Government with the reconfigured Socialist Party and the Left Radicals. One can restate all this more abstractly. Circumstances favored a new Left alliance, as the PCF understood, so the PCF took the most logical steps to promote it, in the hopes of profiting from it eventually. To do so it went as far as it felt prudent to go in calling a truce in the intraleft political warfare that had characterized twentieth-century French Left history.

In this new political context national political matters eclipsed international issues for a time. The CGT shifted its own line accordingly, moving to promote broader trade union "unity in action" in serious ways. Just as the PCF was willing to spike its guns in the political Left's century of internecine warfare, so the CGT was willing to hold its fire against union competitors. The political ulterior motives of this were clear. Greater labor mobilization against the policies of the Gaullist administration would contribute to greater political support for the broad Left. By implication, however, the approach also led to much greater stress on more strictly trade unionist matters rather than overt political issues.

The CGT's timing was good. The new Gaullist regime, bent on rapid economic change and growth, had an authoritarian side in its approach to such matters—General de Gaulle had little fondness for "neocorporatism" and other forms of consulting with intermediary social groups—which was reflected in its monetary and fiscal policies (to limit inflation), its behavior as manager of France's vast public sector, and its antiunion admonitions to private-sector employers. Given practically full employment, pent-up demand, France's sudden explosion of consumerism in the 1960s, and the insecurities flowing from rapid economic change, the moment was propitious, even in the abstract, for the new stimulation to trade unionism that a much less sectarian CGT could provide. The CGT's luck extended even further, however. In the past its chosen target for seduction toward unity in action would have been the FO. And the FO, to which anticommunism was life-blood, was inured to this kind of flirtation. But by the early 1960s the playing field was changing, given the remarkable "deconfessionalization" and radicalization of the bulk of French Catholic unionism, eventuating in the formation of the Confédération Française et Démocratique du Travail (CFDT).

The CGT thus followed an analogous path to that of the PCF—rethinking, opening up, deemphasizing divisive international themes, and, most important, building on such things to reenergize the French labor movement in a broader sense. Thus the decade after the miners' strike of 1963 was one of the very rare moments when trade union pluralism worked for, rather than against, French unionism. In this period the leadership of Georges Séguy, Frachon's successor as secretary-general, was essential. The most important set of initiatives were contained in the unity-of-action pact with the CFDT, which was signed in 1964. The importance of this accord and the unified mobilization that followed, very often led by the CGT, in laying the foundations for the great strikes of May 1968 is all too often underplayed. Equally underestimated, in all contemporary and retrospective fantasies about students in 1968, was the essential role of the CGT in winning the substantial concessions for French workers that came out of "the events."

All was not sweetness and light, of course. The CGT's mobilization in this period was not without political objectives, albeit indirect and more tactical than strategic, which created an ambience of persistent prickliness between it and the CFDT. The CGT sought constantly to turn labor mobilization away from local issues toward large, public, and national demonstrations that might embarrass governments. The CFDT preferred decentralized, local mobilization and, in so doing, for a time promoted *autogestionnaire* (worker control) themes that annoyed the CGT no end (even though the CGT itself would adopt such themes later, after the CFDT had abandoned them).[18] Buried in the CGT's tactical predilections at this point was that fact that it could not shake out of traditional mobilizational habits, rather "Fordist"—that is, appropriate to the industrial unionism of the 1930s—and not terribly creative, despite a great deal of new thinking about creativity going on in the confederation, particularly in the cadres union (the UGICT) and in the Confederal Center for Research.[19]

It is also important to note here that this CGT shift toward France, away from the Cold War, and toward united action, away from go-it-alone competitiveness, also was accompanied by new questioning about the CGT's prior international outlooks. In August 1968 Louis Saillant, secretary-general of the WFTU, condemned the Warsaw Pact invasion of Czechoslovakia. (Ironically he then died of a heart attack before he could resign or be forced to so do. He was succeeded by Pierre Gensous, also of the CGT.) There was widespread discussion inside the confederation about the wisdom of actually leaving WFTU, as the Italians were preparing to do. At this point the CGT made a critical and fateful choice. Rather than leave the WFTU, it opted to try to use its considerable influence to *reform* it from within. Why this choice was made remains a mystery. We know that its most prominent public advocate was Henri Krasucki, who would later succeed Georges Séguy as CGT secretary-general, and that this succession involved something of an internal factional fight. To be sure, it was much easier to stay in the WFTU, both in terms of the internal dynamics of the CGT (particularly given the unreflective pro-Sovietism of most PCF members of the CGT Confederal Bureau, which replicated similar outlooks in the PCF leadership itself) and in terms of international continuity.[20] An educated guess about the underlying causes for the decision, however, would go as follows. Those who had a voice in the CGT were not completely agreed about what to do with the WFTU, but those favoring remaining inside were in the majority; because PCF and CGT leaders firmly believed, despite some awareness of existing problems, that the Brezhnevite reformulation of Soviet politics was positive and, more particularly, that Brezhnevite definitions of the international situation were correct. In these formulations the "Socialist" side in important contemporary Cold War matters (perceived, once again, to exist mainly outside the advanced "North") was essential in constraining American ambitions to subordinate the entire planet to their form of capitalist hegemony. Staying in the WFTU to "reform" it was thus staying on the correct side of history.

Whatever the reasons, the costs of such an approach were already evident at the time the choice was made and increased geometrically thereafter. Virtually everyone except those who made the CGT's decision knew that the members of the WFTU (mainly the Socialist bloc and pro-Soviet Third World) were almost all the antithesis of "free" trade unions and that the organization itself, if it had any useful purpose, was dedicated to advancing Soviet diplomatic goals. Thus staying in the WFTU meant announcing that the CGT either supported this kind of unionism or was too unaware of its surroundings to know that it was doing so. In either case, the CGT was setting itself up for great difficulties.

The deeper logic of this choice was that the CGT would be unable, and probably unwilling, to begin reconsidering its position on Europe. European integration continued to be considered as primarily an American-capitalist plot to be struggled against. This, in turn, was premised on the idea that the Socialist bloc would survive and thrive and that the Common Market, then in the throes of Eurosclerosis, would fail. Although this idea seemed plausible, it turned out to be completely mistaken. European integration would flourish while the Socialist bloc would fail. The position left the CGT with an anti-European nationalist line, which would later cause it to misunderstand the revitalization of European integration in the 1980s. It also placed the CGT at odds with virtually all trade unions in Europe itself. Finally, the pro-Soviet international position that underlay the position completely avoided recognizing clear signs of the decadence of "existing socialism."

LEGACIES AND DECLINE, 1978 TO 1991

What happened thereafter, through the end of existing socialism in the early 1990s, is somewhat murky in its processes but crystal clear in its meaning. The CGT got stuck. Its rethinking and reform disappeared in both national and international realms. At the same time massive political and social changes occurred both nationally and internationally. At the end of the process the CGT was in precipitous decline. The changes in the domestic environment around French unions—the Left's renunciation of its electoral commitments after 1981, the turn to deflation, restructuring and the use of renewed European integration as an instrument to impose neoliberal reforms on France—were huge and disorienting. All unions suffered accordingly.

The CGT suffered, and declined, relatively more, however. In the 1960s it was generally recognized to represent half of a unionized French labor force, upward of 20 percent of the labor force in general. By the mid-1980s the unionized labor force had been cut in half, to 10 percent, and the CGT had dropped to a position of rough equality with each of the other major components of the French union movement, the FO and the CFDT. French unions thus had entered a danger zone in general, but the CGT's fall was most striking of all.

The CGT's shifts away from rethinking and reform are easy to describe. In domestic terms the key to almost everything that the CGT did was undoubtedly what happened in the PCF. Domestically the PCF turned away from what one might call its united front–"Eurocommunist" line when it became aware that the Socialists were benefiting disproportionately from Union de la Gauche. Beginning in 1977 this involved a wrenching turnaround for the party, which made quite clear that Union de la Gauche, which was leading the PCF to decline, was probably a better strategy than any other that the party leadership could invent, which led to decline even more rapidly. In fact, the party leadership tried a number of different approaches. Most prominent were attempts to reestablish the PCF's "identity" and political distinctiveness, on the theory that the Socialists would fail to deliver on their promises (a safe bet), thereby increasing potential support for the Communists. Unfortunately, reasserting Communist identity often meant mindless and sectarian militancy rather than constructive new ideas, and this approach proved costly.

It is probable that a major determinant of these ineffective PCF strategic shifts was a pro-Brezhnevite analysis of the direction of international events, which turned out disastrously. The party correctly concluded at the end of the 1970s that the era of détente was ending and that the Cold War was heating up again. In response it doubled its efforts to support the Soviet side. Georges Marchais's famous formulation to the PCF's Twenty-fourth Congress in 1979 that "the balance sheet of existing socialism is globally positive" illustrated the dilemma. This assertion might incorrectly have been understood to mean that the Soviet experiment was a success, and it was used in this way to considerable effect by the PCF's opponents. In fact, its meaning was more subtle, or perhaps obscure. For some time the PCF had been criticizing the Soviet Union's lack of democracy, and it would continue to do so. At the same time, however, the "balance sheet" position evaluated the role of the Socialist bloc positively *in international affairs* as a counterweight to the Americans. The "bottom line" of the balance sheet position, fateful in its implications, was that *despite* serious deficiencies of existing socialism, particularly in the realm of democracy, its positions had to be defended because of the return of Cold War conditions.

The PCF is not directly our business here, but given the "prominence" of Communist leaders in the CGT, these options proved terribly important for it. Suffice it to say what everyone knows, that the Marchais-induced line shift after 1977 failed to block Mitterrand's success in 1981. Its influence over the CGT, however, led to a dramatic turnaway from efforts at reform after the CGT's Fortieth Congress in 1978, perhaps the most open and promising in the CGT's postwar history. Unity in action with the CFDT broke down into vituperation, and the worst sides of French competitive union pluralism reemerged. Henceforth virtually every gesture by any one union organization would be followed by a competitive countergesture by the others in flagrant disregard of the broader needs of French unionism as a whole.

The CGT played this game with as much, if not more, enthusiasm than its competitors. At a time of rising unemployment and critical political change when the French union movement was already in a down cycle, the results were dismal. While this approach has characterized French unionism for nearly two decades now, a brief interlude of calm occurred during the first three years of the Mitterrand administration after 1981. The calm did French unions and the CGT very little good, however, because following the

PCF's hat-in-hands entry into Leftist governments (after having excoriated the Socialists and Mitterrand in every conceivable way between 1977 and 1981), the CGT became something of a hostage to the Socialists until 1984, when the Communists left government.

Just as important, from 1978 onward the party, and to a lesser extent the CGT, were the sites of incessant internal struggles over lines and positions of power in which connections with the real world of politics and people were very often lost. The PCF's messages were almost always unclear, and when they occasionally and momentarily became clear they were sectarian. In international terms, the PCF consistently misread the reemergence of the Cold War in the 1980s, as we have underlined. This may have been excusable, but it involved the party in an energetic defense of a set of decadent, authoritarian regimes that were on their last legs—from supporting the repression of Solidarity in Poland to Marchais's brilliant political choice to attend the Romanian party congress in December 1989, a few days before Nicolae Ceaucescu fell.[21]

Marchais's pregnant phrase about the positive "balance sheet" of existing socialism had catastrophic consequences for the PCF and the CGT. In a little over a decade the party liquidated most of the credibility and heritage of half a century; the CGT's decline was commensurate. Today's conventional wisdom views this demise as inevitable: Communism was in decline everywhere and the PCF was certain to follow. While this analysis has merit, in the case of the PCF and the CGT inept strategic choices also must be added to the explanation. Marchais and his team will bear a great deal of responsibility. French communism was as much a victim of their political brutality and lack of vision as it was of international causes. The stewardship of Henri Krasucki over the CGT—from 1981 to the early 1990s—deserves parallel blame.

The CGT's internationalism is our subject, of course, even if its domestic and international positions were, during this pivotal period, so closely interconnected and tied to the organizational politics of the confederation as to be difficult to untangle. Seen from a distance, it looks as if the CGT followed the PCF *in general,* but with a slightly greater openness to experimentation. Already during the Union de la Gauche period the CGT's position had begun to decline from its high point in the mid-1960s. The fact of decline meant, however, that there was a serious contradiction between repoliticizing union action to accentuate the CGT's specificities after 1977 (that is, following the PCF away from Left unity) and struggling against further decline. The breakdown of unity in action with the CFDT and the reemergence of virulent competitive pluralism among French union organizations, connected with repoliticization, were thus tragic turns.

The important point is that the international choices that the CGT had made in the 1970s were hardened in this new period. The choices—to stay in WFTU, allegedly to reform it from within, and to continue opposing European integration—both proved disastrously inappropriate. They pushed the CGT into an international wilderness while also undermining its domestic positions. Choosing the WFTU had been the easier thing for the CGT to do, of course. Despite the WFTU's liabilities it was a traditional affiliation, and at least since the 1940s the CGT's principal international contacts had been with the unions of the Socialist bloc. Moreover, there may well have been some prospects for internal WFTU reform in the mid-1970s, although we await much more evidence and analysis before asserting this with confidence. We know that the CGT did act publicly within the WFTU for reform, and we have been told that it did so even more in private. Henri Krasucki, certainly someone of influence, even became vice president in 1986. Finally, the WFTU had important affiliations with important Third World union movements. This dimension of CGT internationalism, alignment with Third Worldism, deserves to be taken seriously.

The collapse of the Socialist bloc after 1989 nonetheless demonstrated that the CGT had bet on the wrong horse. Taking the easiest course was a mistake, even with the revived Cold War in the 1980s. The domestic costs of this choice are worth underlining. The CGT's attitudes about Poland in 1980–1981, although not as stridently anti-Solidarity as those of the PCF, provide a very good illustration. Whatever the realpolitic behind the CGT's de facto support for the regime and General Wojclech Jaruzelski against Lech Walesa and the renascent autonomous Polish labor movement, it was grotesque to see a major Western labor organization helping an authoritarian government in its efforts to squash a genuine mobilization of Polish workers. By so doing the CGT thereafter left the high ground on the issue in France to the CFDT. The CGT's de facto alignment with existing socialism in the 1980s gave its organizational rivals a large club with which to beat the CGT into the ground. The larger mystery of why—even after the collapse of existing socialism in 1989—the CGT was so slow to find its way out of the WFTU orbit remains. A low point was reached in the early 1990s, after existing socialism had collapsed, when it was about to find itself in the privileged company of the Iraqi and Cuban union movements.

The CGT's choice in the 1980s not to rethink its attitude toward Europe complemented its stance toward the WFTU. In the mid-1970s making a strategic bet on a posture of complete opposition to European integration might have seemed reasonable. With Europe mired in post–oil shock crises, other union movements might have withdrawn their lukewarm allegiance to Europe. The European Community might even have collapsed. In the early 1980s, the period of deep Eurosclerosis, opposing European integration was a logical complement to opposing the new Cold War coming from the United States. We all know what then happened, however. European integration revived in the mid-1980s with the program to complete the Single Market.

What followed made obvious the foolishness of the CGT's choices in the 1970s and 1980s. The EC was always a reality whose permanence the CGT's positions denied. The renewal of European integration in the 1980s, by strengthening the EC immeasurably, ought to have underlined the absurdity of these positions. The EC by then had become a unique integrated regional economic bloc whose basic irreversibility was evident to virtually everyone except the CGT (and PCF). However one felt about this, denouncing it altogether was worse than baying at the moon. What labor, particularly French labor, needed were intelligent ways to mobilize that might make the European Community less neoliberal and more "social." The CGT simply opted out of responding to these needs.

There is much more to the European Community–European Union story, however, than the consolidation of a unique regional bloc. Economic integration has had important spillover effects on European trade unionism, effects from which the CGT has excluded itself completely. The Delors Commission, at least, tried to promote their versions of "social Europe" through the social charter and other initiatives. These initiatives can be evaluated in a number of different ways, but it is clear that they do not go very far. At best they are precedents, although they are real ones—in the areas, for example, of European health and safety legislation, the structural funds, and the European Works Committees. The important thing is that social Europe is on everyone's real agenda. There is no plausible action agenda for any European union simply to reject European integration. The urgent tasks involve humanizing and regulating it.

The evolution of Europe since the mid-1980s also has granted considerable new life to European-level trade unionism through the European Trade Union Confederation (CES) and through the sectoral European Industry Committees. The CES is in large part a creation of the Delors Commission as well as the CFDT, the German Union Confederation (DGB), and more recently the British Trade Union Congress (TUC). This achievement serves only to illustrate what can happen in the absence of the CGT, and at its expense. For one thing, the CGT has left to others the credit for laying the foundation stones of what may well become an important dimension of a European-level industrial relations system. Just as important, to this day its enemies have used the CGT's alignment with the WFTU and its complete rejection of European integration to prevent its entrance into ETUC. The CGT has the dubious distinction of being the only Western European union movement of consequence not to belong. And whatever its limitations, and it has many, the ETUC has become the legitimate and active Euro-level organization of Europe's different national labor movements. The CGT can no longer afford to be outside it.

This strategic blunder had deeper implications. By simply rejecting European integration without reflecting on its inner logics, the CGT rendered its own appeal almost completely national, if not nationalist. At a time when one of European trade unionism's fundamental tasks is to figure out a division of labor between what can be done at the national level and what needs to be done at the EC/EU level, the CGT essentially avoided serious thought about either problem. It is no longer feasible to claim, as the CGT has tended to do, that it is still possible for national social and political forces to regulate and control such vital economic and social parameters as employment levels, monetary policy, the structure of investment and the nature of the nation's economic "mix." While proponents of the European Union may exaggerate the extent and meaning of "globalization" for their own purposes, to proclaim, as the CGT almost always has done, that it is possible to revert to the high degrees of national economic and industrial policy autonomy that may have prevailed decades ago is quite absurd. The central problem for unions—all unions—in the current period is to use resources to make regulatory and market areas coincide in a transnationalizing world, at least not to deny that there are any real logics to transnationalization. With the European Union there exist some institutional possibilities for establishing regulatory frameworks beyond the nation-state. Unremitting economic nationalism, on the other hand, will play into the hands of the kinds of dangerously illiberal national populism that one sees cropping up virtually everywhere.

CONCLUSIONS: THE POSITION OF ALL THE DANGERS

We thus have come full circle. The CGT began in the 1920s as the CGTU with what it claimed to be a superior form of internationalism, which it justified because other union movements had de facto abandoned any real internationalism. Today, because its most recent internationalist claims are largely devoid of serious content, the CGT looks, from the outside, to be more nationalist than anyone else. What are the CGT's choices, and tasks, at this point?

It must take seriously, perhaps for the first time, the phenomena of European integration. Whatever one makes of European economic integration—and from a trade union point of view the balance sheet is far from positive—Europe will be the CGT's major theater of action beyond France itself over the medium term. Existing socialism is dead and, moreover, however much it suffered at the hands of militant Western opposition, it was a failure in its own terms. Moreover, the whole brand of progressivism that was associated with it is both a fading phenomenon and a losing bet. The CGT can make no significant future by maintaining fictions about the past.

What will it mean to take Europe seriously as a theater of trade union action? It does not mean, first of all, a beatific acceptance of the logics of integration as presently set out. Voices like that of the CGT could weigh in significantly on the side of opposition to such inventions like the Maastricht convergence criteria. But to be credible in these debates, one has to have European legitimacy, which involves some general acceptance of the realities of Europe. The matter of the ETUC is crucial. The CGT *must* find its way into the ETUC; it has little choice here. Indeed, if this does not happen soon, the CGT will find itself in the ironic position of being outside an organization that some of its erstwhile Eastern European WFTU colleagues already have joined. Moreover, if the CGT does not find its way in, soon it could well be excluded for good. The international isolation of the CGT is too inviting a matter to escape the attention of the CFDT and the FO, which could use this isolation effectively against CGT at home.

The official ETUC line on CGT membership has two dimensions. The CGT should first fully renounce WFTU and WFTU-ist progressivism. Second, it has to make a serious and sincere change of its positions on Europe. The CGT is at a fundamental crossroads. It must change on international matters or pay a very large price. The changes demanded need not be experienced as renunciations. Indeed they should be seen as genuine opportunities. Recognizing Europe as an important theater for CGT action need not mean recognizing Europe *as it stands*. Europe clearly needs a more thoughtful and effective conscience defending European workers. The ETUC, which itself seems to be caught in a strategic logic of advocating the future of European integration in almost the same terms as EU heads of state and government, in particular on the issues of Economic and Monetary Union, needs just the kind of push the CGT could provide. Were it to proceed intelligently, the CGT might even find allies in the task of struggling for a European model of society marked by the conscious political assumption of social solidarity to "frame" the market.

Recognizing Europe as a significant theater for action should not involve any renunciation of the quest for national and local control over market workings. There is no reason whatever to believe that choices are only between advocating autarky and complete deregulation, even if at times current debates imply this. Since the collapse of the neocorporatist dreams of the postwar boom, redefining what can be done on the national and local level has become an open task. Once this task has been faced, then deciding what needs to be done transnationally will be easier. Moreover, none of this need involve renouncing concern with the development of north-south inequalities. One of the central tasks of trade union internationalism in the future should indeed be the development of new ideas and practices to raise the labor standards and living standards of workers outside the triad orbit. The CGT could play an important role here.

There are solid reasons for thinking that the CGT now may be prepared to confront these vital problems of recentering its international outlooks. First of all, even those most refractory to contemporary realities have had— often belatedly—to recognize that the CGT's older international positions no longer make sense. There is no "existing socialism" to defend anymore, anyone who today would argue that its "balance sheet" is positive would be laughed at, and, finally, the WFTU is a completely empty shell. There is, happily, some evidence that all this has been understood since Louis Vian-net's assumption of leadership in 1992. Rupture with the WFTU finally oc-curred in 1995–1996. There have been demonstrations of considerable new energy, mainly creative, applied to international matters inside the confed-eration. Recognizing the European Union, which may be under way, could quickly bring the CGT up to speed about the real trade union problems in a globalizing capitalism and help it to enter the ETUC. Finally, the Cold War is genuinely over. There is no longer any reasonable (or unreasonable, for that matter) international political justification for other unions to avoid cooperating more with the CGT.

These positive movements are promising. But the changes the CGT makes have to be real, not simply cosmetic. And the opportunity for mak-ing such convincing changes may not last forever. The major dangers in the situation today come both from inside and outside the CGT. As anyone who has observed organizational biographies knows, organizational reflexes and habits die hard. The CGT has to reflect creatively and act on such reflections very quickly. This should involve a wide range of theoretical, strategic, and tactical innovations on both international and national matters. Yet there is no reason to think that the CGT is any better prepared for rapid change in outlook and practice than any other organization. Moreover, in the organi-zational realm, it is probably true that trade unions, which are profoundly reactive, change only when the pressures to do so become practically irre-sistible. Inertia is easier than change for them otherwise. Finally, the CGT has long been structured so that the defense of political traditions of all kinds are an easy vocabulary for gaining and maintaining power. Thus it is probably easier to veto and/or frustrate the kinds of innovations that are nec-essary than to promote them.

There are many reasons to be pessimistic, therefore, and they are rein-forced by the broader mechanisms of competitive pluralism in the French union movement. The destructive game of beggar-thy-union neighbor seems alive and well in France. Acting to change the rules of the game and, if possible, to end it altogether should be the major task of all French unions, before it is too late. But it should be the CGT's task above all.

NOTES

1. Donald Sassoon's magnificent *One Hundred Years of Socialism* (London: I. B. Tauris, 1996), without doubt the best comparative history of labor and socialism in the twentieth century that has been written to date, demonstrates this beyond controversy.

2. The use of "CGT" over the long period we are reviewing—1921 to 1996—is fraught with difficulty. Our real concern is with the CGTU-communisant faction, which was in fact in and out of the CGT until 1945 or so, when it managed to take control of the name and organization.

3. The WFTU, which ultimately located in Prague, was led most often by a French general secretary, beginning with Louis Saillant, a CGTer who was its first leader.

4. I have written about this relationship in the past in George Ross, *Workers and Communists in France* (Berkeley: University of California Press, 1982).

5. The best source on this critical moment remains the late Annie Kriegel's *Aux Origines du communisme français,* 2 vols. (Paris: Mouton, 1964).

6. As Martin Schain and others correctly point out, this success was multidimensional. The secret of PCF organizing was that it produced dedicated and skilled operatives who were able to exploit the failures of other organizations as France rapidly modernized. Thus the party created geographical *bastions* that became the backbone of its local political strength in areas like the new suburbs around Paris and among immigrants which were neglected by the Socialists and others. See Tyler Stovall, *The Rise of the Paris Redbelt* (Berkeley: University of California, 1990), and Martin Schain, *French Communism and Local Power* (New York: St. Martin's Press, 1985).

7. This period saw the emergence of the formidably skillful Benoît Frachon as leader of the CGTU and then of the ex-CGTU faction in the briefly reunified CGT. Frachon, who never lost his very French anarcho-syndicalism and his concern with the need to maintain a real union base, was a good fit with the CGTU's international mission. He was conscious of the need for the CGT to maintain relative autonomy from more sectarian international lines. Frachon was also tough and independent enough to stand up to the PCF leadership on unionist grounds while also maintaining his position as a key party leader himself. He was critical in the survival of the CGT during the Cold War. There is no definitive biography of Frachon, but Jacques Girault's *Benoît Frachon: Communiste et Syndicaliste* (Paris: Presses de la Fondation Nationale des Sciences Politiques, 1989), is a useful source.

8. Antoine Prost's book *La CGT à l'époque du Front Populaire* (Paris: Armand Colin, 1964), remains the best analysis of this.

9. The PCF suffered similarly from this.

10. On this period consult Annie Lacroix-Riz, *La CGT de la Libération à la scission: de 1944–1947* (Paris: Editions Sociales, 1983); also Ross, *Workers and Communists,* chap. 2.

11. The FEN's autonomous existence thus came to be characterized by constant conflict among different internal tendencies, including one closely tied to

the PCF. This arrangement turned out to work reasonably well until the 1980s when the FEN, like the rest of French unionism, fell into crisis.

12. See René Mouriaux's essays in Guillaume Devin, ed., *Le Syndicalisme, Dimensions Internationales* (La Garenne-Colombes, France: Editions Européennes-Erasme, 1990).

13. For a clear view, see Irwin Wall, *French Communism in the Era of Stalin* (Westport, CT: Greenwood Press, 1983).

14. For data gathered at the time, see Jean-Louis Guglielmi and Michelle Perrot, *Salaires et revendications sociales en France, 1944–1952* (Paris: Centre d'Etudes Economiques, 1953).

15. The PCF had decided that the danger in France was a rebirth of Fascism, leading the CGT in February 1952 to mobilize around the theme "le fascisme ne passera pas." The problem was that very few people beyond PCF insiders shared this judgment. The "Ridgeway" moment, in which the CGT called strikes to support a PCF action, led to one death and nearly 1,000 arrests.

16. The author heard this secondhand on several occasions in interviews with CGT leaders in the 1970s.

17. One should not exaggerate the CGIL's success. Still, both the PCI and the CGIL took much greater distance from Soviet operations beginning early after the war. This created a "path dependency" that, if it did not modernize either organization sufficiently rapidly, allowed them to play in their national arenas much more successfully. The evidence is clear. The PCI is now the PDS, social democratized and a key factor in Italian politics, while the CGIL is still the major union confederation in Italy.

18. All of this is shrewdly analyzed in Guy Groux and René Mouriaux, *La C.F.D.T.* (Paris: Economica, 1989). See also W. Rand Smith, *Crisis in the French Labor Movement* (New York: St. Martin's Press, 1987). Hervé Hamon and Patrick Rotman's *La Deuxième Gauche* (Paris: Ramsay, 1982) and Pierre Rosanvallon's *L'Age de l'autogestion* (Paris: Seuil, 1976) give sympathetic accounts of the CFDT's doctrinal changes.

19. For greater detail, see Ross, *Workers and Communists,* chaps. 6 and 7.

20. The standard response of Georges Marchais, who dominated the PCF ever more in these years, to critics of the party's continued friendship with the Soviets was to announce that it was much more effective to work "from the inside" to correct the lack of democracy in the Soviet system and, more specifically, to argue the causes of dissidents and greater freedom. Whether much of this kind of "working" actually happened or whether the line was simply a way of shutting up annoying people is not clear.

21. The grotesque nature of this occasion is hard to overemphasize. Recently it has been revealed that the *conducator,* the soon to be deposed and executed Ceaucescu, made all Romanian speakers to this congress record their speeches prior to the congress itself and then, on the congress floor, lip-synch their recorded words. The great leader clearly did not like surprises.

CHAPTER FOURTEEN

The New International Trade Unionism

Jean-Pierre Page

After the events of November and December 1995, will social issues only be an alibi, or a challenge that must be faced? This is the question raised by an unprecedented and original movement that sparked considerable discussion and comment. It was part of a long process of social struggle in France, throughout Europe, and all over the world. In varying ways, all the social, economic, and political players were forced to respond, including the trade union movement whose options, practices, and behavior were strongly challenged, forcing it to make its position clear. Although initially expressed very strongly in the national context, this requirement has taken on an increasingly European and international dimension.

The struggles in France were described immediately as the first major social movement against the Maastricht Treaty and the ultra-liberal criteria of globalization. Although economic, scientific, and cultural internationalization has become a manifest reality, the worldwide social situation has become critical, and many observers rightly speak of the risk of explosion. We cannot agree, however, with those who say that such an explosion is unavoidable. The strength of the social movement in 1995 resulted from a refusal to accept or listen any longer to the siren voices calling for "necessary adaptation." Using the only weapons available to employees, the movement helped to achieve important results concerning retirement pensions, public services, wages, employment, and freedom.

This movement achieved autonomy and became aware of its strength in its day-to-day action, thus helping to modify the existing "order," and will go down in history as a major factor in revealing changes, particularly the democratic requirements for employees to have their say, to be listened to, and to be respected.

Just a few years after the fall of the Berlin Wall, in the heart of a major industrialized country, this unprecedented social movement gave new credibility to the virtues of collective action, the need for trade union membership, solidarity, and unity. As well as winning concessions, it shook the determination of the "elites," whether in Paris, Brussels, or Washington. It attracted considerable interest, sympathy, and support in French public opinion, and particularly among employees in Europe, but also internationally, notably in the United States. The support expressed by several federations in the AFL-CIO as well as the declarations by AFL-CIO President John Sweeney, the leaders of the largest German and Italian trade union confederations, and many others, are proof of this. In Belgium, striking workers referred explicitly to the action by their French comrades, sharing their intention to challenge Maastricht and neoliberalism.

Obviously we should beware of overestimating the significance of this event. But the considerable anxiety expressed by the government, French and European employers, the European Commission in Brussels, the financial markets, and even German Chancellor Helmut Kohl show the extent of what is at stake. The international press gave considerable prominence to this anxiety. On all sides, Jacques Chirac and Alain Juppé were encouraged not to yield in the name of the sacrosanct law of the convergence criteria. This was because, for their promoters, the defeat of the plan to reform the French social protection system meant that it would no longer be possible to meet the conditions for the establishment of the single currency. But it was also because such a resounding success for French employees probably would have social and political consequences throughout the European Union. Many employees in Europe and throughout the world understood this, and events since have shown them to be right.

It is interesting to note that, when the government gave in on the question of taxing family benefits, strong partisans of the single currency such as Jean Gandois or Jacques Delors also began to drift with the tide of Euroskepticism. This was clearly one of the consequences of the social movement. Michel Camdessus, director of the International Monetary Fund, may have proclaimed that there is no reason to panic, but one thing was clear, as many observers agreed: There is growing awareness of the fact that the form the construction of the European Union has taken is not an inevitable part of our time but a choice of the forces of neoliberalism that is in no way ineluctable. In this sense, the progress of united trade union action in France involving the CGT, Force Ouvrière, the FSU (independent trade unions), and parts of the CFDT, combined with action coordinated at the European level for the intergovernmental conference in Turin, is of considerable significance. The same applies to the success of the trade union day of action and protest organized on June 25, 1996, to mark the Group of Seven summit in Lyons. Similarly, recent declarations by distinguished intellectuals are conclusive evidence of a maturing process as well as an important stimulant for intellectual debate in France, Europe, and worldwide.

The fact that this need for larger-scale convergence has progressed is worthy of note. Obviously, this observation does not mean that an irresistible process has begun. By its very nature, the development of the social movement is much more complex, particularly when the movement is attempting to move to the European or worldwide level, but such a move remains urgent. The great merit of the action in December 1995 is to have contributed to its expression.

Although the specific French aspects obviously should not be ignored, it is difficult not to see more general significance: A new cycle of social and political struggles involving massive multiform refusal of neoliberalism is apparently beginning in Europe and worldwide.

Capitalism is a worldwide system, as is the ultra-liberal offensive. It is therefore essential to act in concrete terms to try to modify the balance of power. It is clear that the possibilities vary from one country to the next. They are the result of extremely diverse situations that determine, particularly in trade union terms, identities, conceptions, and choices. But because the structural adjustment plans in the southern hemisphere and the plans for convergence in the northern hemisphere are the product of the same logic, producing the same results and the same social disintegration, there is an objective basis on which we can and indeed must develop peoples' and employees' internationalism against the internationalism of capitalism.

As the economist Samir Amin has pointed out, the challenge today involves reconciling the interdependence that this globalization implies and the inequalities of power in the face of this globalization which characterize the social partners situated in different regions and economic positions. There will be no solution to the crisis without strengthening the position of the weak segments of the system—groups in the peripheral zones and subordinate social classes in all the central and peripheral countries—which means leaving global colonialism and the neoliberal myths behind.

These are the major principles on which we can base our thinking to help to develop a humanist, universalist counterplan that attempts to respect diversity. Such a view helps to boost confidence and also encourages the development of a type of union cooperation that is different from what has prevailed up to now. Obviously, there are obstacles and delays that result essentially from a short-sighted, partisan approach to international trade union relations. There is still a strong tendency in the international trade union movement to base reactions on received wisdom and exclusion, tendencies that paralyze the spirit of initiative and go against any form of innovation.

What are the reasons for this? The fundamental reason is that the international trade union movement has suffered historically from significant divisions, that often have led it to forget the very reason for its existence! These divisions were structured around two major ideological poles, which led people on the two sides of the divide to support the strategy of the two blocs. It must be conceded that the CGT shared this approach, as evidenced by its membership in the WFTU—although it made clear from 1979 onward its disagreements with an organization of which it had been a founding member 50 years before. However, despite the withdrawal in 1978 of Pierre Gensous from his post as general secretary of the WFTU, in the 1980s the CGT once again became involved in this organization whose whole approach and orientation continued to take its inspiration from a bipolar model.

This organization of the world trade union movement around two antagonistic options in the context of the Cold War structured its behavior, practices, and thinking. Despite all the evidence, at a time when the need for solidarity was growing in the context of globalization and the responsibilities of the world labor movement were more crucial than ever in historic terms, the International Confederation of Free Trade Unions (ICFTU) and the WFTU continued to defend what had been the basis of their legitimacy for half a century. Today this obstinacy affects the very concept of their usefulness and reduces their credibility. Their recent congresses are evidence of this.

The question of the overall approach to social action leads us to take a new look at Europe and this continent that was the cradle of the trade union movement. Will Europe help to meet the need for renewal since it expresses both the permanence of trade union traditions and a high level of social protection obtained through struggle? The establishment of the European Trade Union Confederation (ETUC) is without any doubt a positive factor since it groups almost all Europe's trade unions, even if the CGT continues anachronistically to be excluded from it. However, since 1995, considerable progress has been made towards CGT affiliation, which benefits from near-unanimous support from the European trade union national centers. The only obstacle to CGT membership left to overcome is the reality of the division of the French labor movement.

The ETUC had major plans and ambitions for European construction. The fall of the Berlin Wall and the acceleration of the implementation of the single currency at the core of the logic of Maastricht significantly modified the problem. What it cruelly lacks is the affirmation of a more offensive, unitary spirit of initiative, leaving partisan exclusion behind and aiming to bring people together.

The CGT must contribute to achieving this goal. After much debate and as a result of the changes in its conception of trade union activity in Europe and worldwide, the CGT is more active in consultative European institutions as well as in more concrete bilateral and multilateral activity. When it took the decision, ratified by its congress at the end of 1995, to disaffiliate from the WFTU, the CGT chose to work for the construction of a new trade union internationalism. Although this decision between its forty-fourth and forty-fifth congresses sparked lively debate, since it was a question of its history and identity, the CGT can now take initiatives together with other trade union forces.

Like every organization, the CGT is faced with the challenge of how to act in concrete ways. Looking beyond set formulas, the urgent need to renew the international trade union movement requires an approach that is more global, more concrete, more independent, more flexible, and more targeted on bringing people together.

A MORE CONCRETE APPROACH

A more concrete approach is necessary, particularly at the level of the industrial groups and transnational companies. They play a dominant role in the remodeling of the world, calling into question the coherence of its economies and threatening the very principles of bilateral and multilateral cooperation. After all, do not the four most powerful multinationals possess resources greater than the gross national product of a country like China?

In such a situation, the codes of conduct recently set up, notably by the United Nations, have been totally ineffectual. Today the damage reflects the absence of a sufficient counterweight. The New Order has provided a historic opportunity for the transnationals to expand without any constraints, threatening the sovereignty of nations, freedom of choice, human rights, and fundamental liberties. Crushing responsibility for nondevelopment has been assumed by the transnational companies, industrialized states, and international financial institutions who have chosen to support this predatory strategy. The phenomenon of relocation is not new, but it has accelerated with globalization. Here too the policy of forcing employees to compete with one another has become a formidable weapon in a labor market that is increasingly global. According to a recent survey involving 260 leaders of transnational companies, infrastructure, distribution, and telecommunications sectors, all activities that require considerable skills, are set to become the priority areas for investment by transnationals in the next few years. The main reason for such relocation of activity lies in the possibility of imposing low wages and reducing social rights to their lowest possible level, which affects the managerial staff and political and social stability.

Relocation also enables effective blackmail to put pressure on labor costs. Relocation is thus part of a worldwide offensive, in both the north and the south, against labor costs (mainly wages). Why not therefore demand the right to intervene in companies' affairs and act in favor of innovation in international social legislation, so that we dispose of instruments to force multinational companies and even countries to toe the line? If companies relocate their activity to countries with very low wages, why not tax their reimportations in proportion to the extra profits made by overexploiting the countries in question? The product of this tax then could be used to aid the development of these countries.

Furthermore, the need to extend and apply trade union rights and liberties, the right to meet periodically, the obligation to provide information on the groups' strategies, the formulation of opinions, and the assistance of experts are now objectives that would give the trade union movement concrete involvement in the choices and decisions, so that an appropriate framework for negotiation could be set up. When Michelin bought Uniroyal or when France Telecom took a 20 percent stake in Sprint, the employees and trade unions were not consulted in any way. The question is worth raising, particularly when groups operate with a total lack of transparency. The experiment already begun in European Works Councils can be extended, strengthened, and developed to cover the whole of Europe, particularly with the prospect of enlargement, but also internationally.

And what about a social clause that would guarantee union rights, the abandonment of prison work, and the prohibition of child labor? These apparently praiseworthy preoccupations sometimes hide a questionable view of north/south relations. Can trade be the preferential way to advance human rights, particularly when it is controlled internationally by an organization (the World Trade Organization) whose operation and practices are far from democratic? In fact, we risk seeing the unilateral imposition of conceptions internationally.

We also risk following a neoliberal conception of societies where universal rights are reduced to a few principles that abandon a universal conception of social right for all peoples; we risk linking social rights too closely to business activity, excluding whole continents such as Africa from the development of human rights because investors cannot see any prospect of profit in it. We risk favoring even further domination by the multinationals.

We should therefore not forget the dangers to universal rights in international labor law in which the prospect of a social clause is reduced to a basic minimum. This would represent using the law as a selective, discriminatory tool of the commercial policies of the countries in the north against those of the south. Do we not really need a wide-reaching debate on international social rules?

This more concrete approach also must be reevaluated in regional terms, including the regional institutions set up in the context of globalization. It is a fact, for example, that the European trade union organizations are finding it difficult to draw up a strategy concerning the defense of their demands and the means of achieving them or contributing to working out alternative proposals. This fact affects the credibility of the European trade union movement. It is obvious that an unequal balance of power means that the only harmonization currently perceptible involves evening everything out at the lowest possible level. Although the details remain to be worked out, the emergence of the concept of a Social Europe should represent a basis for the progress of trade union demands, particularly those for full employment, the reduction of working time, training, and the extension of new rights and liberties favoring intervention by employees and unions in company affairs.

Doing so means examining the concrete consequences, going beyond a simple statement of the situation, and doing so together, by means of a trade unionism that brings people together. From this point of view, the ETUC can contribute to the renewal of the trade union movement, by proving that all the trade union organizations can come together in a single European organization, whatever their approaches or conceptions, with the sole aim of defending employees' interests effectively.

Current events confirm this necessity, particularly in the public services, which face the deregulation that some wish to impose in the name of Europe and the single currency. It is also true of the choices concerning social protection and full employment. More generally, the trade union movement's approach to the regional problems must take into account all the regional developments, such as the vast free-trade zones that have been set up throughout the world. Designed in terms of domination, they go against any sort of cooperation. This is true of the European Union's relations with the countries of Central and Eastern Europe, as with the countries around the Mediterranean and with regional trade associations throughout the world.

The orientations of the Euro-Mediterranean partnership, for example, are troublesome because they obey the principles of competition and aim more for a southward extension of the European market than genuine codevelopment. Trade unions can organize wide cooperation in terms of action and can contribute to the search for proposals to support other types of cooperation between rich and poor countries by spreading the idea of codevelopment.

A current demand involves cancellation of the debt and redefining a policy on the prices of raw materials as well as acting to increase public development aid and to spread the idea of dissuasive taxation of financial movements. World trade may represent $3 trillion a year, but the volume of international floating capital movements is 30 times greater.

Last, we need more concrete action to impose genuine reforms on international institutions based on the demand for transparency and democracy, and for the promotion of new forms of consultation. This is particularly true when considering the evolution of an institution like the International Labor Organization (ILO), its capabilities and the means of continuing the elaboration of the norms and conventions that are so essential nowadays. The reconsideration of the role of the United Nations' Economic and Social Council or the renovation of the institutions resulting from the Bretton Woods system, such as the International Monetary Fund, requires concrete thinking, particularly now, when structural adjustments and shock therapies are spreading. The G7 conference of heads of state that was held at Lyons in 1996 had full employment on its agenda. For whose benefit were they discussing it, and to do what? That is the question.

To back up the social struggles and advance along the road opened up by the Copenhagen world trade union forum, which brought together all the world's trade union organizations for the first time in 50 years, we should aim to cooperate at the international level in all appropriate forms: contributing to the elaboration of alternatives in favor of full employment for all in a context of north/south co-development and active intervention in cooperation with all those who act against neoliberalism.

A MORE FLEXIBLE APPROACH

I have written about concrete intervention based on real needs, from the workplace right up to international level. This also means that the trade union movement must follow a more militant, better-designed, and more flexible approach in its intervention.

More than new structures, what have to be constructed are forms of organization that are more in tune with reality and the real experience of employees. This different approach must aim to bring together a wider range of people: not just employees protected by collective statutory guarantees, but the vast mass of those who experience exclusion, unemployment, job insecurity, and the various types of temporary, informal work, or teleworking, where the absence of social regulation is the rule.

Thus the trade union movement faces a formidable challenge, one that requires a genuine change of behavior. Such a change is crucial, since its credibility is at stake. To make the change, it must shrug off the forms of institutionalization and bureaucracy that are so often perceived as external to the preoccupations of employees. The essential thing is to establish a more direct relationship with members and nonmembers. The trade union movement is having to face globalization in a troublesome state of weakness. No organization is spared, and no one can claim to be capable of facing this challenge alone. This is one of the paradoxes facing the trade union movement. Indeed, since the neoliberal offensive has never been so brutal, the need for solidarity has never been so great.

By being more concrete, militant, and flexible in its forms of intervention and organization, the international trade union movement must leave behind the culture of the Cold War and siege mentalities.

Partisan prejudices, rivalries, and political or ideological postulates have all become anachronisms in view of trade union needs, questions, and, above all, responsibilities. For a trade union movement bringing people together on an international scale, taking into account and respecting their multiple differences, to boost effectiveness by a unitary approach is without any doubt one of the ways of rebuilding its current reduced credibility. The international trade union movement must be capable of fighting for all employees, whatever their affiliation or options.

Today almost 50 percent of the world's trade union organizations are not affiliated to international organizations. This situation is damaging and an additional handicap, and it is a major question that the affiliated trade union movement has to address. The stakes are important. The CGT is not against the idea of joining an international organization. But it does not want to be affiliated just for the sake of it; it wants its international activity to be genuinely useful.

One of the reasons for the current wait-and-see policy and paralysis of the international trade union organizations is that they have failed to respond to such requirements. Having lost what they considered the basis for their legitimacy—a legitimacy that often had little to do with trade union preoccupations—the international organizations now urgently need to realign their activity on the sole basis of the needs and interests of employees faced with the effects of globalization. To do so, they must leave behind strategies artificially mirroring the policies of blocs, parties or institutions.

To be truly free, the international trade union movement has no alternative but to strengthen its capability to shape the orientations it intends to follow. It also must work out an approach more in tune with the movements taking place in modern societies and not be afraid to confront problems where the interests of employees are at stake, both in companies and in the wider community. This is notably the case with the environment and action against all forms of discrimination, particularly against women and migrant populations.

After the collapse of the Soviet Union and the failure of a doctrine that trade unions should submit to the party's leading role in the countries of Central and Eastern Europe, paralysis and incompetence have continued to affect the trade union movement. This, despite a high level of unionization. The trade union movement still faces an urgent need to develop its own specific conception.

Although the trade unions of Central and Eastern Europe have proven to be giants with feet of clay, social democratic trade union organizations, which for years based their strategy on close collaboration with the social democratic parties in power, are also facing crises and social regression.

The spread of Euroskepticism, particularly in the Scandinavian countries, and the contradictions that this has caused in trade unions between the grass-roots membership and the leadership is significant in this context. How can we ignore, for example, the lively debates inside the Spanish General Union of Workers (UGT) concerning the Spanish Socialist Party, or those in Britain, where many trade union activists have expressed doubts about the Trade Union Congress' (TUC) close ties with the Labour Party?

Something similar is happening in the United States, as shown by the recent evolution of the AFL-CIO. The need to pursue a more autonomous approach, to clarify relations with the Democratic Party, and even to seek other alternatives are all involved in this trend. This tendency is likely to grow in the light of grass-roots experience. History has proven that capitalism has, at certain times, shown sufficient intelligence to meet a few of trade unions' demands, only to impose a total U-turn on them later, when the balance of power has shifted. The social reality of Great Britain is a clear example of this.

The scope of the need for renewal is so great that the trade union movement cannot stay in the background. There is no doubt that the international trade union movement also must continue the combat that is inherent to its identity and vocation. I am thinking particularly of the struggle for peace and quality of life. Indeed, it is difficult to act for social progress without opposing the obstacles to it, when there are dozens of bloody local or regional conflicts in various parts of the world at the present time.

At the same time, the security conceptions that continue to prevail in many countries give priority to policies of force and military power. In the last 50 years, the world has devoted 5 to 6 percent of its gross national product (GNP) to a senseless arms race. Today, more than $9 trillion is spent on arms worldwide, whereas the major powers devoted only 0.026 percent of their GNP to human development in the third world.

Such waste must be stopped. Despite the progress promised by the Non-Proliferation Treaty, the Conservative government of France in 1996, for example, was preparing to spend $16 billion to continue its weapons testing in the laboratory. The trade union movement also must take into account the situation created by the existence of a military industry that employs millions of people throughout the world. The labor movement must not allow itself to be trapped by the dilemma of the arms race versus unemployment. Switching military production to civilian uses represents a major battle that must be fought. There are numerous possibilities for conversion and there is no lack of proposals from the workers themselves. Such thinking should be adopted by the ILO and the United Nations.

The same applies to our handling of issues concerning the quality of life. The fruits of growth must be used to improve the quality of life, to protect the environment, to create environmentally safe transportation, to ensure the right to housing and the security of individuals, respecting their customs and cultures.

The full employment of the twenty-first century will be very different from the full employment societies have known before. It will be based particularly on skills and new relationships among work, education, and civic or community activities. The implementation of new technologies already involves a considerable training effort, with the transfer of technologies and know-how. The challenge of a new type of productivity is relevant everywhere. To be effective, it must be based on radical improvement of living and working conditions, higher wages, a shorter working week without reducing wages, and the development and improvement of social protection systems, which play a major role in the dissemination of advances in medicine. This requires the development of democracy and workers' rights at all levels of society, particularly in companies.

The 1995 United Nations conference in Beijing was a step toward recognition of the major role played by women in social development. In all countries, such recognition cannot exist without equal rights, the promotion of women, giving them full access to responsibilities in all fields, and the suppression of all sexist discrimination against them.

Young people are the main victims of the crisis of unemployment, the absence or imperfections of training systems, the crisis in urban areas, and the type of town-planning that characterizes the major cities. This situation cannot be ignored. It cries out for genuine consideration by the trade union movement followed by suitable action.

The world is experiencing an increase in migratory pressures. The geographical mobility of men and women will only increase if the problems of development and employment are dealt with. Faced with this migratory pressure, the major receiving countries are implementing repressive measures that are a source of tension, promoting ethnic confrontation, violations of social rights, racism, and intolerance. The international trade union movement must come out in favor of the respect of migrants' rights and against any discriminatory measures concerning them, demanding full application and reinforcement of the measures regulating human rights and the guarantees in favor of refugees and migrants.

This has not always been the case. At times trade unions have been divided about the approach to follow. We should not forget that in France at the turn of the century, a CGT congress even planned to send a delegation to Italy to dissuade people from migrating. Even if today there is no longer any ambiguity involving the concept of putting a stop to immigration, some are still in favor of this. Such behavior remains influenced essentially by the rise in unemployment and is not unconnected with workers' xenophobic attitudes.

This takes us back to the need for the trade union movement to take on the challenge of full employment in the world in the context of harmonious, noncompetitive development of genuine cooperation between north and south as well as between developing countries. If we take into account the needs expressed in all fields of social affairs as well as in terms of infrastructure, transport, energy, telecommunications, health, education, and training, we will find that the interests of employees in industrialized countries and developing countries are convergent.

The trade union movement has a job to do that it is uniquely qualified to handle: promoting solidarity between all employees through the convergence of their interests, whatever their nationality, sex, color, or religion. This has been true since the birth of the trade union movement. Today it is even more crucial because millions of men and women can no longer wait. All elements of the international trade union movement must respond to this challenge.

About the Authors

Herrick Chapman is Associate Professor of History and French Studies at New York University. He is the author of *State Capitalism and Working Class Radicalism in the French Aircraft Industry* (Berkeley: University of California Press, 1991) and (with Peter N. Stearns) *European Society and Upheaval: Social History Since 1750,* 3rd Edition (New York: Macmillan, 1991). He is also editor (with Reid George Andrews) of *The Social Construction of Democracy, 1870–1990* (New York: New York University Press, 1995).

Mark Kesselman is Professor of Political Science at Columbia University. He is the editor (with Guy Groux) of *The French Workers' Movement: Economic Crisis and Political Change* (George Allen and Unwin, 1984). He has written many articles on French Labor, political parties, local politics, and public policy. His most recent article on French labor is "Where It Stops, Nobody Knows: The Troubled Trajectory of the French Labor Movement," in John T. S. Keeler and Martin A. Schain, eds., *Chirac's Challenge: Liberalization, Europeanization, and Malaise in France* (New York: St. Martin's Press, 1996).

Martin A. Schain is Professor of Politics and Director of the Center for European Studies at New York University. His is the author (with Henry Ehrmann) of *Politics in France* (New York: HarperCollins, 1992) and editor and author (with John Keeler) of *Chirac's Challenge: Liberalization, Europeanization, and Malaise in France.* He has written many articles on the French labor movement, as well as on the politics of immigration and the rise of the National Front in France.

Roland Cayrol is Director of the Opinion Poll Institute C.S.A. and directeur de recherche at the Centre pour l'Etude de la Vie Politique Française (CEVIPOF) at the Fondation Nationale des Sciences Politiques. He is the author of (with Thierry Moreau) *Les médias: Presse écrite, radio, télévision* (Paris: PUF, 1991) and *Le grand malendendu: Les Français et la politique* (Paris: Seuil, 1994).

Anthony Daley is the author of *Steel, State, and Labor: Mobilization and Adjustment in France* (Pittsburgh: University of Pittsburgh Press, 1996) and has written numerous articles on the French labor movement. His current book project examines organizational and ideological cleavages with the French working class movement.

Laura Levine Frader is Associate Professor of History at Northeastern University and Senior Associate at the Center for European Studies at Harvard University. She is author of *Peasants and Protest: Agricultural Workers, Politics, and Unions in the Aude* (Berkeley: University of California Press, 1991) and (with Sonya O. Rose) *Gender and Class in Modern France* (Ithaca, NY: Cornell University Press, 1996).

Guy Groux is a Research Associate at CEVIPOF at the Fondation Nationale des Sciences Politiques. He is the author of numerous books and articles on the French labor movement. His most recent book (with René Mouriaux) is *La C.G.T.: Crises et alternatives* (Paris: Economica, 1992). He has also edited (with Mark Kesselman) *The French Workers' Movement: Economic Crisis and Political Change*.

Chris Howell is Associate Professor of Politics at Oberlin College. He is the author of *Regulating Labor: The State and Industrial Relations Reform in Post-war France* (Princeton: Princeton University Press, 1992). He is currently completing a book on British trade unionism.

Jean Magniadas is Director of the CGT's Trade Union Research Institute (IS-ERES). He is the author of *Le patronat* (Paris: Éditions Messidor, 1991) and "La vie difficile des travailleurs en cette fin de siècle," in Claude Willard, ed., *La France Ouvrière, vol. 3, De 1968 à nos jours* (Paris: Les Editions de l'Atelier, 1995).

Bernard H. Moss is Professor at the Institute of European Studies in London, and co-editor and author of *The Single European Currency in National Perspective: A Community in Crisis?* (London: Macmillan, 1998).

René Mouriaux is Directeur de Recherches at CIVEPOF at the Fondation Nationale des Sciences Politiques. He is the author of numerous books and articles on the French and European labor movements. He is the author of *Le syndicalisme dans le monde* (Paris: PUF, 1993) and (with Guy Groux) *La C.G.T.: Crises et alternatives* (Paris: Economica, 1992).

Jean-Pierre Page is head of the CGT's International Department. He is also a member of the Executive Committee of the CGT. He writes frequently on the international trade union movement and maintains contact with trade unions throughout the world.

George Ross is Morris Hillquit Professor of Labor and Social Thought at Brandeis University, and Acting Director and Senior Associate at the Center for European Studies at Harvard University. He has written *Workers and Communists in France* (Berkeley: University of California Press, 1982) and *Jacques Delors and European Integration* (New York: Oxford University Press, 1994). His most recent book project is (editor, with Andrew Martin) *The Changing Place of Labor in European Society: The End of Labor's Century?*

Georges Séguy is former national General Secretary of the CGT. He is the author of *Le Mai de la CGT* (Paris: Julliard, 1972; new ed., 1988).

W. Rand Smith is Professor of Politics at Lake Forest College. He is the author *Crisis in the French Labor Movement: A Grassroots Perspective* (London: Macmillan, 1987) and, most recently, *Dirty Job: Dilemmas of Industrial Restructuring in France and Spain* (Pittsburgh: University of Pittsburgh Press, forthcoming). He has published numerous articles on French and Spanish political economy.

Index